A FUNNY THING HAPPENED ON MY WAY TO HEAVEN

To Borys, Trudy + Bianca

I hope you will enjoy + be blessed by this book.

Thanking you for your kindness towards us!

God Bless

Terry + Ginny

Nov 18, 2015

TERRY BRIDLE

A Funny Thing Happened on My Way to Heaven

Library and Archives Canada Cataloguing in Publication

Bridle, Terry, 1948-, author
   A funny thing happened on my way to heaven / Terry Bridle.

Issued in print and electronic formats.
ISBN 978-1-896213-69-9 (bound).--ISBN 978-1-896213-78-1 (pdf)

   1. Bridle, Terry, 1948-. 2. Christian biography--Canada.
I. Title.

BR1725.B75A3 2014   **248.4**   **C2014-905922-1**
                                                  C2014-905923-X

Publisher: byDesign Media, Uxbridge, Ontario, Canada L9P 2A5
www.bydesignmedia.ca
Copy editors: Stephanie Beth Nickel and Ginny "eagle-eye" Bridle
Cover: Adam R. Terrio
Back cover photography: Reynold Mainse, Mainse Media Group www.reynoldmainse.com
Illustrator: Adam R. Terrio
Interior layout and design: Diane Roblin-Lee

Unless otherwise noted, scripture quotations are from
1) The Holy Bible, King James Version. Copyright © 1977, 1984, Thomas Nelson Inc.
2) and from the New King James Version. Copyright © 1979, 1980, 1982. Thomas Nelson Inc.

A note from the author: While I have been necessarily frank and honest, I do hope that nothing I have written has offended anyone. I cannot imagine how any of it could have, but one cannot be sure these days. So let me say that if anyone takes umbrage with anything written in this book, I do most sincerely apologize and trust you will believe me when I say that it was never my intention to offend. ~ Terry Bridle

byDesign
MEDIA

CONTENTS

DEDICATED TO GINNY

On January 27, 1979, exactly one year to the day after I arrived in Canada, I walked down the aisle at The Peoples Church, Toronto, Canada and began a journey that I could not have imagined.

I made two promises that day: one to God and the other to the most beautiful girl in the world, Virginia Lynn Ambrose.

God has never left my side and Ginny Lynn has been my constant friend, lover and companion. Neither of them has ever let me down.

Without Ginny, this book would never have been written.

To say I love her with all my heart is totally inadequate.

Each morning when I wake up I love her more than when I went to sleep the night before and I thank God she is still here with me.

INTRODUCING "REP"

As I began the writing of this book, I was challenged by the fact that although I am the central character, this book is not really about *me*. It is all about what can happen when an ordinary, flawed human puts his life into the hands of God.

In an attempt to deflect attention away from myself, we have created the character named Rep. While neither a cartoon nor caricature of me, he represents me here and there throughout the pages of this book.

Every story is absolutely true and unembellished, so come on the journey with us. I am sure you will enjoy it.

INTRODUCTION

Each person's life is like a journey.

Some people plan that journey meticulously; education path, career course, marriage, family, children's education, retirement: all planned and executed, with almost military precision.

But for some people—like me—their life journey more resembles the course of a river. There is no apparent plan and all the twists and turns seem to have no logic.

Sometimes this river of life meanders casually through pleasant, wooded fields or across barren flat plains. At other times, it can thunder dangerously through narrow gorges and tumble painfully over shallow rapids.

Although each twist and turn seems random, to the river itself, they are all extremely logical and make a great deal of sense as the river reacts and responds to whatever barrier is placed before it, always finding a way around, over or under each challenge.

And although this river can often seem to be going nowhere, it is, in fact, moving with relentless persistence in a specific direction towards a specific, but as yet unseen and unknown, destination.

This book chronicles stories gleaned from the river that is my life journey. Rather than being in chronological order, they meander around the joys and challenges.

Many of the stories are funny; others are thought-provoking. Some, I hope, will make you laugh, whilst others may cause you to shed a tear or two. Some may challenge your thinking. Still others may encourage your faith.

All the stories are true and accurate. I have guarded against allowing the passage of time to embellish them.

This book is volume one, because I have not yet reached the end of my journey.

I believe that my ultimate destination is heaven. I can say this with certainty, not because of anything I have done, but because of a Man I met. His sacrifice made it possible for my name to be written in His book. He promised He would go ahead and prepare a place for me, a place where He awaits me at the end of my journey.

So, I invite you to join me. Laugh, cry and marvel at what has happened—so far.

Terry
Ajax, Ontario, Canada
www.terryandginny.com
terenceb@rogers.com
www.afunnythinghappenedvolumeone.com

1

DEAL OR NO DEAL!

Be careful of making deals with God.

Note: Some of the situations in this true story may surprise you; and some of my actions may even shock you, but please remember that I was in a desperate situation where surviving was my paramount thought. At the time, I was running away from God.

It was an incredibly clear, cloudless night. The sky was flooded with so many stars, it felt as if I could reach out, gather a handful and, like the old Perry Como song says, "put them in my pocket."

Looking down into the valley, the full moon cast a strange blue hue on the scene below, like one of those paintings in which you feel that the artist's imagination has gone far beyond reality. But this was *real*.

Broken down haciendas. Tumbleweed rolling and skipping gently across the valley floor. The dried up riverbed meandering on its course looking like an eerie river of blue milk. Yes, this was real. And so was the pack of two or three dozen rabid, wild dogs snarling around me, their teeth bared, long tendrils of saliva swinging to the ground and the smell of death in their nostrils.

My dad had always told me that dogs can smell fear, so it must have been confusing for this pack of wild canines that were circling me and snapping at my feet. Their prey was giving off the stench of fear whilst, at the same time, yelling at them and periodically swinging a duffel bag in their direction, causing them to scatter temporarily. They would immediately regroup and edge even closer, their courage growing as my fear increased .... It really did seem as if they had a well-orchestrated plan of attack. I guessed they had done this many times before.

And so we were locked into this macabre dance that seemed so out of place, so incongruous in this otherwise tranquil, beautiful moonlit setting, high in the mountains of southern Spain.

How on earth did I come to be here in the first place? What bizarre series of events had brought me to this beautiful place, surrounded by instruments of a potentially horrible death?

To answer that question, we need to go back several weeks, to a destitute young man in a steakhouse in Brighton, on the south coast of England, spending his last £5 on what he expected to be his last decent meal for some time. I was that young man.

A year or so after becoming a Christian I became disillusioned with it and went back to my old life. With three good friends I sang and played double bass (later bass guitar) in a band called Romany Brew. We wrote much of our own music and were very popular locally. We really thought we had a shot at the big time.

Unfortunately, we had a manager who stole our money and

Original Romany Brew in BBC TV Studio

Romany Brew—Version 2

our equipment. The group disbanded to lick its wounds, the reason I was in that restaurant ordering my "last meal." Just then, in walked a couple and sat at the table next to mine.

The fellow was very distinguished and looked to be from the Mediterranean. The woman looked like she had spent too much time in the sun eating health food. She had no discernible shape. Her skin was leathery and she had long, dry, slightly greying hair.

During the meal, they asked me if I knew anything about cars, as apparently a man was coming to the restaurant to show them a car that they hoped to buy. After that, they would need someone to drive them down to their summer home in the south of Spain and work for them as their chauffeur for about three months.

Well, my total knowledge of cars could have been written on a postage stamp—with space left over—but I *did* know about the south of Spain. The idea of spending three months down there was very appealing. I gallantly offered to give an unbiased, independent appraisal of the car—of course, not admitting that my appraisal would be worth even less than the aforementioned postage stamp.

When the car arrived, it was a classic old Rover with plush leather seats, a sunroof and all the bells and whistles you could imagine in a old, stately, almost vintage car. While the "odd couple" (as I tagged them in my mind) continued with their meal, I proceeded to give a very good impersonation of someone capable of giving the car a thorough inspection.

Needless to say, I did not fool the salesman and he quietly asked what was going on. I explained that if I gave approval, the couple would buy the car. At this point, the salesman slipped £100 into my hand—and so the deal was done.

The couple bought the car and hired me as their chauffeur.

I informed some close friends of what I was going to do and they expressed some concern, as I really didn't know anything about these people, but being young and foolish, I cast aside their concerns. In my mind, it was like I had fallen into a garbage pit but had come up smelling like roses. Spanish señoritas, here I come!

It was not long before I realized that the odd couple were, indeed, a little strange.

They always acted very aloof, sitting in the back of the car while I was alone in the front; and they were always giving the impression that they were in total control of their emotions, while at the same time, the atmosphere around them was strained, awkward and frosty.

As we drove down through France, I was instructed to never take the main highways but to always take the small back roads. Every day, I had to find an empty field and stop there. They would get out of the car, walk to the middle of the field, shout and scream for about twenty minutes and then calmly get back into the car as if nothing had happened. Very strange!

At every food stop, I had to sit at a different table from them. They paid for everything—even supplied me with cigarettes—but they gave me no actual money. At every overnight stop, they would take the best room available at whatever hotel we stayed at, whilst I was given the cheapest room possible—once, quite literally, in a stable. To be honest, I did not mind this, as I was glad to get some time away from them.

At one point, the man accused me of "looking at" his wife. He actually accused me of lusting after her. It was all I could do not to laugh in his face at this suggestion. In my previous description of this so-called lady, I gallantly neglected to add that her body sagged in all the wrong places. What once may have been an hour-glass figure, was now most definitely a bone rack—but oddly pear-shaped.

The fact was she always sat in the very middle of the back seat, so every time I checked my rear-view mirror, I was unavoidably looking in her direction. Despite my protestations of innocence, I was given a firm warning to not look at her (as if she was Medusa;[1] perhaps she was, so it's just as well I didn't look at her) and so henceforth, I never looked in the rear-view mirror; I used only the side mirrors outside the car and studiously avoided looking in her direction at any time.

It really was a bizarre situation.

One night we stayed in the southern French town of Toulouse. At that time, I was reading a paperback called *Jaws* (long before it was made into a movie) and as I settled down in my cheap closet room to read an exciting part of the book, there was a gentle knock on my door. When I opened the door, there, standing before me, was a beautiful young French girl. I do not understand French, but she very quickly made it clear what services she was prepared to offer me.

I was a long way from God at the time, a healthy young man, and this girl was exceptionally beautiful in every way. You can imagine my surprise when I found myself declining her offer. I remember thinking, even after I closed the door, "Terry, are you nuts? Go and call her back." And yet something inside restrained me.

I did not appreciate, until many years later, that it was God who was protecting me from myself. I know that when we stay close to God, He will not allow us to be tempted beyond the point that we can resist—and yet here was God protecting me even though I had strayed far away from Him.

The next day I was in big trouble with the odd couple as apparently, they had arranged for the girl to visit me. When she went back to receive payment for

---

[1] In Greek mythology, Medusa was a once beautiful Gorgon, who was punished by Athena for her rebelliousness. The punishment involved Medusa's hair turning into snakes and anyone who looked into her eyes was turned to stone.

"services rendered," an argument ensued at the discovery that I had declined any actual services. Nevertheless, the girl had demanded to be paid anyway. This only served to convince the man, all the more, of his absurd notion that I fancied his wife.

The decision of these people to use only back roads meant that our journey south was not proceeding as fast as they wanted, so they were continually demanding that I drive faster to make up time. I was happy to oblige, but the local French police were not so happy about it. Consequently, I was stopped a few times for speeding, the fines for which they had to pay immediately. According to the odd couple, because I was *thinking* about the police, I was attracting them to our vehicle. It never seemed to occur to them that driving in excess of the speed limit has a tendency to trigger radar guns and attract unwanted attention.

The situation worsened considerably every day, to the point that, for the only time in my life, I found myself considering whether or not it would be worth my while to kill these two ridiculous people and dispose of their bodies. I very quickly dismissed the idea, but it frightened me that the thought had actually entered my mind.

During the next few days, there were several other bizarre incidents, but to relate them all here would only make this story long-winded. I think you get the picture.

I was somewhat trapped in the situation. I was obligated to drive the odd couple to their destination and the thought of spending three months in southern Spain was still very attractive. Furthermore, I never had any cash of my own, so my options were somewhat limited.

Finally, late at night, five days after that fateful meeting in the Aberdeen Steak House in Brighton, England, we arrived at the large villa owned by the odd couple, just outside of Mazarron, very near the south coast of Spain.

After putting my duffel bag in the small bedroom allocated to me, I casually walked into the lounge, where I was gruffly informed that the only two rooms that I was allowed in were my bedroom and an equally small guest bathroom. Banished to my room, I settled down to read my book, when there was a gentle knock on my door. Again? This time when I answered, I found a tray on which was a glass of lukewarm water (no ice) and a tired looking cheese sandwich. I think they had bought it originally on the cross-channel ferry from England and it had somehow survived the journey.

After an hour or so in my solitary confinement, I was summoned to the lounge where the odd couple proceeded to inform me that they had decided to dispense with my services and that I was to leave their property immediately.

I did not mind, as in our original verbal agreement, they were supposed to pay my way back to England. However, they reneged on that agreement and told me they would give me nothing and I was to leave immediately.

Upon my threat to go to the local police, they laughed, asking who I thought the police would believe: them, an upstanding, well-off couple, fully conversant in Spanish or me, a long-haired English youth who didn't understand or speak a word of the language?

They pointed out to me that in Spain (at that time over thirty-five years ago), if the police had cause to arrest a person and they discovered that the person had no money, the person could be imprisoned as a vagrant and placed in a cell for 14 days, without even the right to call a lawyer or anyone else. When released, the police could immediately arrest the person again, knowing that he or she was still penniless—and so, technically, still a vagrant.

It all sounded very draconian. I had no way of knowing if there was any truth to their threat, but I did not feel inclined to put it to the test, so cutting my loses, I took my duffel bag with my few possessions and walked out into the dark, still night, penniless, not knowing exactly where I was nor how I was going to get back home to England. My potentially idyllic time in the south of Spain had quickly morphed into a nightmare.

Fortunately, it is not in my character to panic. Upon seeing a sliver of ocean twinkling in the light of the full moon, I walked towards the coast and soon found myself sitting on a hill overlooking the Bay of Mazarron.

It was a totally cloudless night and the moon cast a sliver-white line across the still waters of the bay. It was beautiful and serene as I sat there, taking stock of my situation and my life in general.

I realized that I had been running away from God and He had just let me get on with it. Somewhere in my subconscious, I had tried to be like Cliff Richard—a very famous English pop star who, after he had reached the pinnacle of his profession, had become a Christian. His consistency of faith was a shining example to people as to what Christianity was all about.

I can laugh now at my youthful audacity. I was certainly no Cliff Richard. He was extremely good-looking, very talented, rich and famous—all of which I was not. Well, maybe I shouldn't be too hard on myself. After all, my wife thinks I'm good-looking and talented. But then, she would think that, wouldn't she?"

The realization that hit me, like a blow from a heavyweight boxer, was that the plans God had for Cliff Richard were not the same as the plans He had for me.

I had come to the end of the rope—or I had reached the proverbial crossroads in my life. You can choose whichever metaphor you like, but I realized that God had brought me to this place. He had allowed me to go my own way, while never completely abandoning me, and now I had a major pivotal decision to make.

It is interesting how people will shun God and arrogantly follow their own path until something goes wrong. Then they turn to Him—often to blame Him—but sometimes, to contritely ask for His help. It rankled me to be in this position. It offended my pride, but in my desperation, I made a deal with God, not knowing where it would lead.

Before I go on, let me say this: be very careful of any deal you make with the Almighty, especially if you make it during a time in your life when such a deal seems to be your only option. You see, when the situation improves, you may forget the deal, but God, in His love for you, does not.

So what was my deal? As I looked over the tranquil beauty of the Bay of Mazarron at about 11:30 p.m. on that still summer night, I bargained with God that if He would get me safely back to England, I would recommit my life to Him. It was an easy deal for me to make. After all, I was asking everything from Him and all I was offering in return was a wasted failure of a life.

As it turned out, it was a deal that, amazingly, was acceptable to God.

But things got worse before they got better. In my state of mind, I was determined to not let the odd couple off the hook. I thought I had to somehow make them pay for their unfair treatment of me. So I went back to where their cherished car was parked and I did three things to it.

First of all, I slashed the tires; then I removed the rotor arm from inside the distributor cap and, finally, I poured sand into the gas tank. I figured they wouldn't discover the distributor wasn't working until after they replaced the tires and the sand in the gas tank would eventually cause great damage to the engine, but only some time after the tires and distributor cap had been fixed—progressive revenge.

I have pondered whether or not to include this (as it was wrong for me to have done those things), but in staying faithful to the story, I felt I should tell the whole truth, as it affected my future actions. You see, I realized I needed to get as far away from that place as I could, as quickly as possible.

With my duffel bag slung over my shoulder, I set off on my journey north, back to England—little knowing that, in the mountains, I had an appointment with a large pack of rabid, hungry, wild dogs. I was not exactly "dancing with wolves," but for two hours, I quite literally fought off the wild dogs as I inched my way across those low mountains.

Quite suddenly, as dawn was breaking and I was starting to descend into a small town, the dogs were simply not there anymore. That is how it happened: one minute they were there snapping at me, the next minute they were gone.

Call it coincidence if you like. Certainly, at that time, I was too exhausted to consider the possibility that God had literally "called off the dogs." I stumbled wearily into the sleepy little Spanish town and into the next chapter of this bizarre journey that, in five days, took me up the Mediterranean coast of Spain, up through central France, across the English Channel and then along the south coast of England, back to where my own car was waiting for me.

To help in my repatriation, the British Consulate in Valencia gave me £50. Because I had no money and had no access to any funds, the consulate would give me money only if someone would stand surety for me, by first sending it to the British Consular Department in the UK. At the time, I was totally lost without the help of friends. Martin Pusey came to my rescue. Now we joke about the fact that I still owe him the £50, despite the fact that he doesn't want me to repay it. He likes the fact that I am still beholden to him and that, whenever we meet, I have to buy the first round of drinks. In truth, I have probably paid the £50 back many times over! But £50 was nowhere near enough, considering I had to make a journey of about 1,100 miles (1,800 kilometres) across three different countries, plus cross the English Channel.

Photo taken in Spain for temporary travel document

For most of the journey, I bought platform tickets at train stations and bluffed my way as far as I could. I spent quite a lot of time in the washrooms on the trains, avoiding the ticket inspectors. My genuine lack of understanding of French and Spanish helped in bluffing my way out of many tricky situations.

Almost all of the £50 went on buying platform tickets and a ticket to cross the English Channel. I knew I would not be able to bluff my way past the British rail ferry police.

There was a multitude of small incidents en route that, if included, would make the telling of the story tedious, but there was one notable incident in Barcelona.

All of my train journeys were done at night, so I could sleep on the train. When I arrived in Barcelona, I decided to take a walk down the famous "La Rambla," a tourist attraction in Barcelona.

La Rambla is a wide street, stretching from midtown Barcelona to the ocean at the port. Down the entire length of the street is a tree-lined boulevard littered with cafés, coffee shops, souvenir stalls and all kinds of performing artists, singers, jugglers and—the cause of my next 'international incident'—sidewalk shoe shiners.

Let me set the scene for you. It was a beautiful, sunny day and La Rambla was packed with its usual crowd of boisterous tourists from many nations, all looking for a bargain from local traders, who were, in turn, looking for easy money from naive foreigners. The foreigners were seen as easy prey because generally, they had too much money in their pockets, too much alcohol in their blood or had spent too much time in the sun. This was a potentially lethal combination for the tourist but a profitable one for the local traders who could spot an easy target from a great distance.

Into this scene walked little ole' me, having left my duffel bag in a luggage locker at the Estacio-Sants, the main train station in Barcelona.

Yes, I had hair to my shoulders, but I did not look destitute. In fact, I probably looked like a good mark. I was wearing blue jeans; a three-quarter length, lightweight, maroon leather jacket; and two-tone, brown leather shoes with one-inch thick soles and four-inch heels. (Don't laugh; they were very fashionable back then.)

As I was sauntering down La Rambla, enjoying the ambience and anonymity, to unwittingly add to the illusion of affluence, I was smoking one of my favourite brands of cigarettes, a Sobranie Black Russian. I had not spent the £50 wisely. These cigarettes are black, with gold coloured filters and a little longer than usual.

My appearance most certainly belied the reality of my predicament and a couple of sidewalk shoe shiners decided I would be their next meal ticket. They approached me in a very friendly animated manner, indicating that they would like to shine my shoes.

I tried to decline politely, explaining that my shoes did not need to be shined and I had no money. Remember, however, they spoke no English and I neither spoke nor understood Spanish. Our gesticulating pantomime continued until, with reluctance, they seemed to give up. With a disheartened shrug, they indicated that maybe I could give them one of my cigarettes.

To be honest, I did not want to give away two of my precious Black Russians, but neither did I want to upset these two excitable, volatile men, so I magnanimously gave them each a cigarette, causing them both to come alive again, jabbering in excited Spanish with exaggerated pantomime actions, indicating that they would now shine my shoes.

Well, it seemed to me to be a fair exchange: two expensive cigarettes for a shoe shine. Although they were getting the better of the deal, at least it would get them out of my hair.

These two men were an incredibly entertaining double act, elevating the simple task of shoe-shining into a highly entertaining spectacle that quickly attracted a large, laughing, high-spirited crowd. I was happy to go along with it and did not object when my two "new friends" apparently decided that my shoes needed more than just a shine. As the shoes were, quite literally, down at heel, my new benefactors proceeded to hammer on steel toe-tips and heel-tips. This may seem strange to my North American readers, but it was quite a common practise in Europe back then to increase the longevity of expensive shoes.

All of this was done as the shoes were still on my feet. The audience was loving the show as these two guys performed for the crowd, turning me around and making me look like a horse being shod.

When the performance was over, after giving their audience a flourishing bow, the men turned to me and asked for the equivalent (in pesos) of about $20 for their work.

But I didn't have it!

To be honest, if I'd had the money, I probably would have given it to them, but I simply had no money left. I pulled out my pockets to show them that I had nothing, and that's when things started to turn very nasty.

The transition from friendly, animated new friends to malevolent adversaries was startlingly fast. Both of them started to try to remove both of my shoes. I guess they figured they had an investment that they wanted to recoup.

The crowd became unfriendly towards me as they unquestionably sided with the two shoe-shiners, and the commotion attracted the attention of two Spanish policemen standing about fifty yards away.

The threat by the odd couple echoed in my mind. I had no money, so I could be arrested for vagrancy. This was *not* a good situation, so on the spur of the moment, I made a decision. I ran!

As I bolted, I heard the crowd and the shoe-shiners yelling at me, but I did not have time to look back to see if they were following me or not. The shrill blasts from the policemen's whistles confirmed that they were in hot pursuit.

Running away from the scene of a crime is a sure sign of guilt, and although I did not believe I had done anything wrong, this was not the time or place for diplomatic discussion. I hightailed it into the labyrinth of the cobblestoned back streets of Barcelona, with no idea where I was going. The only thought in my mind was to put as much distance between myself and the Spanish Policia as possible. However, I had a distinct disadvantage—the steel heels and toe tips on my shoes.

First of all, the noise my shoes made was like a homing beacon for my pursuers. Plus, trying to navigate quickly around corners in steel-tipped shoes was akin to trying to run on ice in a pair of leather-soled dress shoes. There was no traction. I felt like a character in one of those old "Road Runner" cartoons: going nowhere as my feet were spinning, trying to get a grip on the street's surface.

I did the only thing that came to my mind in that moment of despair: I took off my shoes and headed off through the back streets of Barcelona with just my socks on my feet. Believe me, the grip was barely any better, but at least I was running silently.

Several hours later, exhausted and with my socks shredded and my feet killing me, I found my way back to the train station where I quickly retrieved my duffel bag. Having bought a platform ticket earlier, I boarded a train heading north.

The next two days were a bit of a blur. The only legitimate ticket I had was the one for the ferry from Calais, France, to Dover, England. The rest of the journey involved a mixture of subterfuge, lies, feigning ignorance, lack of understanding of the language and sheer luck in avoiding ticket inspectors. Nevertheless, I eventually got back to Southampton to pick up my car.

I was physically and mentally exhausted, penniless and had no idea what to do next. I decided to go back to Brighton to see if I could salvage something of my life there, but as I had not eaten a proper meal for a week, the first order of business was to eat a good nutritious meal—and I knew just how to solve that problem.

Little did I know that this would take me exactly where God wanted me so that He could cash in on our bargain. I was now safely home in England, so it was time for me to keep my side of the deal.

Driving from Southampton to Brighton entailed driving along the English south coast and would necessitate driving past Portsmouth, where I knew I could get a free meal.

About a mile north of Portsmouth was the little community of Cowplain. Years earlier, as a practising Christian, I had attended the Cowplain Evangelical Free Church, a small church where I had met a very generous older couple. Dudley and Jan Paterson were known affectionately as "Uncle Dud and Auntie Jan." They were renown for having many guests over on Sundays to enjoy their wonderful roast beef lunches, complete with mashed *and* roasted potatoes, a variety of vegetables and Yorkshire pudding.

I knew if I were to pop by right before lunchtime they would invite me to stay. Since it was Sunday, I "just happened" to drop in to say hello. Sure enough, they invited me to stay for lunch, along with whatever other guests they had that day.

They knew I was no longer going to church and that my lifestyle had strayed far away from that of a committed Christian. While my appearance betrayed the circumstances of my heart, they were that kind of non-judgmental couple who oozed love for people and demonstrated it in practical ways. I planned to take advantage of that.

I knew how to conduct myself properly in their company and thoroughly enjoyed a magnificent Sunday lunch, with apple pie and custard for dessert ("afters" as we call it in England). I was enjoying myself so much that I stayed on for the afternoon. When it came time for tea—the late afternoon meal of sandwiches and tea—I stayed for that, too. However, I knew if I did not extract myself before about 6:00 p.m., they would invite me to join them in going to church that evening. Sure enough, I didn't (extract myself) and they did invite me to go to church.

Looking back, I think I was being a little bit mischievous, wanting to see everyone at that church again, especially as I was in a rebellious, arrogant frame of mind. Let them see me now with my cool clothes and long hair. So I went to church with Uncle Dud and Auntie Jan and it caused a bit of a stir when I, the prodigal, walked in.

The pastor, Rev. Leslie Edgell, was speaking that night, but I have no recollection whatsoever of what his message was about; I just endured the service, feeling numb and bored. Then came the closing song, that well-known song, used so often by Billy Graham.

> Just as I am, without one plea,
> But that Thy blood was shed for me,
> And that Thou bidst me come to Thee,
> O Lamb of God, I come, I come.
>
> Just as I am, and waiting not
> To rid my soul of one dark blot,
> To Thee whose blood can cleanse each spot,
> O Lamb of God, I come, I come.
>
> Just as I am, though tossed about
> With many a conflict, many a doubt,
> Fightings and fears within, without,
> O Lamb of God, I come, I come.
>
> Just as I am, poor, wretched, blind;
> Sight, riches, healing of the mind,
> Yea, all I need in Thee to find,
> O Lamb of God, I come, I come.
>
> Just as I am, Thou wilt receive,
> Wilt welcome, pardon, cleanse, relieve;
> Because Thy promise I believe,
> O Lamb of God, I come, I come.
>
> Just as I am, Thy love unknown
> Hath broken every barrier down;
> Now, to be Thine, yea, Thine alone,
> O Lamb of God, I come, I come.[2]

As that song was being sung by the congregation in that little church, I suddenly started to sob, not just quietly crying, but wracked with deep sobbing convulsions,

---

[2] Original words by Charlotte Elliott in 1835. Public domain.

so much that I had to sit down to try and hide what was happening from those around me. My stubborn foolish pride did not want them to see me like this, but I could not control what was happening to me. I tried to fight it, but I could not.

As I sat there with my head in my hands, I distinctly felt the Lord remind me of the deal I had made with him a week earlier, when overlooking the Bay of Mazarron in southern Spain. To my heart the Lord said, "Well Terry, I brought you home safely, so are you going to keep your side of the deal?"

No one had to convince me; I just knew God was calling me and I had to respond. Years later, my wife Ginny recorded a song called "He's Been Faithful"[3] the words of which most perfectly describe what I was going through.

The lyricist, Cathy Goddard, writes of the faithfulness of God through every moment of fear and pain. Her words, "When my strength was all gone, when my heart had no song..." seem to have been written expressly for me, because in those days, I was in the very place she described. Like Cathy, I found every word He promised to be true and I've seen Him do things I was sure were impossible. Looking back, I can see His love and mercy, even though my heart was full of doubt. He never abandoned me when I was selfishly reaching out for what pleased me. He let go—let me learn from painful experiences how very much He loved me. He was faithful to me even though I had not been faithful to Him. When I found His arms still open, I understood the depth of His love and mercy and recommitted my life to God.

Uncle Dudley said wisely that if I continued my journey to Brighton I would get pulled back into my old life. I knew good people back then—friends who I still cherish very much—but God had another plan for me. I had to make a choice to either follow Him or return to my own ways. I am glad I chose to follow the Lord. I am grateful, too, that the friendships I cherished from those days are still as strong as ever. I'm also grateful that my old friends still love me and indeed respect me for the path that I have taken. Brian and Grahame remain two of my most cherished friends.

So it was that Uncle Dud said I should stay with him and Auntie Jan for a couple of weeks, just to decide what to do in the future.

The "couple of weeks" turned into just under two years. I remember Uncle Dud saying that if I lived in his home, he would treat me like a son (he had

---

[3] Lyrics by Cathy Goddard

two daughters). However, since it was a Christian home, I would have to live accordingly: no smoking; no alcohol; no dating non-Christian girls; no going to nightclubs, bars or pubs; be home by 11:00 each night; maintain an appearance befitting a Christian. That was how Uncle Dud saw it.

Now remember, I was twenty-seven-years-old and had just spent the last four or five years living how I pleased. No one told me what I could or could not do, where I could or could not go, and whom I could or could not date. Yet now I was being presented with this set of what were in my opinion, draconian rules. My head said, "You've got to be kidding!" But in my heart, I knew this was where God wanted me to be at that time.

I even had to get a proper job and pay for my room and board, and I had to pay it each Friday before 6:00 p.m. If I was late in handing the money over I was left in no doubt that was unacceptable.

Uncle Dudley's tough love saved me.

Yes, I had many struggles. I broke the rules sometimes, and on a few occasions, I was caught, for which I received a stern but loving reprimand. But that tough love literally yanked me back to where I needed to be and set me on a course of redemption that led me to where I am today.

I cannot take credit for any of this. God never gave up on me. He worked through good people such as Uncle Dudley and Auntie Jan, Rachel and Tom Dale, Terry and Janet Wiseman and many others. All of them were God's instruments who, in different ways, set me back on the right path and helped me stay there.

As you read this, you may be one of those who have strayed from God. Perhaps you know someone, even a loved one, who has turned their back on Him. Maybe you have never come to a place of recognizing your need to surrender your life to Jesus Christ.

Ginny sings another wonderful song by Hillsong that speaks so clearly of the fact that there's nothing we can do to make God love us any more than He already does. Nothing we could ever do would make Him close the door on us. He loves us so much that He sacrificed His Son so that we would be able to come to Him.

Ginny chooses songs that connect deeply with the hearts of those who hear her, and that certainly includes me. Another of these is a song by Ralph Carmichael.

It begins, "The Saviour is waiting to enter your heart" and goes on to ask, "Why don't you let Him in?" The lyrics challenge the listener to consider the reality that there's really nothing in the world that could keep anyone apart from God.

The song is called "The Saviour is Waiting" because the main point is that God makes Himself real to people, giving them opportunity after opportunity to respond to His great love. He continues to wait, hoping they will open the doors to their hearts and let Him come in. If we will take just one step towards Him, we'll discover His arms are wide open, waiting to receive us. The darkness in our lives will vanish when we allow Him to live in our hearts. "Time after time He has waited before, and now He is waiting again..." The words go on to press for a response to Him.

The rest of this book testifies to the fact that this was, by no means, the end of the story. In fact, it just marked the beginning of an exciting and eventful journey that I am still on. Indeed, *A Funny Thing Happened On My Way to Heaven*.

But as for now?

Well, one day I hope to go back to that hill overlooking the Bay of Mazarron, to sit again in that place where I made the best deal I could ever have made.

And it was a deal that God, thank goodness, kept me to.

2

THE RELUCTANT EMIGRANT

THE THREE FLEECES

It was 1977. I was sitting in a stuffy office in Canada House in London, England, when a rather bored looking bureaucrat said to me—not even looking at me as he spoke and speaking so quietly that I barely heard him—"You can go now."

I am almost totally deaf in my left ear, so it is possible I misheard him, but at the time, it really did sound as though he said, "You can go now."

So I stood and turned to leave, which caused the official to look up in surprise and say, "Where are you going?"

"I am going, like you said," I answered, equally surprised.

To which the bureaucrat actually smiled and said, "Sit down, please. I did not mean for you to leave this office now. I meant that you can go to Canada now. I am granting you emigration status."

To many people, those words would have been music to their ears; but to me, those were the last words I wanted to hear. You see, I had no desire whatsoever to emigrate to Canada.

What, then, was I doing, having a meeting in Canada House—this beautiful, Grade ll listed, historical Greek Revival building, situated in Trafalgar Square in London, part of the High Commission of Canada in the UK—with this government official?

Well, as I have posed the question, I suppose I had better answer it.

Back in 1970, my parents and only other sibling, an older brother, had emigrated to Canada, but I had stayed back in the UK. As I said, I had no desire to go and live in Canada. Somewhat at the last minute, I had announced to my family that I would not be going. I have always been grateful that my parents respected my decision and did not put any pressure on me to go with them. If they were disappointed, they hid it well.

To my shame, I have to admit that, in the following years, I was not good at keeping in touch with my family in Canada. None of us were prolific letter writers, and the Internet had not been invented yet, so there was no such thing as e-mails. As they got on with forging a new life for themselves in Canada, I got on with carving out a life for myself on my own back in the UK.

To begin with, I lived in a tiny attic room in my Auntie Joan and Uncle George's bungalow in Southampton, but then moved out on my own, quite soon, into a rented bedsit (bachelor apartment).

For the princely sum of £6 a week (about $12 Canadian at that time), I had a good sized room with a bay window, with a coin meter to pay for any electricity I used. I shared bath and toilet facilities with about ten other people whom I rarely, if ever, saw, and talked to even less.

I was working for a company called Olivetti as a typewriter engineer, going from office to office, servicing and repairing manual and electric typewriters. To help finance my new freedom, however, I had to take a second job pumping gas four nights a week. But I was now totally independent, living as my own boss. I could come and go as I pleased. I could make decisions based on what I wanted in life. I could take risks.

During this time, my life took two dramatic turns. The first involved quickly drifting away from going to church and anything remotely related to a Christian lifestyle.

I am not saying I became a bad person, and indeed, during this time, I formed friendships with three people: Brian Stansbridge and his wife Angela (who is beautiful inside and out) and Grahame Pusey (an extremely talented musical enigma). I had a sort of older brother (me)/younger brother (Grahame) relationship with him.

Romany Brew in a night club in the UK

It is a long story, but Brian, Grahame, another guy whose name was Malcolm and I ended up forming a group called Romany Brew, which became very popular in the south of England. With tight vocal harmonies, we sang mostly songs we had written ourselves. We would spend countless, wonderful hours working on intricate harmonies. A bond of friendship was formed whereby I still consider Brian, Angela and Grahame (Malcolm sadly passed away some years ago) to be amongst my most cherished friends.

My contribution to Romany Brew was partly my singing ability (especially finding unusual harmonies), partly my contribution to the lyrics and, perhaps, a pragmatic talent and discipline for organizing.

Whilst Grahame and Malcolm were excellent songwriters, it was Brian who had a gift for writing incredibly incisive words.

Please indulge me as I share two brief examples of the lyrics he wrote. We worked together on creating the harmony arrangements.

This particular song was about a young man who was caught up in a life of crime.

> *Hunted like a fox run to ground in blind confusion*
> *Strung up like a dog, the reward for revolution*
> *He's no Che Guevara or some latter day Mata Hara*
> *Just a kid in his old man's coat and trousers*

And then there was this one about the advertising industry:

> *I'm a Rat Man Rat Man, I'm a parasite*
> *You can earn your bread I only want a little bite*
> *I'll tell you what you want and then supply it if I can*
> *I'm the ultimate in marketing, I'm the Rat Man.*
>
> *You work hard for your money*
> *To buy all the things that you need.*
> *Oh, and though it may sound funny*
> *The things that you need have already been agreed.*
>
> *You don't get much say in it,*
> *You don't get much choice—and why?*
> *Because through all kinds of double-talk advertisements*
> *I'll tell you want I want you to buy.*

We had good voices, great creative harmonies and incisive original lyrics that were fun but also made pertinent social comments that resonated with people.

Grahame's artistic temperament would sometimes clash with my more pragmatic approach to life and we would sometimes fight, but this was done with a little, soft, fluffy teddy bear that Grahame used to hit me with. We are not psychologists, but that teddy bear enabled frustrations to be vented that could otherwise have been more damaging.

It was a time of doing my own thing, but stubborn independence is not always fun.

Grahame, Teddy & Terry reunited after 25 years

I remember one Christmas when I was out of work and we were trying to make a go of it as professional musicians. We were "gigging around" in folk clubs, pubs, bowling alley clubs, working men's clubs and anywhere that would pay us to sing to mostly drunk patrons.

We played in one club in Newcastle where the manger said we had to do three forty-five-minute sets. He would pay us after each set was completed. This seemed very strange, so we asked why.

He explained that his customers got progressively drunk as the night went on, and if they didn't like us at any time during the evening, we would know. Pointing to a balcony directly over the stage upon which we were to sing, he said, "See that balcony? If they don't like you, they'll pour beer on you from that balcony."

Oh really?

We survived the first set unscathed. By halfway through the second set, the crowd was getting restless, so we pulled out the three aces we had up our sleeves. Fortunately, in our repertoire, we had three very popular songs that had been written and recorded by a local Geordie group who had become famous in the UK; and so, as we sung "Fog on the Tyne," "Lady Eleanor," and "Meet Me On The Corner," the crowd went wild—singing along, dancing, cheering and drinking even more heartily.

For our third set, we basically sang those three songs over and over again, as the crowd kept requesting them. By now, they were so drunk we could probably have song "God Save The Queen" and they would have been happy. But that was a scary experience.

Another, completely different, experience involved a very lonely Christmas. I had been invited to spend Christmas with some friends in Brighton, a two-hour drive from where I lived in Southampton. My car was a dilapidated piece of junk, and I was so broke I had only enough money to put petrol in the tank for the drive to Brighton and back. When, on Christmas Eve, I tried to start the car to drive to Brighton, it would not start.

I knew nothing about the mechanics of cars. I could not afford membership in the AA; and anyway, even if I had had the money for the car to be repaired, no one would be working on Christmas Eve.

There was no phone in the building where my bedsit was, cell phones had not yet been invented (this was the mid 70s) and I had no coins for a public phone booth.

Somewhat deflated, I trudged back to my little bedsit room, with no money and no food or drink.

I sat on my bed, watching my little black and white television, until the pay-as-you-go meter ran out and the electricity in my room turned off. As I had no money to put in the meter, I sat alone in the descending darkness.

After a fitful night's sleep in the cold, I awoke the next morning to the happy sounds of local children playing outside with their new Christmas presents, but for me, there was no joy, nothing to be happy about.

I spent the rest of Christmas Day cold, tired and hungry.

Midway through the next day, Boxing Day, I swallowed my pride and walked about an hour to the house of some friends. When they heard what had happened, they castigated me for not having come to them sooner, but I had been too proud, not wanting to bother them on Christmas Day. Silly of me, but there you are!

Despite everything, I do still look back on those years with great fondness.

The second dramatic turn occurred when God, having given me the freedom to try and make it on my own, reaffirmed His love for me and led me back to Himself. (This I shared in detail earlier, in the chapter "Deal or No Deal.")

In 1977, my life began to turn in a positive direction.

I knew that my parents and brother still wanted me to join them in Canada, but (having abandoned the pursuit of trying to become a pop star) I had, in the previous few years, worked hard and become the manger of an employment agency, which found permanent jobs for people and employed about 200 people each week in temporary placements.

The UK gospel group, Eleusis

I earned good money, drove a nice new company car, was happily involved in a local church where I had lots of friends, and lived in an upstairs, four-room flat rented to me at a reasonable price by a dear old lady by the name of Mrs. Christmas.

Life was good. Why would I want to join my family in Canada?

Around this time, a couple of the elders at my church spoke to me separately, unofficially asking if I was likely to go and live in Canada. Apparently, they were sounding me out as possible leadership material in the church.

I figured that if I applied for landed immigrant status in Canada and was turned down, that would settle the issue once and for all and I would stay in England.

I discovered that in the pre-application process, an applicant would be sent a ten-part questionnaire they could answer and mark themselves. Each question carried a maximum of ten points. If one didn't achieve at least seventy points, there was no point in applying for a personal interview in London. In the section concerning immediate family, I scored ten out of ten because my only immediate family members were already all in Canada. In the section on age, where a person scored one point for each year he or she was under the age of thirty-five, I scored seven points. But in all the other categories, I scored very few points, as I had left school at sixteen, had no trade qualifications, no educational credentials, no job to go to and was not prepared to go to any other part of Canada except Toronto. The total number of points I scored on the self-assessment was thirty-two—nowhere near enough.

As far as I was concerned, my low score was great. I did not want to go to live in Canada, and now I could legitimately blame the system. However, just to make my inability to go to Canada rock solid, I decided to take the day trip up to London so I could be officially turned down in person. My parents and brother would be sad, but the elders at my church would know for sure that my intentions for the future were to stay in England.

All of that led to my being stunned when the emigration official said those words, "You can go now."

Apparently, the landed emigration permit lasted for just three months. If I didn't go almost immediately, I would have to go through the entire process again.

As I walked out into the bright October sunshine, into the hustle and bustle of Trafalgar Square, I was in a world of my own thoughts. I could easily have done nothing and simply let the permit expire—or I could do something to try to determine what God wanted for me in all this.

I sat near one of the lions in Trafalgar Square, oblivious to the fact that the pigeons were flapping noisily about me. I came to the conclusion that I should not deliberately sabotage my chances of going to Canada, but should at least make an honest attempt to qualify.

I gathered all the best references I could, both personal and professional, and arranged to visit Toronto over Christmas and New Year of 1977-1978.

I arranged for five interviews with different employment agencies and I wrote to the pastors of four churches, letting them know I might be going there to live.

Whilst I still did not want to go to Canada, I would at least give it my best shot, to settle the issue once and for all.

But there was one other thing I did! I put out three fleeces to God.

For those of you who don't know what it means to "put out a fleece," and for those who would benefit from a reminder, I've included the following, as it pertains to my state of mind at that time.

GIDEON'S FLEECE

The following is an article by Alexander Maclaren *in "Expositions of Holy Scripture"*

Behold, I will put a fleece of wool in the floor; and if the dew be on the fleece only, and it be dry upon all the earth beside, then shall I know that Thou wilt save Israel by mine hand, as Thou hast said" (Judges 6:37).

"The decisive moment had come, when Gideon, with his hastily gathered raw levies, was about to plunge down to the plain, to face immensely superior forces trained to do warfare. No wonder the equally untrained leader's heart beat faster. Many a soldier, who will be steadfastly brave in the actual shock of battle, has tremors and throbbings on its eve. Gideon's hand shook a little as he drew his sword.

I. Gideon's Request:

"His petition for a sign was not the voice of unbelief or of doubt or of presumption, but it spoke real, though struggling faith, seeking to be confirmed. Therefore it was not regarded by God as a sin. When a 'wicked and adulterous generation asked for a sign,' no sign was given it, but when faith asks for one to help it to grasp God's hand, and to go on His warfare in His strength and as His instrument, it does not ask in vain.

"Gideon's prayer was wrapped, as it were, in an enfolding promise, for it is preceded and followed by the quotation of words of the Angel of the Lord who had 'looked on him,' and said, 'Go in this thy might and save Israel from the hand of Midian: have not I sent thee?' Prayers that begin and end with 'as Thou hast spoken,' are not likely to be repulsed.

II. God's Answer:

"God wonderfully allows Gideon to dictate the nature of the sign. He stoops to work it both ways, backwards and forwards, as it were. First, the fleece is to be wet and the ground to be dry; then the fleece is to be dry and the ground wet. Miracle was a necessary accompaniment of revelation in those early days, as picture-books are of childhood. But, though we are far enough from being 'men' in Christ, yet we have not the same need for 'childish things' as Gideon and his contemporaries had. We have Christ and the Spirit, and so have a 'word made more sure' than to require signs.

"But still it is true that the same gracious willingness to help a tremulous faith, which carries its tremulousness to God in prayer, moves the Father's heart to-day, and that to such petitions the answer is given even before they are offered: 'Ask what ye will, and it shall be done unto you.' No sign that eyes can see is given, but inward whispers speak assurance and communicate the assurance which they speak.

III. The Meaning of the Sign.

"Many explanations have been offered. The main point is that the fleece is to be made different from the soil around it. It is to be a proof of God's power to endow with characteristics not derived from, and resulting in qualities unlike, the surroundings.

"Gideon had no thought of any significance beyond that. But we may allowably let the Scripture usage of the symbol of dew influence our reading into the symbol a deeper meaning than it bore to him.

"God makes the fleece wet with dew, while all the threshing-floor is dry. Dew is the symbol of divine grace, of the silently formed moisture which, coming from no apparent source, freshens by night the wilted plants, and hangs in myriad drops, that twinkle into green and gold as the early sunshine strikes them, on the humblest twig. That grace is plainly not a natural product nor to be accounted for by environment. The dew of the Spirit, which God and God only, can give, can freshen our worn and drooping souls, can give joy in sorrow, can keep us from being touched by surrounding evils, and from being parched by surrounding drought, can silently 'distil' its supplies of strength according to our need into our else dry hearts.

"The wet fleece on the dry ground was not only a revelation of God's power, but may be taken as a pattern of what God's soldiers must ever be. A prophet long after Gideon said: 'The remnant of Jacob shall be in the midst of many peoples as dew from the Lord,' bringing to others the grace which they have received that they may diffuse it, and turning the dry and thirsty land where no water is into fertility, and the 'parched ground' into a 'pool.'

"We have said that the main point of Gideon's petition was that the fleece should be made unlike the threshing-floor, and that that unlikeness, which could obviously not be naturally brought about, was to be to him the sure token that God was at work to produce it. The strongest demonstration that the Church can give the world of its really being God's Church is its unlikeness to the world. If it is wet with divine dew when all the threshing-floor is dry, and if, when all the floor is drenched with poisonous miasma, it is dry from the diffused and clinging malaria, the world will take knowledge of it, and some souls be set to ask how this unlikeness comes. When Haman has to say: 'There is a certain people scattered abroad and dispersed among the peoples ... and their laws are diverse from those of every people,' he may meditate murder, but 'many from among the people of the land' will join their ranks. Gideon may or may not have thought of the fleece as a symbol of his little host, but we may learn from it the old lesson, 'Be not conformed to this world, but be ye transformed by the renewing of your minds.'"[4]

We must be very careful if we decide to put out a fleece to the Lord. We must not demand anything or think we can bend God's will towards our own.

At that time, my faith was weak; I would say *very* weak. And I was certainly confused. I did *not* want to go to Canada to live, but I *did* want to know what God wanted for me. Although my faith was weak, at least I was smart enough to know that I had reached a very important juncture in my life. I was facing a decision that I had better get right.

I knew that my fleeces needed to make sense. I should not make a mockery of God by saying, for example, "If a 4'11" Japanese admiral knocks on my door at 3:00 a.m. in the morning ..." That would be facetious and disrespectful. So each of my fleeces to the Lord would directly connect to my life and situation.

---

4. *Expositions of Holy Scripture*, by Alexander Maclaren—used by permission

Fleece #1:

A good place to live, preferably in a Christian home, would need to be revealed to me.

My brother and his wife were moving to a town about two hours east of Toronto, so obviously I couldn't live with them. Apart from them, I knew no one else in the city. I felt this was a sensible request pertaining to my social well-being

Fleece #2:

A church where I felt at home would have to be found.

I really liked my church back in Portsmouth, England. Of course it wasn't perfect, but it was vibrant and moving forward with excitement. I think this was a reasonable request pertaining to my spiritual well-being.

Fleece #3:

I did not want to have to work my way up through the ranks again to become a manager, so a managerial position in Toronto would need to be found.

This may have been a little selfish, but I had worked hard to become the manager of an employment agency back in England and I did not want to have to work my way up from a lower level again. I needed to find a job as a manager and it needed to be in Toronto. I think this was a reasonable request pertaining to my physical and professional well-being.

My flight from London to Canada in December, 1977, was delayed for two-and-a-half days, so I did not arrive at my brother's home in Markham until Christmas Eve.

It was then I learned that my brother, Doug, had talked to his wife's sister about my need for lodging. Her boyfriend's brother and wife attended The Peoples Church and they had a room I could rent for $100 a month in the Beaches area.

So, fleece #1 was answered.

Of the four churches I had written to, only one had reciprocated by writing to me at my brother's address. The pastor of that church even phoned my brother a couple of times to see if I had arrived safely. That pastor was Rev. Ralph Rutledge of Queensway Cathedral—so I went to his church on Sunday and slipped in, unobtrusively, at the back. Queensway Cathedral had a very vibrant music ministry. During the worship time, I closed my eyes and experienced the wonderful recognition of the same Holy Spirit in Toronto as I experienced back in England. I felt at home.

Fleece #2 was ticked off.

That left only the third fleece, but I was not too worried as I was sure I would not be able to land a managerial position at a Toronto employment agency.

I attended interview after interview after interview, and found it interesting to be interviewed with zero stress, as I didn't want a job anyway. Nevertheless, in the same spirit of honesty, effort and integrity I had applied to the previous processes, I did not, in any way, sabotage the interviews, but because I was completely relaxed, I guess I exuded confidence.

However, the agencies were either not hiring at that time or saw my lack of experience in Canada as a hindrance. I have since learned that this is the biggest stumbling block for people from overseas trying to land jobs in Canada. It doesn't seem to matter what one's qualification are or how much job experience one has. If he or she has not worked in Canada, one can't get past the front door.

The conundrum was that I couldn't get a job unless I had Canadian experience, but the only way to get Canadian experience was to get a job ... but I couldn't get a job unless I had Canadian experience ... and so the merry-go-round went round and round.

Yes, there was one company, Drake Personnel, who called me back, no less than five times, to be interviewed by five different people, but by Friday evening (I was flying back to the UK on Sunday) when I had heard nothing more from them, I began to feel relieved and safe that I would not be going to have to live in Canada.

But then it happened!

That Friday evening, my brother, his wife and I were due to go out for a meal, but we were delayed in leaving by about an hour. Just as we were going out the door, there was a telephone call. Pausing to consider whether or not we should answer, we answered and my life changed completely.

The caller was a Mr. Earl Matthews from Montreal. He was the Canadian National Manager of a company called Technical Overload. As a division of Drake Personnel International, they dealt with permanent and contract placements of people in highly skilled professions—everything from mining engineers to the people who operate the Hubble telescope.

Mr. Matthews had been working late, reading the transcripts of the five interviews I had had with people in his organization. Apparently, he was hugely impressed. Even though I did not have specific experience in the areas that were needed, he felt that, because of my track record, I would be quickly assimilated into the Canadian culture and quickly become a valued member of "his team," as he put it.

My brother was waving at me to hurry, as we were late for our dinner reservations, but Mr. Matthews wanted an immediate answer. I was thinking, "It has to be a managerial position, and it has to be in Toronto"—the final fleece.

I closed my eyes and asked Mr. Matthews exactly what job he was offering me, and where it would be.

He said, "I would like to offer you the job as Manager of the Toronto office of Technical Overload, situated in the Manulife Centre in downtown Toronto."

I was stunned! This was *not* what I wanted. But what could I do? All three fleeces had been answered.

My brother and his wife were thrilled for me, but all I could feel was a numbness mingled with fear. It all overwhelmed me. Nevertheless, I did not have time to dwell too much on it, as Technical Overload wanted me to start as soon as possible. Within one week, I was back in Canada, having angered my former employers in England and dumbfounded my friends, most of whom thought I was crazy to do what I was doing.

This was the first time in my life that I had dared to ask God to show me, in a specific manner, exactly what His will was for me. Strangely, there has never again been an occasion when I felt it was right to lay out a fleece before God in that same way.

I think, as my faith has grown stronger, I have felt more able to discern God's will for me. Certainly my wife and I have faced several situations where we have had to make firm, pragmatic decisions after much prayer—and often fasting.

It seems to me that the older we get and the stronger our faith becomes, there is less likelihood of needing to do something like putting out a fleece in order to determine God's will.

Nevertheless, I am thankful for that experience and how it built up my faith at a time when it was badly in need of a boost. People may want to criticize my decision-making process, but they can never deny the results. Personal experience trumps the impersonal opinions of other people.

So now I was in Toronto. Other than my brother and his wife, I knew no one.

On my first Sunday in the city, I attended the morning service at Queensway Cathedral. There, God was gracious in showing me more evidence of His love.

I found myself seated beside a lady who had a very good singing voice. During a time when the congregation was encouraged to greet whomever they were seated next to, I (perhaps audaciously) commented to this lady that, as her singing voice was so good, perhaps she should join the choir; whereupon she laughed heartily and, hearing my very pronounced English accent, asked if I were in Toronto for a holiday and whether I was at the church with friends.

I said, "No, I am here alone and this is my first Sunday."

The service continued. It was very good and confirmed my earlier feeling that I was going to enjoy attending that place of worship.

At the end of the service, as we rose to leave, the lady turned to me and said, "My husband is away preaching in Vancouver. My brothers and their families are coming over for lunch and my eldest daughter is bringing over her fiancé[5], to whom she has just become engaged. Why don't you come and join us?"

Well, I had no plans and, although I knew nothing about these people and they knew nothing about me, I could see no reason to decline this kind offer. So, in my nice, new, silver-grey Pontiac Grand Prix (a perk of my new job), I followed the lady to her home in the suburbs of Toronto, a place called Mississauga. (While Mississauga is really a city in it's own right, the greater Toronto area—the GTA— melds into one big metropolis.)

From what I was accustomed to, by English standards, the lady's home was rather

---

[5] I have just discovered that, when referring to a man, the word is spelled with one 'e' as in 'fiancé,' but when referring to a female, the word is spelled with two 'e's,' as in 'fiancée. I never knew that! It's good to discover new things, however trivial they may be.

large; although, in the coming weeks I realized it was not exceptionally large by Canadian standards. Nevertheless, I was very impressed.

When I walked into the house, I was introduced all around by the lady and welcomed with a warmth and enthusiasm that I had never experienced before. It was as though I was the returning, long-lost prodigal son. Maybe I am exaggerating a little bit, but these people made me feel instantly at home. It was exactly what I needed at that time in my life, as I was feeling somewhat "all-at-sea," having launched off into the great unknown.

And then I made an amazing discovery! One of this lady's brothers was none other than Rev. Ralph Rutledge, the only pastor who had called my brother to see if I had arrived safely for Christmas.

Needless to say, there was much rejoicing as we all realized the hand of God at work. You may call it a coincidence if you wish but, as for me, there were way too many disparate pieces coming together for this to be a coincidence.

So, who was this lady who invited a perfect stranger to her home for Sunday lunch—albeit with the safety of her large family all being there?

Some of you may have already guessed. It was Norma-Jean Mainse, the wife of Rev. David Mainse, the founder and host of a daily Christian television ministry that is highly respected for its integrity, professionalism and faithful adherence to the Word of God. David and Norma-Jean's genuine humility is such that they would not like me to say this, but to the Christian community, they are almost like royalty. They have weathered many storms of adversity but have shone forth as worthy examples of Christian love, compassion and humility.

It was interesting because when they were telling me about their flagship television program, *100 Huntley Street*, it really meant nothing to me. Coming from England, I had no concept of what a daily Christian television program was.

Arriving later that afternoon, Norma-Jean and David's eldest daughter, Elaine, and her husband-to-be, Bruce Stacey, were introduced. Bruce and I became firm friends and he ended up being my best man when I was married.

Exactly one year after my January 27, 1978, arrival in Canada, I married Ginny Ambrose on January 27, 1979, at The Peoples Church in Toronto.

And what had happened in the intervening year?

The work at Technical Overload was overwhelming. I felt totally out of my depth. Every day, when I drove to work, I would say to the Lord, "Lord, I'm scared. I don't know what I am doing here, but because I know You brought me to Canada, I'm going to trust You to help me." My dependence on Him was total.

One day, a rather cheerful, very overweight man walked into my office in the Manual Life Centre at Bay and Bloor in downtown Toronto. He was a political analyst who, whenever there was a major national or provincial election, was in great demand because of his vast knowledge. He had no particular political affiliation, so he would work for whatever party grabbed him first, offering the best money. Between elections, he would hire himself out as a consultant to whatever employment agency was willing to take him on. To me, he was an answer to prayer; so I hired him as a consultant.

Through his extensive contacts, he learned (before it hit the news) that some mining operations in Northern Ontario would be laying off some highly skilled mining engineers. At the same time, he knew of some mining operations in Saskatchewan that were expanding and needed men of exactly the same skills and experience as those who were being laid off in Ontario.

At that time, back in 1978, employment agencies such as Technical Overload could not get a license to operate in Saskatchewan; so, working with the mining companies in Northern Ontario, the mining companies in Saskatchewan and the Saskatchewan Provincial Government, we constructed a deal that satisfied all the requirements of the provincial laws, making everyone winners—especially those miners who would have lost their jobs.

Sadly, my consultant was so large that he could not fly out to Saskatoon for all the negotiations. However, he prepped me well and I learned quickly about the intricacies and pitfalls of such complex, potentially lucrative deals.

It would have been easy to take the credit for this, but I was well aware that my only contribution was being in the right place at the right time. Who had put me there? God.

At the church, Queensway Cathedral, I planned to join the orchestra, playing the trumpet I had brought over from England, but at the first rehearsal, sitting between two horn players who were so good they blew me away, I knew I would never reach their standard—even if I practised for several hours each day—so I joined the choir.

At that time, the choir was under the direction of Don Newman, a truly wonderful man. To my surprise, I was invited to audition for a six-person singing group called "The Third Day." The services at Queensway Cathedral were broadcast on television weekly in southern Ontario, and this group was formed to play an integral part in those broadcasts.

To my surprise, I was selected as the second tenor. My ability to blend, which I had learned as a youngster in the Salvation Army, undoubtedly helped. What I was totally unprepared for was that we would meet on a Thursday night, at which time a brand new song would be introduced. Three days later, we would sing that same song, live on television, with no words or music in front of us.

Again, it was a case of, "Lord, I am completely out of my depth. Help!"

Another challenge in the church was contending with those wonderful ladies whose marriages were so good they felt it was their duty to pair up any eligible candidates. I became a prime target of the church's unofficial matchmakers.

In their defence, their interest was probably natural. I was twenty-nine; in good shape; good looking (according to my wife) with a good job; earning great money; and driving a cool, two-door Pontiac Grand Prix, a mid-sized sports car. Okay, I'm exaggerating, maybe the car wasn't exactly a sports car, but it was new and it was cool. Add what they called an "adorable" English accent to the mix and they had the recipe for "good husband material."

Seriously, I had no intention of getting married. Holidays to exotic destinations such as Hawaii had been out of reach for an Englishman earning a modest salary in the UK. But now I was geographically closer and earning the kind of money that would make a holiday in Hawaii doable. I didn't want to complicate my life with marriage; well sure, one day, but not now. There were a lot of beautiful girls in Toronto from many different countries. I didn't feel any need to hurry. It was Honolulu, here I come!

How quickly, when things start to go well, we can forget that if God's hand has been clearly evident in our lives, there's a reason.

In my mind, I was happy to be involved in church—up to a level that did not demand too much. While singing in The Third Day was musically demanding, it brought me a certain notoriety and I enjoyed the attention. I knew I definitely did not want to be involved in full-time ministry. The idea of becoming a missionary was not for me.

But God had other plans.

At that time, the auditorium at Queensway Cathedral was semi-circular. One night, at a training meeting for counsellors who would be involved in an upcoming Billy Graham Crusade, I looked across the auditorium—and saw an angel. It was love at first sight.

Her beautiful, smiling face was framed by gorgeous long, thick, blonde, wavy hair. My attraction to her was all the more amazing to me because I always thought I would marry a dusky-skinned, dark-haired Brazilian type—but again, God had other ideas.

The way we were

First of all, I needed to make sure she was not taller than me. Standing at a compact five foot, seven-and-a-half inches tall (don't forget the half inch), I could not go out with a girl who was taller. Allowing three inches for shoes with heels, I had to find someone who was under five foot, four inches—not that I was looking!

So, when we were invited to go to the foyer of the church to sign forms to be counsellors, I went back there and waited until I could stand beside her. Even though I had a row of pens in my inside jacket pocket, I asked if I could borrow her pen. She flashed me a heart-melting smile and I was done. Anyone who has seen Ginny's smile will know exactly what I mean. It will light up any room.

At that time, I had no clue that only six months later, we would be walking down the aisle together. Five days after our first date, I asked her to marry me; she said yes.

The story of our whirlwind courtship will have to wait for another day because, for the purpose of this chapter, I need to stay within the context of my first year in Canada.

In the September of 1978, I had arranged for Dave Pope, a gospel singer friend of mine from the UK, to come and do a mini tour of Toronto. Bruce Stacey helped me put together a live band.

I was unaware that David and Norma-Jean had been quietly observing me. The result was that I was invited to join the television ministry of *100 Huntley Street* in several capacities, including booking the television audience and organizing live rallies and crusades to be held in hockey arenas across Canada.

I started to work for *100 Huntley Street* in October of 1978. Ginny started to fill several roles there in November: secretary to the head of production, head make-up artist and staff singer, singing frequently on the program.

Then came our wedding at The Peoples Church, January 27, 1979, exactly one year to the day since I had arrived in Canada. Dr. Paul Smith officiated, assisted by Rev. Ralph Rutledge.

What a year! What a change!

Why me? Honestly, I sometimes still ask myself that question.

Everything I *didn't* want, came to pass:

I was living in Canada.	• I became a citizen. I now have dual citizenship.
I was married.	• As I write this, I've been married over thirty-five happy years.
I was married to a blonde.	• But oh, so beautiful! And Ginny loves me to an extent that I still don't think I deserve.
I was in full-time ministry.	• Our ministry has, so far, taken us to over thirty countries on three continents.

As I look at my computer screen, after reading what I have written, I have a fresh recognition of how awesome God is. There is so much more I could tell of His goodness, but no words could ever be enough. He is faithful to those who will truly put their trust in Him.

There is a saying, "God doesn't call the qualified, but He qualifies the called."

I left school when I was sixteen-years-old. I had no further education other than life itself. If God can use me, He can use anyone. If I were to tell of some of the tasks He now has me fulfill for Him, many would find it hard to believe. But those stories are for another day.

3

RUSSIAN HOSPITALITY

It is sad but true, that stereotypical views about the peoples of certain nationalities abound.

We English are pompous. The Scottish are tight with their money. Canadians are always apologizing. Americans are loud. The French are rude to foreigners. And the list goes on.

Let me be honest and say right now that I just don't like the French—but let me add quickly that every French person I know is a really nice person. I have wonderful friends who are French. Personally, I have never actually met a French person who I had cause not to like. So why do I say I do not like the French? Is it in my DNA? Or have I been conditioned by someone else's opinion?

In the film *French Kiss,* starring Meg Ryan and Kevin Kline, there is a scene where Meg is dealing with a concierge in a hotel in Paris. It is a very funny scene, but it says it all where the general opinion of the French and Americans are concerned.

The French concierge comes across as rude and uncooperative, whilst the American (Meg Ryan) comes across as loud and demanding. Each falls neatly into a preconceived slot.

As for me? Well, historically, England and France were at war for the infamous One Hundred Years' War, but that ended in 1453; surely that cannot be the source of my instinctive dislike towards the French—could it?

Well, from an article in *HistoryToday* referring to that One Hundred Years' War, I quote, "The long struggle powerfully strengthened the sense of national identity in both England and France, and created a mutual antagonism which has lasted ever since."

Lasted ever since 1453? That's over 560 years ago! Should we not have grown up and buried the proverbial hatchet by now?

I hate to say it, but I am aware of this antagonism lurking somewhere in the depths of my psyche. It lies dormant almost all the time, and yet, sadly, the slightest reaffirmation of my deeply ingrained, predispositional dislike of the French brings this antagonism bubbling—unwanted and unbidden—to the surface.

Okay. I have to confess that I feel the same way about Germans, too, despite the fact that Ginny and I have many German friends, all of whom are wonderful people. We even worked in Germany, on one occasion, for over two months, and we had a wonderful time. Sure, they have their quirks, but don't we all?

Actually, my disdain for Germans has nothing to do with the two wars in which my grandfather, and then my father, fought. It has everything to do with the fact that the Germans have this nasty habit of seemingly always beating England at that beautiful game that we invented and gave to the world: football (soccer). Those German soccer players have no respect. You would think they would let us win once in a while.

And—whatever you do—don't get me going on the subject of the Argentineans.

Ever since the Falklands/Malvinas war in 1982, a seventy-two-day conflict that saw Britain retake the Falklands Island during an Argentinean invasion, I have an unreasonable aversion to people from Argentina. That brief war cost at least $2 billion and the lives of 236 British and 655 Argentine troops—and Argentina has never formally surrendered. Because it was a war that was never 'declared' by either side, there is no mechanism for surrender. It remains a festering sore between the two nations, a sore that is reopened every time England and Argentina face each other in competition on a football pitch.

Which brings us to the 1986 World Cup football match between England and Argentina, when the Argentinean player, Maradona, scored a goal clearly by punching the ball with his hand, a clear infraction of the rules seen by, apparently, everyone in the world except the referee. To add insult to injury, Maradona claimed it was "the hand of God." My goodness! What bare-faced sacrilegious audacity!

But, once again, despite all this, I do know several Argentineans and they are amongst the most gracious people I have ever met.

I think we can discern from this that people in themselves are good and decent, but when herded and manipulated by political agendas, they can, collectively, become obnoxious. If we were to scratch under the surface of most people, we would discover that everyone has a certain nation whose people irritate them.

But what about the Russians? Ah yes—the Russians—perhaps everyone's whipping boys. To understand Russia and Russians, one has to understand its size, its population density, and its geographical position in relation to other nations. As by far the largest nation on our planet, the land mass of Russia is almost double that of Canada (the second largest nation in the world). It is approximately double the size of China, of the USA, of Brazil and three times the size of India.

Next, compare the population density of Russian with that of other countries. It has eight people per square kilometre compared to Brazil's twenty-two, the USA's thirty-one, China's 136, and India's 329. Canada trails a long way behind with just three people per square kilometre. Russia has a lot of land but, relatively speaking, not a lot of people.

Now consider that there are an amazing seventy-two—yes, seventy-two—languages spoken in Russia. It is an isolated, fractured nation that has seen only a modicum of prosperity and self-respect when ruthlessly governed by a dictatorial, iron hand.

We in the West think we know Russia, but we don't.

Let's face it, the opinions of many of us concerning Russia are tainted by James Bond and other such films, espionage books and snippets in the news.

Instead of asking the question "What are Russians really like?" let me rearrange the words a bit and ask this question: "What are *real* Russians like?"

I had an utterly amazing experience a few years ago, that gave me profound insight into what a real Russian can be like.

While presenting the drama "Heaven's Gates and Hell's Flames" all over Europe, on many occasions, I had to travel to those countries first to meet potential organizers.

On the occasion in question, I was in Moscow meeting with such people. I then had to fly down to a city called Krasnodar, way down south, almost on the Black Sea, for a few days of meetings. I was scheduled to then fly to Vienna via Moscow. From Vienna, I would be driving to Bratislava, the capital city of Slovakia.

My connecting flight from Krasnodar through Moscow to Vienna necessitated an overnight stay in Moscow; so my flights were arranged to get me to Moscow by late afternoon.

Hailing taxis from any of the Moscow airports was a very precarious proposition because most of the taxis were controlled by the local mafia and they would charge whatever they wanted. They would take greatest advantage of the Western tourists or businessmen who always had plenty of US dollars, the favoured foreign currency. (This was in the days before the Euro supplanted the US dollar as the most favoured foreign currency in Eastern Europe.)

From experience, we had learned that it was best, before flying out of Moscow, to find a trusted, private taxi driver (one who was not controlled by the local mafia) and arrange for him to meet my incoming flight and take me to the hotel where I had booked a reservation. This was done, the price negotiated ahead of time, and the collection point and time arranged.

However, my return flight from Krasnodar to Moscow was badly delayed because of mechanical problems with the plane. Consequently, I did not arrive in Moscow until just after twelve midnight—over eight hours later than I had arranged for the taxi driver to meet me. As my flight neared Moscow, my anxiety increased as I contemplated having to try to deal with mafia taxi drivers.

You can imagine my amazement when I walked out of the arrival hall of Sheremetyevo airport to discover that my taxi driver had patiently waited for me. With no fuss, he loaded my suitcase into his rusty, dilapidated cab and we drove off towards the centre of Moscow, where I was booked into a hotel on the Garden Ring, one of the inner ring roads that circumvented the centre core of Moscow.

As we approached the hotel some thirty minutes later, I thought the front looked a little dark; it appeared to be devoid of any lights. It was not a very welcoming sight and we soon discovered that, in fact, the hotel was closed.

Apparently, in those days, the hotels, unless one were staying at one of the very expensive international chain hotels, would close at about 11:00 p.m. and if any of the guests were not in their rooms—well, that was just too bad.

So there I was, stuck in Moscow after 1:00 a.m. with a taxi driver who spoke no English—and I spoke no Russian. Going to one of the expensive hotels was out of the question. What was I to do? I had to be back at the airport at 7:00 a.m. for an 8:00 a.m. flight to Vienna.

I briefly considered going back to the airport and sleeping on a bench, but that was not an attractive idea, as I had heard, and read, of people doing that in the Moscow airport and being mugged as they slept.

As it happened, the decision was taken quickly out of my hands as my taxi driver, jabbering at me incoherently, had obviously made a sudden decision. Without consulting me, he proceeded to carry out his plan. I soon realized I was being driven away from the city centre and way out into the Moscow suburbs—whether it was north, south, east or west, I had no idea.

I remember thinking, "Better the devil you know than the devil you don't know." But I could hardly wait for a traffic light to jump out of the taxi. Now I knew that could well have been a case of jumping out of the frying pan and into the fire, so I stayed in the relative safety of the taxi cab.

So it was that after twenty minutes of hair-raising driving, we drove into what I can only describe as a forest of high-rise buildings, twenty to thirty stories high.

In Eastern Europe, behind the Iron Curtain, they seem to have this strange ability to build instant slums. They try to make them look bright and modern, but the finishing work on the buildings is so awful that, even as new buildings, they still look dilapidated.

There was no landscaping; the lower windows were mostly broken; and the sidewalks and poorly marked streets were littered dangerously with leftover building materials. There was a pervading, unpleasant smell hanging in the air from a neighbouring factory that—even at night—was belching forth yellow smoke.

The only colour to this scenario was provided by the ever-present graffiti plastered on the buildings in indecipherable Russian with a few choice expletives in English. It's funny how certain words seem to transcend culture and language.

Pulling up outside of one of these architectural monstrosities, with other similar buildings looming dangerously close, my taxi driver motioned for me to get out of his car while he proceeded to remove the wiper blades, which he then locked in his boot (trunk). He then urged me to follow him quickly, as he staggered under the weight of my suitcase that he insisted he carry for me.

My options had disappeared; I was fully committed to whatever was going to happen, although I had no idea what that might be.

When we entered the apartment building, the smell that assaulted my nostrils was a strong urine smell that made me gag and almost throw up. Fortunately, there was nothing in my stomach, the last food I had eaten being a hard bread roll at Krasnodar Airport, some ten hours earlier.

The taxi driver ran past the broken, caved-in elevator doors, racing out of sight up the stairs. What was the big hurry?

The stairs were dangerously chipped and unsafe. Lit only by the ambient light of moonlight that was intermittently shrouded by passing clouds, there was nothing to warn of the human detritus littering the stairs, amongst broken furniture and discarded toys.

The man forged ahead, dragging my suitcase with him, while I huffed and puffed behind. Although he was out of sight, I had to make sure he never got out of earshot.

Although, in my naïveté, it did not cross my mind that, as I was told later, while we were running from the car to the twenty-seventh—yes, twenty-seventh—floor, we were exposed to danger from any number of marauding gangs—either those organized by the local mafia or those independent gangs who competed with the mafia for the available spoils.

If I had known that at the time, I think I would have run up those stairs even faster.

Nevertheless, totally out of breath, I stood, finally, at the door to his apartment. I doubled over, gasping to refill my lungs with the putrid, probably toxic, air. The door itself looked like a prop in a horror movie. It was at least twelve inches thick, studded, covered with quilted imitation leather, and sported a peep hole.

But that door was important to this man. It was the demarcation line that separated the world of chaos outside, in which he fought to survive, from the relative peace and safety of the home he had created; an inner sanctum where he kidded himself about the communist authorities not being able to reach. It was an illusion, but it was the best he could come up with, considering his meagre resources.

The next few moments were like a scene in a slapstick comedy routine.

As the taxi driver urged me into the apartment so he could close and secure the door, he was shouting in agitated Russian (which, of course, I could not understand). Then another voice—a high-pitched, agitated, female voice—joined the cacophony. As the outer door slammed behind me, there suddenly appeared a barely-clad lady with huge rollers in her hair. Upon seeing me, her voice changed from mere agitation to an ear-piercing scream; at which time, she leapt back into the bedroom.

I was left standing there, wishing I could wake up from this nightmare.

The man ushered me into his combined kitchen/dinning-room/lounge. After seeing me safely seated, he went off to placate his wife. I heard a lot of muffled, excited discussion before he finally returned with his wife in tow. She had made a valiant effort to fix her hair and put on some make-up. I say "valiant," but the word should probably be "unsuccessful." At least she was now fully clothed, affording her some reasonable dignity.

The three of us sat there for a few moments, looking awkwardly at each other, until finally the lady decided I needed something to eat. She started pulling pots and pans from her cupboards and food from her pantry and tiny fridge.

By now, it was close to two o'clock in the morning. All I wanted was to sleep, as we would have to leave in about four hours to get to the airport. But no, the lady was determined that this total stranger was going to be shown some Russian hospitality—whether he liked it or not.

And wouldn't you know, out came the Vodka. I don't mind the occasional glass of white wine, but from my misspent youth I had a healthy dislike for vodka.

But I was in a difficult situation.

This Russian couple were showing me extraordinary kindness. Not wanting to be culturally offensive, I felt the least I could do was show my gratitude by not declining their hospitality.

As the man and I each downed our measure of vodka in one gulp, with great gusto, he said something to me in Russian. Although I had no idea what he was saying, I replied, "Na zda-ró-vye!"

I don't think that was quite the right 'thank you' to use, but after a brief moment of shock, the man and his wife roared in laughter. They were so pleased that I could speak some of their beloved language beyond "da" and "nyet." He slapped me on the back, so hard I thought my teeth would fall out, and before I knew it, he had poured two more measures of vodka.

The food—fried eggs, potatoes, some kind of meat, cheese and sweet dumplings—and vodka—flowed and mingled with lots of laughter as we used pantomime to try and communicate.

The first vodka felt like it would burn a hole in my stomach; the second sent a surge of warmth all over my body; by the third and fourth, I began to understand why people who live in such poverty and desperate political climate, with no hope, would retreat into drinking vodka to give them temporary release from the harsh reality of their lives.

We laughed until our sides hurt as we pantomimed what we all did for a living. It turned out that the man drove a taxi only because, after serving in the Russian military, he was unable to get a civilian job as a trained electrician. The wife was a qualified hairdresser, but because she could not get a job in an official hair salon, she did hair in her home for ladies in the area. Sadly, she lived in constant fear that if the authorities found out—if someone told on her—she would spend years in prison as punishment. Corruption is rife in Russia and everyone seems to live in abject fear of something.

But then something quite amazing happened.

When it came my turn to communicate to them what I did, I really didn't know how to explain it—not until I noticed a religious icon prominently displayed on the wall. At the time, I was an ordained minister in the UK, so I thought the simplest thing would be for me to declare that as my profession—without trying to go into the complexities of all the things I did as an ordained minister.

I pointed at "the holy person" in the picture and then pointed at myself. The couple at first looked shocked, but then started to treat me with a deference that was almost embarrassing. In their minds, "a holy man" was in their apartment. Then they blew me away by indicating that they wanted me to pray for them.

I sobered up real fast!

Seated at the kitchen table, we held hands and I prayed for them in English. Then they said a little prayer in Russian.

When I looked up, after ending the prayer, I could see they had been crying. We hugged and cried together some more.

Then Hebrews 13:2 came to mind. *"Be not forgetful to entertain strangers: for thereby some have entertained angels unawares"* (KJV).

That simple Russian couple had shown extraordinary kindness to a stranger in need. The twist ... could it be that on that day God used me, flawed as I am, to be His angel in that situation?

As I am writing this, a thought has come to me that I cannot substantiate. But wouldn't it be wonderful if, way in the future when I get to heaven, I discover this dear Russian couple is also there? My, what a celebration we would have. And we wouldn't need any vodka.

Well, I have no idea how late I went to sleep that morning on the bed they made up for me on their couch, but it seemed no sooner had my eyes shut, than my taxi driver friend was shaking me so I could wake up and get ready to go to the airport. He got me there in good time for my flight to Vienna.

Before I left their apartment that morning, I tried to pay my new friend for his taxi rides and their kind hospitality, but he vehemently declined any money.

During the ride to the airport, I slipped some US dollars in an envelope and insisted that he take the envelope. I managed to communicate to him that the envelope was from God—not from me. It was my hope that he would be thrilled at how the Lord had, in return, blessed him and his wife.

And that will forever be my endearing image and memory of Russia and some wonderful Russian people.

UKRAINIAN HOSPITALITY

In the heat of one summer, we were pulling our equipment trailer behind our van from Poland (where we were living at the time) to Krasnodar in southern Russia to present the drama "Heaven's Gates and Hell's Flames."

Our good friends Czarek and Jola Wojtasik, the Polish "Heaven's Gates and Hell's Flames" team, were travelling with us. Also with us was another guy who would guide us through the Ukraine. He knew some Christians there, in whose homes we would be able to stay on the two nights we would need overnight accommodation.

It was a challenging drive through Ukraine, as the roads were not good and gas stations were very sparse. In the early evening of the first day, we drove into a Ukrainian village that looked like a movie set for the film *Fiddler On The Roof*. The local people were dressed from that bygone era, to the extent that we half expected to see a cheerful, beefy man come walking around the corner singing "If I Were A Rich Man."

Our Ukrainian hosts insisted we drive the van and trailer right into the muddy yard of their little farm so the high wooden gate could be closed, thus obscuring the van and trailer from prying eyes. When we were safely parked, there was not much room left in the yard, much to the dislike of an unbelievably ragged old dog who had only one eye and who drooled constantly. His incessant yapping left no question that he did not appreciate us invading his territory. Thankfully, he was safely chained at the far end of the yard, but as it was a small yard, it was still too close for my liking.

We went into the farmhouse, which was situated on the right of the yard, and enjoyed a wonderful, home-cooked, Ukrainian meal. I don't know what it was, but it was hot and it tasted good.

We were told that the toilet facilities were in the barn situated across the yard. We would see the door with the wooden latch and should be prepared for the bad smell, as it was basically a hole in the ground.

So we prepared for bed.

Ginny and I, with Jola and Czarek, would be sleeping in the same room where we all ate. Apparently, it doubled as the bedroom and the main living room. We had no idea where our hosts were sleeping.

We gave Czarek and Jola the tiny bed, while Ginny slept in a large chair and I slept (or tried to sleep) on a flat, sheet metal table. At least it was naturally cold, so it served as a kind of air-conditioning for me, providing a slight respite from the summer heat.

During the night I had to answer a call of nature, so I stepped out of the farm house and into the yard. It was one of those moonless, starless, black nights where one could hardly see anything beyond one's own nose.

I was very conscious of not wanting to awaken the wild dog, which I knew to be off to my right. I most certainly wanted to "let sleeping dogs lie."

Here is an aside. Have you ever wondered where that saying comes from?

> *Like one who grabs a stray dog by the ears is someone who rushes into a quarrel not their own* (Proverbs 26:17 NIV).

> *He that passeth by, and meddleth with strife belonging not to him, is like one that taketh a dog by the ears* (Proverbs 26:17 KJV).

> *"It is nought good a slepyng hound to wake"*[6] is said to be a phrase originated by Chaucer around 1380, in *Troilus and Criseyde*. The NIV and the KJV say it somewhat differently, but are echoed by Chaucer in meaning one shouldn't stir up a potentially difficult situation when it's best left alone.

Leaving that dog well alone was uppermost in my mind as I inched my way as quietly and carefully as I could in the dense blackness of that night ... around the left side of the yard, past our van and trailer.

---

[6] Chaucer, *Troilus and Criseyde*, around 1380 (The spelling back then was strange.)

When I reached the barn, I felt my way around it until I came to the door with the wooden latch. It was even blacker inside than it had been outside ... but, oh my ... the smell. They had definitely not exaggerated about how bad it was.

It was impossible to breathe. I started to gag ... and it was then, as my eyes slowly adjusted to the dim light, I saw I was standing with my nose no more than an inch from ... the rear end of a cow!

I had gone through the wrong door.

My concern now was to not wake up this cow, which, if disturbed, could have done me way more harm than the dog. Very slowly, very carefully, very quietly, I backed out of that place and gently re-latched the door.

Quite some time had elapsed since my initial call of nature, so when I eventually found the correct door, one could say I was relieved, indeed.

I was always amazed by the hospitality of these simple Ukrainian people, and I use the word *simple* in the most affectionate, respectful way.

Our second night, now in Crimea, was no different, as the people opened up their homes, their hearts and their kitchens and welcomed us with genuine, generous warmth.

This, too, was an old farmhouse, the doors of which were so narrow that we had to turn sideway to get through them. This night, Ginny and I were sleeping in another living room/bedroom on chairs that folded down into small, cramped beds. Jola and Czarek were with another family. Again, we had no idea where the host family slept that night.

The toilet facilities consisted of the customary hole-in-the-ground outhouse at the bottom of the garden.

On this night, it was Ginny who had the call of nature, but she woke me up somewhat frantically when she discovered that we were, in fact, locked in the farmhouse.

At first we could not believe it, but we soon realized there was no way we could get out. We were locked in the farmhouse—alone.

What could we do?

Well, a girl's gotta do what a girl's gotta do. When the forces of nature "press on," one has to improvise. Finding a large bowl in the kitchen, she lined it with toilet paper, a well-known missionary staple we always carried with us. Then Ginny— well—filled it and then covered it with more of our toilet paper.

Wrinkling your nose? Well, what would *you* have done?

The bowl stayed with us until we were "released" in the morning. At which time, Ginny surreptitiously took it to the outhouse and emptied it. She then took it back into the house and thoroughly cleaned it in hot water and the detergent which she always carried in our van.

At one point, Czarek came by and asked Ginny what she was doing. To which, she replied tersely, "Don't ask."

We laughed a lot about that later.

Coming the night after my exploits in the barn, these were two eventful days.

With lots of smiles and hugs, we finally said our goodbyes to these wonderful people whom we shall likely never see again this side of heaven. Although we may not remember names, we shall never forget how they showered God's love on us, giving what little they had to give.

Christians belong to a truly amazing family.

The next time missionaries share at your church, you can be sure there are things they cannot share from the platform—or in the restaurant over a meal, or in your home should you be billeting them.

Actually, the best stories I've ever heard are those shared when missionaries and pastors get together for a meal after a meeting. You have to be careful with some of them. There is a guy I know well (we'll call him John to protect the guilty) whom I stop before he starts. I say, "John, please wait until next year—or even the year after that—before you tell me the story. By then, it will be much better."

However, please be assured that, when you commit your stories to print, you have to be sure the facts are accurate and the details are correct.

There's no allowance for "evangelasticity."

5

BE AN ENCOURAGER!

My early years were spent in the north of England just outside of Manchester. When I was about six, we moved down to live in Southampton on the south coast. It was almost like moving to a different country, especially as my thick Lancashire accent could barely be understood by the southerners.

One day at school, the teacher announced that we were to stand up, one at a time, and state what we wanted to be when we grew up. The girls wanted to be nurses, teachers or secretaries; whilst the boys wanted the usual macho professions, such as soldier, fireman, policeman and, of course, football player (known as soccer among my North American friends).

Imagine my excitement as I waited for my turn. You see, I wanted to be something completely different from everyone else.

My Auntie Iris had married a man from Holland at the end of the Second World War. My Dutch cousins amazed me at how, even though they were young, they could speak English very well (thanks to the progressive policy of the Dutch education system). Consequently, as a little boy, I decided that I not only wanted to learn the Dutch language, but I wanted to learn other languages too. I had found the word, "linguist" to describe the person I wanted to be.

So when my turn came and the teacher said, "Well Terry, what do you want to be when you grow up?' I stood up with great excitement, puffed out my chest with pride and declared in my thick northern accent, "I want to be a *linguist*."

Well, the teacher threw her head back and roared in laughter, saying, "You could never be a linguist; you can't even speak English properly."

I slumped back into my seat with the laughter of the teacher and the other children ringing in my ears. I was humiliated and devastated. My dream had been crushed.

I have often wondered what might have happened if that teacher, instead of ridiculing my accent, had spoken a word of encouragement.

I did not think ill of that teacher, but I do recall determining that I would never crush anyone. Somewhere in my subconscious, I decided I would be an encourager of people rather than a destroyer of dreams. I didn't want to be a positive thinking guru, but rather a quiet encourager.

I never did learn another language, but I do find that I like to quietly and unobtrusively encourage people for, as it says in Proverbs 25:11, "The right word at the right time is like golden apples in silver jewellery."

I hope this book, while entertaining and even challenging you, will also encourage you on your journey.

In Continental Europe they like to tell this joke:

Q. What do you call a man who speaks three languages?

A. Trilingual.

Q. What do you call a man who speaks two languages?

A. Bilingual.

Q. And what do you call a man who speaks just one language?

A. An Englishman.

That's me ... an Englishman to the core!

6

THE MAN WITH NO NAME
GUARDING HANDBAGS

It's amazing how the smallest, seemingly most innocuous, event can set into motion a line of thinking that produces a story such as this. Stay with me and you will see how all the dots connect.

As the fog rolled gently in off the Adriatic Sea, October 14, 1944, it was a cold day in the once beautiful town of Rimini, which lay on the northern Adriatic coast of Italy. The town lay in ruins after a fierce battle a few weeks earlier between the retreating German Army and the British Eighth Army under the command of General Montgomery. Montgomery was most famous for his defeat of the German General Rommel—the Desert Fox—at El Alamein in the North African desert.

The Germans were in a full but highly disciplined retreat up the entire length of Italy, making the Allies—in this instance, British, Canadian, and Greek soldiers— pay dearly for every mile surrendered.

But in the lull of battle, life went on, typified by a simple marriage ceremony that day that took place in a battle-scarred farmhouse just outside of town. There it was, that Charles, from Southampton, Hampshire, England, and Dorothy, from Ashton-Under-Lyne, Lancashire, England, were married.

Charlie and Dot were my mum and dad.

How did two people who lived 220 miles apart in the UK find each other and get married over 900 miles away in Italy in the middle of a war?

My father, Charles Frederick James Bridle, was the son of a Channel Islander who was one of eighteen children, from an island called Guernsey, situated just off the coast of northern France. My father left school at sixteen and entered an apprenticeship to become a precision engineer, but a few years later, he was called up as a conscript into the British army.

Although he served willingly, and with distinction, repairing artillery guns while under fire from the enemy, my father could not say that he actually wanted to be there with the Eighth Army in North Africa and then Italy. Like so many men at this time, he gladly served his country but considered his youth had been taken from him.

My mother, Dorothy (nee Squires-Ward) had a difficult upbringing in northern England. Her father died in the First World War and her stepfather was a strong disciplinarian. In those days, the use of a strap or stick to administer discipline, was normal. While the physical scars my mother bore testified to her strong will the psychological marks would become evident only later in life.

My mother was very active in the Salvation Army during a time when that denomination was very strong in the UK. During the Second World War, she volunteered as a driver with the Red Shield.

> The League became known as the 'Red Shield' during the Second World War, as this distinctive symbol appeared on the mobile canteens that provided not only tea; but also chewing gum, soap, toothpaste and sewing kits to military personnel. These canteens arrived in occupied Europe only a matter of days after the 'D-Day' landings and closely followed the advance of Allied troops into Germany.
> ~ The Salvation Army, UK web site

My mother was in the war because she wanted to be. (I think I may well have inherited some of her adventurous spirit.) Apparently, she was not a good driver and, on a couple of occasions, nearly drove right into a German camp. However, she was courageous and beautiful and quickly came to the attention of the good-looking engineer from Southampton.

Apparently, as my mother was closely following the Allied troops, my father closely followed her. Their journey led them to their wedding in that farmhouse with the noise of artillery shells being exchanged between retreating Germans and advancing Allies sounding over the roof on the outskirts of Rimini, on October 14, 1944.

Rimini, today, is a beautiful city—well worth visiting for a vacation. Sadly, the farmhouse was obliterated by a German artillery shell the day after the wedding at approximately the same time the wedding had taken place—so I very nearly did not come into being!

Sadly, while my parents were both very good people, it was not a marriage made in heaven. It would not make for pleasant reading to go into this in detail. Suffice it to say that when they returned to England after the war, it became evident that they came from two different worlds. While there were occasional fights with dishes and cutlery flying around, they quickly settled into an uneasy peace.

My mother was staunchly Salvationist, whereas my father was not religious. While not an atheist, he was indifferent to the very thing most important to my mother.

They were extremely good parents, in that my older brother and I never lacked for anything materially—be it good clothing, food, family holidays, school trips abroad, et cetera—but I have no recollection of ever seeing any affection between my parents. My own reluctance to hug people no doubt stems from never seeing it happen in our family.

My father worked nights and went fishing or gardened on the weekends. His garden was his pride and joy.

My mother, having left the Salvation Army early in the marriage, carried regret and resentment in her heart. While my father never touched me, she would sometimes vent her frustration on me, in the same way her stepfather had punished her—the wooden spoon being her instrument of choice.

I never felt any resentment or thought I was being abused. I thought all this was normal; at least it was for me.

My brother and I were sent to the local Salvation Army, never encouraged nor discouraged by our father. I excelled as a tenor horn player. Even today, I prefer a brass band rendition of classics such as Chopin's Polonaise in A Flat Major, Peer Gynt Suite #1 or Hall Of The Mountain King, by Edward Grieg. Playing that music whilst sitting as a tenor horn player in the centre of a thirty to forty-piece brass band still ranks for me as the best musical experience, the ultimate surround sound immersion.

And now to connect the dots …

Ginny currently sings in the Toronto Mass Choir (TMC), an amazing black gospel choir based in—you guessed it—Toronto. If you ever get a chance to see or hear them, don't miss the opportunity; it will be memorable. (www.tmc.ca)

Gospel choirs such as the TMC sing in three-part harmony: soprano, alto and "enthusiastic men" (a euphemism for tenors). I am enthusiastic and I would dearly love to be able to sing in the TMC, but unfortunately, I am a baritone. I am not quite fully bass nor tenor. I simply can't reach those high tenor notes.

However, I have been happy to serve TMC, fulfilling the very important role of backstage manager. Thirty minutes or so before all the choir members arrived at a venue, I would find out where the dressing rooms and washrooms were, so that I could quickly direct the choir members when they arrived. I would make sure that whatever else had been agreed upon—such as the provision of water, a meal or snacks or whatever—had been provided. If there was one, I would collect the honorarium cheque and, when necessary, guard the handbags of the choir ladies whilst they were on stage singing.

Unfortunately, some concert venues or churches do not have locks on the dressing room doors; so whilst the choir is on stage singing, it is essential to have someone guarding the handbags. It may not seem a very glamorous way to serve, but it *is* important.

It is remarkable what some ladies carry in their handbags. Of course, everything in there is absolutely essential; and whatever you do, don't go into a lady's handbag—even that of your own wife. It is a part of a lady's life that remains totally sacrosanct and forever a mystery to us men. Just don't go there!

Now, before you start to think what a wonderful person I am, willing to serve as such an unsung hero, let me confess that sometimes my thoughts have not been so magnanimous.

There have been a few, albeit rare, occasions when I have found myself thinking, "What on earth am I doing this for? When I consider all the 'great' things I have done for God in the past, why am I now reduced to such a demeaning task as guarding handbags?" Then I'd think back to some of the things that I've been called upon, by the Lord, to do in the past: giving altar calls and seeing thousands of people come forward (the largest event being at Earl's Court in London, England, where, out of a crowd of 20,000 people, more than 4,000 responded) and many other similar situations in countries all over Europe, from Iceland to Russia, from Finland to Spain, in fact, in almost three dozen different countries. Of course, the Lord gets all the credit and glory, but this thought would involuntarily invade my mind: "So why I am now guarding handbags?"

Yes, I know that being a good servant is not about *what* we do, but rather about *how* we do it—our attitude of willingness to do whatever we are asked to do happily and to the best of our ability. But really ... guarding handbags? Not much room for creativity or the showing of initiative!

I did, on one occasion (in order to try and raise some money for a missions trip), try to charge the ladies a fee to retrieve their handbags, but all I got was withering looks that left me in no doubt that I should not try that again.

Well, you've got to at least try, right?

"And what," you may be thinking, "does this have to do with the chapter title, 'A Man with No Name'?"

Well, on the particular occasion in question, the Toronto Mass Choir was doing a concert with a group I really like, Newworldson, and I had been looking forward to seeing them in concert with TMC for a long time—only to discover that there was no lock on the dressing room door and I had to be on guard duty that night. There I was, in the bowels of the church, hearing only the muffled sounds able to seep through many walls and the floor, down into the basement—where I was *guarding the handbags.*

I was disappointed; I was tired. I was *not* in a good mood. As I sat in an uncomfortable chair at the bottom of the stairs leading to the dressing rooms, down the stairs came a cherub-faced little boy.

Undoubtedly the child's parents and family would have described him as being cute, but to me, he was just an annoying little boy who started to ask a string of irritating questions that I was in no mood to answer.

Despite my obvious reluctance to engage in any conversation (each unanswered question led to another question), he was relentless. Could he not take the hint and just go away and leave me to stew in my increasingly bad mood?

My mother always told me that, as a little boy, I drove her crazy always asking, "Why?" and "Who are 'they'?" *They* were the faceless, unnamed people who were responsible for me not being allowed to do many of the things I wanted to do.

They said it was not good for me; *they* said it was not safe; *they* said it would lead me into trouble—and so on and so on. To this day, I have never discovered *their* identity. *They* have a lot to answer for.

So the little boy persisted. "What are you doing down here?" he asked.

I should have just told him, but in that split-second, for some reason, I said, "Nothing," which was partly true.

But the little boy then asked, "Why are you sitting there doing nothing?"

The nasty man inside me wanted to say, "It's none of your business." But as I still had some control over the decent side of my character, I compromised by saying, "Because I am," which is, of course, a non-answer.

My tactic to get rid of this irritating boy was not working out very well at all. In fact, evading a straight answer was like waving a red rag at a bull. The lad came right back at me with more questions. So he stood there in front of me, looking all angelic and innocent, and said, "I'm David. What's your name?"

To my great shame, I have to admit I was quickly developing an intense dislike of this little urchin, with his neatly parted hair and cherubic smile.

I recalled how my mother used to tell me I was such an inquisitive child that I drove her crazy, asking question after question after question. Could it be I was seeing myself in this child?

When the boy asked, "What is your name?" I replied, "I don't have a name," thinking that response would shut him up and he would go away and allow me to wallow in my self-pity in peace. I could not have been more wrong!

"Why don't you have a name?"

"Because my parents didn't give me one."

"Why didn't your parents give you a name?"

"I don't know; maybe they forgot to."

"Why did they forget?"

"I don't know; maybe they didn't like me."

"Why did they not like you?"

"I don't know," I answered a little too sharply, causing the little boy to run back up the stairs.

If I thought that was the end of it, I was soon to discover how wrong I was. Within a few short minutes, the cherub returned with two small girls of a similar age—his sisters, I think. He wanted to show them the "man with no name," like I was some freak in a circus sideshow. The bombardment of questions intensified.

Most of all, they wanted to know my name, but I was in no mood to encourage them by giving it to them. I figured if I could hold the line there and not disclose my name, they would soon tire and go away, but with the support of these girls, the little boy grew bolder and more persistent.

All I had wanted was some peace and quiet, but now the three of them intensified their interrogation. Why, oh why, had I not just given the little boy the straightforward answer and told him my name?

Anyway, as I looked at this cute, little blonde boy, suddenly I thought, "*This* is what it was like for my mother; I am looking at *me!*" I smiled inside and actually started to warm towards the little urchin.

Nevertheless, I repeated my "sort of lie." I told them that I had no name.

Okay, there really is no such thing as a "sort of lie," but when they challenged me, I told them my parents had not given me a name ... and that was "sort of true."

When I was a little boy—about the same age as my tormentor—my mother used to tell people that when my father came to the nursing home after I was born (before he went to see me), she told him I was "really ugly." After seeing me—so the story goes—my father popped in again to see my mother and said, "You're right."

Well, for some reason, my parents could not agree on a name for me. Dad wanted to call me Ian after a Scottish friend he'd had in the British army during World

War Two. My mother wanted to saddle me with the name Cyril after an old boyfriend. Unable to agree, they turned to the nurse on duty in the hospital and asked, "Why don't *you* give him a name?" So, in a technical sense, it was true that my parents had not given me a name.

I was named Terence by a faceless stranger. It was not a family name and she didn't choose it in honour of anyone in particular. I wasn't even given a middle name, not even the name Charles, which had been handed down through the male lineage of the Bridle family. My father bore the regal name Charles Frederick James Bridle, but my parents' indifference was reflected in my name: simply, Terence Bridle.

My brother's name is Douglas Kenneth Bridle. Kenneth was my mother's half-brother's name. When I was very young, I naively thought I also had two names. I thought my name was Terry Terence Bridle.

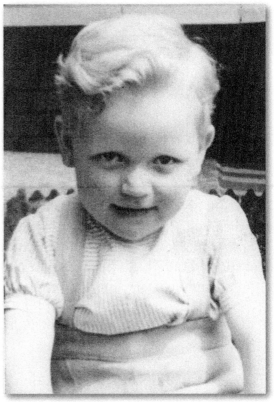
Baby Terry

Everyone called me Terry except my mother, who called me Terence when I was in trouble. I grew to dislike the name, and it was quite a shock when I learned I had only one name. It happened one day at school when I was about eight years old. We were instructed to write our full names, so I wrote, "Terry Terence Bridle." The teacher thought it was so funny that she made sport of it, causing all the other students to laugh, too. It shouldn't have been a big deal, but in my little mind, I was not sure which hurt me most, being laughed at or having only one name.

Having a name is important. It identifies us in the community in which we live.

In the Bible, great significance is given to the names of many biblical characters; while today, most people pick names that simply sound good or may be currently popular. Some parents give their children ridiculous names that may well be in vogue at the time of birth; but ten, fifteen or twenty years later, the recipient has to live with the embarrassment of a name that is out of date or just plain silly.

These days, some celebrities make their brains work overtime to give their children ridiculous names, while others don't seem to think ahead. When I was fifteen, in my class was a boy called Benjamin Bot. Benny Bot was made fun of mercilessly for his parents' lack of foresight. I am sure some of you reading this will know of even more bizarre names.

Some societies place great importance on the meaning of a person's name and how he or she comes by the name.

I am reminded of an old joke. A young First Nations boy asked his father how he and his brother and sister had been named. The wise old chief said, "Well son, when your sister was born, I stepped out of the tepee and the first thing I saw was a shooting star, so I named her Shooting Star. When your older brother was born, I stepped out of the tepee and the first thing I saw was a running deer, so I named him Running Deer. So now, my son, you know why your name is Pooping Dog."

I guess Terence—or its short form, Terry—is not such a bad name after all.

Later, I considered adding Charles as a middle name. Terence Charles Bridle— sounds rather grand, don't you think? I've just never gotten around to it.

As I was contemplating these thoughts and memories, the little boy reappeared, having dragged his father, by the hand, along with him.

"There," said the little boy, pointing triumphantly at me, "that's the man with no name." I guess his father had not believed him.

My heart softened. As the little boy turned to go, I called out, "Hey David ..." He and his father turned. I said, "I'm sorry. I didn't tell you the whole truth earlier. I do have a name; it's Terry."

The smile that lit up the little boy's face was priceless. He looked up at his dad and said, "He *does* have a name!" His delight at this discovery was worth the experience. In fact, it's what led me to write about it.

How I received my name may be inglorious, but now I am known by name to many important people.

The government knows my name.

The tax man knows my name.

The Ontario Health Insurance people know my name.

Credit card people know my name, as do an interminable number of telemarketers who insist on calling me Mr. Briddle rather than Mr. Bridle.

However, the most important thing is that *God* knew me even before I was born.

He knows my name and He has written it down in heaven.

Yes, I have a name and I am loved more than I deserve to be loved. To God Himself, I am a very important person—as are we all—and have great value to Him.

So, if He wants me to guard handbags, I will do so; and I will not only do it to the very best of my ability, but I will consider it to be the very best job that I can have, equal in importance to any other job the Lord has given me in the past—or to any job that He may entrust to me in the future.

All you are reading here started because a pesky little boy wanted to know my name. Thank you, little David; and thank You, Lord for the reminder.

(Note: Since writing this story, I no longer guard handbags for the Toronto Mass Choir; someone else has that privilege. But I honestly miss doing it. Really, I do!)

A PRiNCE OR A PAUPER

I have learned to be content whatever the circumstances. I know what it is to be in need, and I know what it is to have plenty. I have learned the secret of being content in any and every situation, whether well-fed or hungry, whether living in plenty or in want. I can do all this through Him who gives me strength. ~ The Apostle Paul in Philippians 4:11b-13

For Ginny and I, our entire ministry life has involved extensive travel that has taken us all across Canada and the USA, to Africa, all over the four nations that comprise Great Britain and the Republic of Ireland, and to no less than thirty-three countries of Western and Eastern Europe.

For forty-five weeks of each of the ten years when we pioneered "Heaven's Gates and Hell's Flames," we stayed in the homes of people from local churches in thirty-three European countries. These were people we did not know, of varying lifestyles and economic and cultural situations.

From the north of Iceland (near the arctic circle) to near Sochi in south east Russia, from Gibraltar and Portugal in the south-west of Europe to northern Sweden and north-east Finland, from Greece to north Scotland—and all points in between—we depended on local pastors to find accommodation for us for the week (or more) when we would be ministering in their churches.

We have slept in comfortable four-poster beds, beds that were too soft, beds that were too hard, foam beds, old broken spring-mattress beds and on wooden boards, a sheet of cold steel, the floor in kitchens and on the floor in a church boiler room.

In one situation, a pastor showed us a one-inch sliver of a mattress on the floor where we were to "get a good nights rest" and generously invited us to help ourselves to whatever was in the fridge. Later, when Ginny opened it, all she found was a small jug of milk of questionable vintage and a couple of small, silver foil packages that we did not dare open.

Once we stayed in a home in Corpus Christi, Texas, where the cockroaches seemed to be part of the family, scurrying noisily around in every room. The family did not even bat an eyelid. On another occasion we endured a massive ant swarm in Seville, Spain. At an old communist army barracks in Estonia, the resident rats were not happy when we invaded some of their living space, so they invaded ours, examining all our belongings (including our sleeping bags) and kindly sampling our food before we had a chance to try it. Needless to say, we lost our appetites after discovering what had happened.

Of course, we slept many nights in our very own "Toyota Hilton" (our Toyota van). On one two-week trip in Bulgaria and Romania, nine of us (all adults) slept in it for five nights—close fellowship indeed!

Sometimes we were well fed. Other times we had over-loaded platters of unappetizing, unrecognizable food thrust upon us that we could not refuse without insulting our hosts—no matter that it might be unclean or too old to eat safely. Forget any kind of diet or healthy eating.

With Murphy's Law in high gear, when we were hungry there was no food and when we were not hungry we were expected to eat what was offered. Oh yes, travelling in ministry was great fun.

Add to this the fact that the people with whom we stayed usually wanted to talk, and talk and talk—when all we wanted to do was crash and sleep. It was not unusual for them to want to unburden all the problems they were having at their churches, or in their families, on to us.

Two contrasting accommodation stories will serve to illustrate our challenges without going into long, tedious examples from hundreds of experiences.

POLAND DURING COMMUNISM

On one of our early visits to Poland, when the country was still under the thumb of communism, we ministered at a small church in Wroclaw, in western Poland. After the service we were taken to the home of the people with whom we would spend the night.

We followed the pastor to a very old apartment building, probably built at the turn of the century, in an area tightly crammed with similar bleak and foreboding looking buildings. There was no elevator, so we stumbled up creaking wooden stairs, lit only by the moonlight seeping through small dirty windows.

Exhausted after lugging our suitcases up four floors, we stood behind the pastor as he rapped loudly on the door to one of the apartments. It swung open, revealing seven smiling faces. Mother, father, four children ranging in age from about five to fifteen, and the smiling old babushka (grandmother) had been waiting excitedly for our visit. Especially in those days, it was a matter of great excitement for Christians in East Europe to be able to welcome Christians from the West into their homes.

We were invited to leave our suitcases in the hall while we were ushered with a flourish into what we would call the living room. This room had one small window to the outside and was furnished with a three-person couch (which we later discovered was a futon that converted into a bed). There were two matching armchairs and a low, wide coffee table that could be raised to the height of a dining table. A display cabinet took up almost one entire wall of the small room. This was filled with a few plates and dishes and fading family photographs whose crumbling, brown paper indicated that they went back many years.

The coffee table was resplendent with a wide assortment of homemade cakes and a beautifully decorated, six-piece coffee set. These wonderful people were honouring us by sharing the best they had that they could share with us. The cakes were wonderful, but the coffee was awful, partly because, at that time, sugar and milk were unavailable in the stores. Of course, we did not show any reaction to the strong, bitter, grainy coffee.

After a time of laughter and fellowship, the pastor excused himself to go to his home and the mother and father began to prepare the room for Ginny and me to sleep in. In no time at all, the small living room was converted into a bedroom.

When our hosts retreated from the room, Ginny and I were soon cuddled up on the small futon bed. We were so exhausted that, despite the strong coffee, we fell asleep quickly.

Inevitably, probably because of the coffee, I needed to get up in the night to answer the call of nature. So, armed with my little pen light, I opened the door of the room we were in. It opened into a little hallway. To my left was the door to the stairway where we had come in; then there was a door to my right and a door straight in front of me. The question of where three adults and four children were sleeping, if there were only two other rooms beside the one that Ginny and I were in, began to form in my sleep-fogged mind. I was soon to find out.

I gently opened the door to my right and eased slowly into the room. Making sure my pen light was set on its red beam (and shining it first on the ceiling so as not to disturb anyone who might be in there), you can imagine my surprise when, bringing the beam slowly down, I discovered this was the kitchen and the floor was covered with the bodies of the grandmother, mother and father and the youngest child. Yes—sleeping on the cold, bare floor.

I quietly slid out of the kitchen and stealthily opened the only other door.

If I was surprised by what I had found on the kitchen floor, that paled in comparison to what I found in this room. This was the tiniest of bathrooms and there were the three other children, two entwined together in a shallow bath and the other on the floor underneath the sink and toilet bowl. These three adults and four children had only three small rooms in which to live, including the bathroom and the kitchen— and yet they had been willing to share what little they had with us.

It was a very humbling experience.

Mind you, I could not bring myself to actually *use* the facilities, for fear that any of the children might wake up whilst I was doing so. Needless to say, I had to "hold it" all night.

Like the apostle Paul, I have learned the secret of being content in any and every situation.

PORI - FINLAND

It was always a time of slight anxiety when it came time for the pastor of the hosting church to introduce us to our hosts for the next week. Were we going to be treated like princes—or would we find ourselves staying like paupers?

So we had developed a kind of radar.

All of Eastern Europe was pretty much as I have described here already (with a few exceptions) but in Western Europe we might sometimes fare better, not always, but sometimes.

For example: If we were told we would be staying with an older couple, that was usually good because such people usually live alone, their children having grown up and moved out. That usually meant we would have a nice bedroom all to ourselves and sometimes even an ensuite bathroom. However, if we were told we would be staying with a young couple, we would wait with bated breath to see whether or not children entered the equation. If there were no children, that was usually good—but if there were children there could be any number of problems.

In one place, we were to sleep on a bed in the middle of a room that had no doors. The children stood there and watched us get ready for bed. Awkward.

On another occasion, in England, the pastor and his wife gave us their own bed, but they warned us that sometimes their five-year-old daughter would sleepwalk. Well, several hours later, I was wakened by something warm and wet seeping into my pyjamas. Apparently, the child had sleepwalked right into our bed and snuggled herself between Ginny and me (I never even felt her there) and proceeded to wet the bed. That would not have been so bad, had the little girl not strenuously denied doing it. We wondered if her parents actually believed her.

However, back to Pori, Finland.

After meeting the cast who we would be training for the upcoming drama, the pastor came to tell us with whom we would be staying. It was a couple in their early thirties with four young children. Not only that, but they had a recovering alcoholic / drug addict staying with them, who they were trying to help get back on his feet.

We had noticed that Finnish houses did not appear to be very large, so this was not looking good.

It was late as we drove away from the church, following this couple in whose home we would be staying for a week. It was a moonless night, but the sky was crystal clear with thousands of stars twinkling in the sky. From previous experience, I had come to be suspicious of such idyllic nights, as they had often proved to be harbingers of unpleasant things to come. We drove out of the city and then headed north for about twenty to twenty-five minutes, until we suddenly turned left onto a dirt track that plunged into a dense forest. We carried on down this winding and undulating track for a good fifteen minutes as it headed ever deeper into the forest.

Suddenly, the car in front stopped. We could see that its headlights were illuminating the back of a small log cabin. Our hearts sank as it did not look to be anywhere nearly big enough for a family with four children plus the recovering alcoholic, let alone Ginny and myself.

As we reached the front of the cabin and stepped up onto a veranda that stretched all across the front, the husband and wife proudly announced that this was their summer cabin and *this is where Ginny and I would be staying—just the two of us*. Adjacent to the cabin was a fully functional sauna with plenty of logs to fire it up. The location was so remote that we would have all the privacy we could ever want. I am not a sauna person, but Ginny is, and she used it every day— Finnish style!

When we stepped into this beautiful retreat, all made of logs, wood and locally hewn stone, there was a fire roaring in the fireplace. The refrigerator and cupboards were packed with food. There was a telephone, dishwasher, hot water shower and no television (thank goodness). Quaint and charming are the words that come to mind. We were so tired that when we climbed the slate stone steps to the little two-person bedroom, we fell asleep quickly in the peaceful silence.

When we awoke in the morning, there was another surprise awaiting us that we had not noticed when we arrived, in the dark, the night before. The cabin was situated on a promontory, surrounded on three sides by water. Over the surface was a fine mist fog that the sun gradually burned away to reveal a beautiful lake with islands on the other side.

In this idyllic location Ginny and I spent a wonderful week in Finland. Working hard each evening training the cast, there were three nights of actual presentations of the drama. More people responded to the gospel message than that church had seen over the previous several years. We made many good friends as we experienced the upside of the apostle Paul's comments on being content.

> *I have learned to be content whatever the circumstances. I know what it is to be in need, and I know what it is to have plenty. I have learned the secret of being content in any and every situation, whether well-fed or hungry, whether living in plenty or in want. I can do all this through Him who gives me strength* (Philippians 4:11b-13).

Being able to be content in all things is something we have to be willing to learn and that means we have to experience the downside as well as the upside. Indeed, it is in experiencing the down times that we learn to appreciate, all the more, the good times.

Are you willing to let God teach you?

THE TRIGGER

FROM THE GOUDYS TO GUERNSEY

In this true story, I may well employ some British humour which I must explain for the benefit of those readers who may not understand the nuances and delicacies of the British mind, when it comes to what we call humour.

(As I type this, I am fighting a losing battle with the spell checker in my computer that continually rejects the English spelling of "humour," insisting that I use the American "humor." I know I cannot win against this soulless machine, but I shall continue to spell the word the right way, even though I am sure the battle will continue with my editor and publisher. What? Me? Stubborn? Whatever gives you that idea?)

I remember vividly when I first took Ginny, my wife, to England and we visited Terry and Janet Wiseman, who were my friends before I met Ginny. We have continued to be close friends to this day.

When we left the Wiseman's house, Ginny turned to me and asked, "Why were your friends so horrible to you?"

To understand why Ginny said this, you need to know that the welcome mat read, "Oh no! Not you again!" and when it came time to leave, my friend Terry escorted us to the door and said, "I'll see you to the door because we've had a lot of things go missing lately." As we walked down the driveway and Terry was closing the door, he called out to Jan (loudly so that we could hear), "I thought they'd never leave."

It is difficult to make general statements about a nation that is now so culturally diverse, but as a general rule, British people will be extremely polite and courteous to people whom they meet for the first time.

If the relationship is purely on a business level, or does not go any deeper, that courtesy remains intact, but as soon as a friendship develops and they get to know you better and are comfortable with you, look out! You could well become the target of their English humour as the witty insults flow back and forth.

It is friendly repartees—never done behind your back—and it is expected that you will give as good as you get, but whatever you do, don't take it personally. Again, this is a general rule, but if the British like you, they will probably make fun of you.

I know it seems like a contradiction, but that's the way it is.

It reminds me somewhat of when I met a friend's Pekinese dog. I like to think I am good with dogs, but as I tickled this little canine behind his ear, it started to growl and bare its teeth, giving me quite a ferocious look.

Naturally, I started to slowly take my hand away, upon which my friend informed me that it was okay. Apparently, a Pekinese dog growls when it is happy.

So I asked, "What does it do when it is unhappy?"

"It growls" was the reply.

So I asked the obvious question, "If it growls when it is happy and also growls when it is not happy, how will I know the difference?"

"Oh, that's easy," said my friend. "When it is not happy, it will bite you."

And wouldn't you know it, the little blighter chose that moment to do just that: It bit me. I could not believe that such a little mouth could deliver such a painful bite. Needless to say, I am not overly fond of Pekinese dogs.

In case you're unfamiliar with the word "blighter," it is English slang and means "a contemptible, worthless person; a scoundrel or rascal."

So, tuck all that in the back of your mind as you read on ....

Book and movie titles are supposed to grab your attention and stir your imagination in the hope that you will want to find out more. So, what is this title all about? Well, read on and all will become clear.

One of the meanings of the word "trigger" is "anything, as an act or event, that serves as a stimulus and initiates or precipitates a reaction or series of reactions."

As this story unfolds, you will see why I have entitled it "The Trigger," and you will also see why it has been subtitled "From the Goudys to Guernsey."

Let me begin by introducing you to Ray and Nancy Goudy. There have been no words yet invented that could do justice to describe this couple. They are Scottish—but then, no one can be held responsible for where they are born—and Ray carries with him the delusion that Scottish footballers are better than the English. I am not going to get into a full-fledged description of this couple other than to say I love them both dearly.

I consider it a privilege to be able to call them friends. We have a deep and enduring friendship that has weathered the years and the fact that we hardly ever see each other. I have an immense respect for their faith and the incredible pioneering and creative work that they do for God under His guiding hand. If ever they were to write a book on their life's journey I would be the first in line to buy a copy. Please see what they are about at www.ngm.org.uk

Back in 1981 (or thereabouts), Ginny and I were living in the basement apartment of a house owned by our friends, Lynn and Sunit John.

In those days, we lived totally by faith—as we still do—and were ready to go anywhere at any time. So it was that, in the first sixteen years of our marriage and ministry, we lived in no less than seventeen different places. Such was the vagabond nature of our lives in those days.

One day, as I was sitting at my desk paying the monthly bills, I suddenly had a strong impression that we should send $500 to our friends Ray and Nancy Goudy and that they should spend it on a holiday.

I shared with Ginny what I was feeling. Although giving that gift would leave us short of the finances we needed to pay our bills at that time, she agreed that if I felt strongly that it was God who had prompted me, we should do it—and do it immediately, before we changed our minds.

I can't tell you how wonderful it is to be married to a partner who shares the same simple and total trust in God.

So, despite the five-hour time difference between Canada and the UK, I set about trying to contact Ray and Nancy. They worked with Youth for Christ at the time leading a band called "Heartbeat." I called the YFC office to find out exactly where they were.

The nature of their work meant that they were hardly ever in the office, but amazingly, Nancy was there when I called, so I was able to tell her straight away that we would send the $500 gift and that it was to be used towards them taking a holiday.

Well, in her excitement, Nancy nearly came through the phone as she explained that recently, some other people had given her and Ray financial gifts, saying exactly the same thing—that they were to use the money to go on a much-needed, long-overdue holiday.

After getting the details of where to send the money, I asked Nancy if she would please let us know the specific details. I reasoned that if it truly was the Lord orchestrating this vacation, Ginny and I would like to know when and where they were going so we could pray for them to have a exceptionally great time.

Ending the call, I hung up the phone to the sound of our door bell ringing. It was a family member standing there who had never before given anything to our ministry. He said he had felt prompted to give us something and handed me an envelope in which was $500 cash.

What an amazing "coincidence"– that is, if you believe in coincidences.

We had obeyed the Lord's prompting and received instant confirmation that it was, indeed, His will, knowing others had done the same—and then the Lord immediately replenished our finances!

The timing was uncanny, but that was just the start, the trigger.

The very next day, we received a telephone call from a Christian television program, *100 Huntley Street,* which featured many of the host's family members who were all excellent singers. Ginny had been working at the station and had often sung on the program.

Apparently a faithful financial supporter of the program had died and his family had requested that one of the television host's family members sing at the funeral, but the timing was not good, as all the host's family were booked elsewhere.

So it was that *100 Huntley Street* called, asking Ginny if she could sing at the funeral. There was, of course, no talk of receiving any money for doing this, but Ginny gladly agreed and the family of the deceased were very happy as they had seen Ginny singing on the program many times. She was well-liked by the deceased and his family. A few days later, Ginny went to sing "The Lord's Prayer" at the funeral and was invited to attend the wake afterwards.

Later, when Ginny was about to leave, a family member gave her an envelope containing "something to show their gratitude for her coming to sing." Ginny said it really wasn't necessary, but they insisted. With great surprise, Ginny later opened the envelope to discover four crisp new $50 bills.

But, as those infuriating, late-night television commercials say, there's more.

A short while later, we received a phone call from Nancy and Ray informing us of where they hoped to go for their God-given holiday. They asked if they could spend time with us in Canada.

And so it was that, later that summer, Ray and Nancy came over to Canada and we spent an idyllic holiday at Ginny's parents cottage in Wasaga Beach, Ontario. Wasaga Beach, about an hour north of Toronto, is a poplar four-season tourist destination. The beach itself, at nine miles wide, is the world's longest freshwater beach.

Most days Ginny and Nancy worked on their tans while Ray and I played a game we'd created called "Donkey."

Donkey was a simple game, whereby, waist deep in the water, we would throw a frisbee back and forth, trying to make the other person have to dive to catch it. If they missed the frisbee, or fumbled and dropped it, a letter of the word "Donkey" was added to that person's account. The first person to spell out the word lost the game.

You have to understand, however, that when you get a Scotsman playing against an Englishman in any sport—even one as inconsequential as Donkey—the competition becomes serious and fierce. National pride is at stake.

If you have ever seen that excellent film *Braveheart,* you will know there is a history between the English and Scottish—one for which we English cannot be proud—that stretches down through the annals of time, reaching the present day.

It is a fact of history that since the Angles defeated an alliance of Scots, Britons and Picts in the Battle of Raith way back in the year 596, there have been approximately 263 armed conflicts between the English and the Scots. This includes all major battles, cross-border skirmishes and sieges.

In 1603 England and Scotland were joined when King James VI of Scotland succeeded to the throne of England as King James I, and wars between the two nations officially ended.

However, although the wars of the three kingdoms in the seventeenth century and the Jacobite risings of the eighteenth century were technically British civil wars, they were, in fact, Anglo-Scottish conflicts.

This tension between the Scots and the English has carried over into modern times through the "beautiful game" known in Europe and most of the rest of the world as "football." Since the first official game of football between teams representing Scotland and England was played at Hamilton Crescent, Glasgow in 1872 (the game ended as a 0-0 draw), there have been 110 full international matches between England and Scotland, with England winning forty-five, Scotland winning forty-one and twenty-four games ending in a draw.

Many of those matches were in European competition, but a lot of them were called "friendlies" because there was no purpose for the match other than the game itself.

But friendly is most definitely not the word to describe the atmosphere of the 100,000 fans who would pack the stadiums. Something in our collective DNA would rise up, and we would fight the "auld enemy" once again—albeit by proxy.

And so into this historical context started back in 596 at the Battle of Raith, Ray and I embarked upon the 1982 "Battle of Wasaga." Our weapons of choice were frisbees rather than swords, lances, bows and arrows; but our desire to win was no less intense. We were fighting for bragging rights. As I said, national pride was still at stake.

Although my tongue is firmly placed in my cheek as I write, this innate rivalry between England and Scotland remains today.

As for Ray and I, we laughed ourselves silly and had a great time. Let's face it: If one is playing a game called "Donkey," one cannot take oneself too seriously.

In case you're wondering, Scotland won that first Battle of Wasaga, but I'll get him next time.

Come evening, competition resumed with the card game "UNO." No less serious and fierce, it was England verses Scotland all over again. Shortly before Ray and Nancy's visit, England had beaten Scotland 4-0 in a football match and I took great delight in reminding Ray of this—especially when he gained the upper hand.

Ray and Nancy's competitiveness was not limited to games. Even in such a mundane act as sharing a bunch of grapes, woe betide Ray if he should take more than Nancy—or vise versa. Suffice it to say that he never did because Nancy would be all over him like a ton of bricks if he were to try. Even today, if Ginny and I are sharing something and she tries to take more than her share, I'll say, "Hey, hold on there Nancy." It's an inside joke, a reminder of the fun-filled and delightful holiday we had with Ray and Nancy at Wasaga Beach.

Little did we know when we obeyed the Lord in sending that $500 that we would share in the blessing from the resulting holiday.

But there's more. Fast forward one year.

By this time, Ray and Nancy and the Heartbeat band had branched out with their own organization, called "NGM." They were based in the small market town of Malmsbury situated between Bristol and Swindon in west England.

Ginny and I were living in the UK, just outside of Portsmouth on the south coast. We had just spent a very busy and tiring two months singing and preaching all over northern England.

As we travelled home, our route took us near Malmsbury, so we decided to pop in unannounced to the Heartbeat base on the off-chance that Ray and Nancy might be there. It was more likely that they would be away, but we thought we would at least try.

To our surprise, Ray, Nancy and the entire band were all there. We spent a great time that evening: laughing and sharing stories of our respective escapades. We were having so much fun that we did not notice how late it had gotten, so it was suggested that Ginny and I stay overnight with friends of Ray and Nancy in the village. It was planned that in the morning, after a brief visit to the Heartbeat base, Ginny and I would drive back down to Portsmouth.

When morning came, because we had gotten up a little later than intended, I suggested that, perhaps, we should go straight home, but, as is often the case, Ginny was right in feeling that we should visit Ray and Nancy as planned. When we arrived, they were there with the band.

After a short time of laughter and prayer, Ray and Nancy walked with us to our car. Just before we drove off, Nancy handed us a sealed envelope, telling us that everyone in Heartbeat had contributed towards this "little gift," and they wanted us to use it for a holiday in Guernsey. (The beautiful island of Guernsey in the English Channel just off the coast of northern France is where my family comes from. When Ginny and I were married at the end of January, 1979, we had had time to take only a two-day honeymoon in the bitter cold of Niagara Falls. I had always wanted to take her to the home of my ancestors for a proper honeymoon.)

After we had driven a respectable distance away (maybe 200 yards or so, such was our excitement), we pulled the car over and opened the envelope. To our utter amazement, that group of young people, the members of the Heartbeat band—all who lived completely by faith—had given us a total of £1,200. In those days, that was the equivalent of about $2,500 Canadian—way more than the $500 the Lord had asked us to give to Ray and Nancy the year before.

Are you beginning to see how God works? How His blessings multiply towards those who are faithful and who do not twist His words?

Well ... you guessed it ... there's more. Hold on to your seats because you're gonna *love* this, and trust me, what I am about to share with you is *exactly* how it happened.

Ginny and I drove to Waterlooville (just outside of Portsmouth) where we were staying at that time and straight to our local travel agent. She knew us well because of the frequent trips we made to Europe. In those days, we were taking a lot of humanitarian and ministry journeys into, what was then, communist Eastern Europe.

I vividly remember sitting with Ginny across from this charming, young "English rose" of a travel agent.

She was utterly delightful with her Queen's English accent and was very eager to please. However, she had no idea what she was about to face. The conversation went almost exactly like this:

"Good afternoon Mr. and Mrs. Bridle. It's so nice to see you again. What can I do for you today?"

"We would like to book a two-week holiday."

"And where would you like to go?"

"Guernsey."

"Ah yes, an excellent choice."

"Well, it's where my family came from and I've always wanted to take my wife there. I haven't had the opportunity until now," I said.

"That's lovely." The travel agent was beaming. "And when would you like to go?"

"Tomorrow," I said.

The smile on that poor girl's face turned quickly to wide-eyed surprise mingled with consternation.

"But, Mr. Bridle," said the girl, recovering her poise admirably, "this is the peak of the holiday season. There will be no rooms at any of the hotels in Guernsey. All flights will be fully booked, as will all the ferries."

Ginny and I were not at all discouraged. In fact, we had a feeling of mounting excitement, as we sensed God was going to do something here.

"That's okay," I said, a little mischievously. "We're sure something will open up. Will you please at least try?"

With a resigned sigh, the girl gave us some brochures on small hotels in Guernsey.

Because I am familiar with Guernsey from going there on family holidays so many times, one hotel immediately caught my eyes: the Captain's Hotel, La Fosse, Guernsey. The brochure read:

> Nestled in the wooded lanes of rural St. Martins, a few minutes walk from Guernsey's picturesque south coast bays and cliffs, yet only minutes by car from the centre of St. Peter Port town. Ideally situated for those who enjoy cycling and walking, the Captain's Hotel combines Old World charm with modern day amenities. Guernsey's wonderful reputation for enjoyable holidays is based on a combination of its natural beauty, the friendliness of its natives and its peace and tranquillity. All around the coastline, the visitor will be amazed at the variety of natural beauty. The large sweeping sandy bays of Cobo, Vazon and L'Ancresse contrast with miles of magnificent cliff walks on the unspoilt south coast. E-mail us at delali@cwgsy.net or telephone/write for our brochure. We look forward to seeing you!
> Colin and Alison De la Mare Proprietors ~ www.accom.guernseyci.com/captain/

"But, Mr. Bridle," said the girl, "this really is a waste of time."

"I can understand why you would say that," I said, "but you see, God has given us £1,200 for a holiday in Guernsey and God would not do that and then make it not possible for us to go—so would you please indulge us?" (It really is fun when we are completely honest and tell people about our walk with God.)

Furtively looking for help from her manager or any of the other travel assistants, and appearing to fluctuate between pity for us and fear that we were mentally unbalanced, this sweet girl called the Captain's Hotel. I will never forget her look of surprise when she was told that, because of a late cancellation, the Captain's Hotel had one double room available—for the exact dates we wanted.

So far, so good. We had somewhere to stay, but how were we going to get over there? All the flights to Guernsey from Southampton and Gatwick were, indeed, fully booked. We wanted to go by ferry anyway so we could take our car.

Ferries to Guernsey sail out of either Portsmouth, close to where we were, or from Weymouth, about an hour and a half drive down the south coast. All ferries to Guernsey, from both Portsmouth and Weymouth, were, as expected, fully booked as they had been for several months.

We asked our patient travel agent to try again. She pointed out that if we could wait a few weeks, she could probably get space on a ferry, but I explained, "No, it has to be tomorrow, so could you please try a third time?"

At this point, the young lady asked to be excused so she could attend to "a call of nature." It crossed my mind that maybe she was in the back calling the police.

Who could have blamed her? To be honest, with the prospect of having a large portion of egg on our faces, our faith was beginning to waver a little—not that we showed it on the outside, but inside, the thought began to creep in, "Have we got this wrong?"

The girl walked slowly back into the office and sat at her desk facing us. With a look that vacillated between pity and annoyance, her professionalism finally won the day. In her best polite voice, she asked, "Are you quite sure you want me to ask again?"

"Yes, please," we replied sweetly.

93

So she called the Portsmouth ferry office and was told again—not very politely—that they were fully booked and to stop bothering them. With a great, dramatic sigh, she called the Weymouth ferry office again.

If her face had communicated surprise at the discovery that a hotel room was available, now the look on her face was priceless. The ferry booking agent informed her that he had, just that moment, put the phone down from a call cancelling two people and a car. It was exactly what we needed on the exact ferry on the exact date to coincide with our hotel reservation.

That really is exactly how it happened.

We have often mused over the fact that if that young lady had not excused herself at precisely that moment, she would have called the ferry company before the cancellation that opened the way for us to take our car on that ferry.

Could it be that the call of nature was an act of God? I don't know, but I don't believe in coincidences.

All I know is this: Either my life is in God's hands or it's not. If it is, and I do my best to live in dependence upon Him, I know things are going to happen that have no rational explanation.

Ginny and I enjoyed a glorious two weeks in Guernsey with blue skies every day. We were refreshed and rejuvenated and our faith was revitalized.

But remember from the beginning of this chapter the definition of "trigger": "an act or event that serves as a stimulus and initiates or precipitates a reaction or series of reactions."

Consider then this sequence:

Our Part:	God's Part:
1. A simple act of obedience in giving the $500 to Ray and Nancy	1. God immediately gave us the $500 back.
	2. God provided more funds because Ginny unexpectedly sang at the funeral.
	3. We had the fun and blessing of a hilarious

holiday with Ray and Nancy at
Wasaga Beach.

4. God marvellously provided £1,200 through those wonderful young people, who were also acting in obedience and trust in God.

5. God performed the"'miracle" of getting us the last-minute booking at the wonderful hotel in Guernsey despite it being peak holiday season.

6. The Lord opened the way for the ferry booking in an incredible way.

7. The girl in the travel agency, and all her colleagues there that day, saw first-hand God at work. Who knows how many people they shared that personal experience with. Personal testimony is powerful and undeniable.

8. And most wonderful for Ginny and I, we had the honeymoon we previously had been unable to have, in the place I had always wanted to be able to take her.

9. I am able to share with you—and all others who read this—this remarkable sequence of events that proves to us God really does care for every aspect of our lives.

Was divine intervention involved? I know what I think; it's up to you to determine your opinion regarding these events.

Through all these events I learned some valuable lessons that will serve me well as I continue this journey towards heaven in these uncertain times. I never intended this book to contain any sort of theological discourse. Nevertheless, it is a recounting of my own spiritual journey and, as such, it would be unfair to ignore the spiritual signposts along the way. While our society is experiencing a time of continual turmoil and uncertainty about the future and we are being bombarded with conflicting teachings and ideas about how to prosper—or even just survive—in the midst of accelerating cataclysmic world events, I have been profoundly affected by a few verses from the Bible.

In the Gospel of Matthew, Jesus says this:

> *So do not worry, saying, "What shall we eat?" or "What shall we drink?'"
> or "What shall we wear?" For the pagans run after all these things, and
> your Heavenly Father knows that you need them. But seek first His kingdom
> and His righteousness, and all these things will be given to you as well.
> Therefore, do not worry about tomorrow, for tomorrow will worry about
> itself. Each day has enough trouble of its own* (Matthew 6:31-34 NIV).

It is, perhaps, natural to experience worry, but the question is this: What do you do when you start to worry about things? How does your relationship with God affect your response to worry, considering He is your provider?

Unfortunately, for many people, prayer, or communication with God, becomes a shopping list of what they want. Too often we get our wants mixed up with our needs. We say, "I need this or that," but what we really mean is, "I want this or that." We need to get our needs and wants lined up with God's plan for our lives.

We must get to the place where we can say, "What I want is whatever God wants—not what I want" and "What *I need* is to seek *first* His Kingdom and righteousness.

So when my wants and needs are in harmony with what God wants, then everything I need (which is now the only thing I want) is actually given to me by God.

It is so simple. Why do we have to complicate it?

My intention in sharing this story is not to boast about how good I was in being obedient. Frankly, I struggled over giving that $500. My intent is to demonstrate, through this totally truthful, real-life story, just how good and faithful God is to those who can humbly grasp, and step into, this simple teaching of total dependence on Jesus Christ.

Our motivation for giving should not be based on whatever needs we have, whether real or imagined. Contrary to some popular teaching, we don't have to plant a seed for our need. This whole idea of our having to give money to God (via any particular ministry or institution) if we want our needs to be met is a subtle, but dangerous, distortion of what the Bible says.

The only motivation behind giving should be as an expression of our simple, childlike faith and trust in God and not because we want or expect to receive something from God. It should never be an effort to curry His favour. We do not earn brownie points from God from any act of giving or because of the size of our gift.

If we can learn to live in simple humility and dependence on Him, it will become obvious that the only need we have is to *"seek first His Kingdom and righteousness."*[7] God will supply all our needs according to His riches—and His riches are inexhaustible.

In seeking first His Kingdom and His righteousness, we will discover His will for our lives. As we live in total dependence on Him, He is faithful to His promise to give us absolutely everything we need—no need for striving, worrying, manipulating His words, bending His teaching to fit our desires or competing with other people or organizations. Saying we should have simple, childlike faith may trouble people who are proud of their intellect, but that is what God requires.

In this instance, the trigger to God's blessing was the simple act of obedience in giving the $500 with no thought, intent or expectation of ever receiving anything in return.

One can't plan these things, but they don't just happen. God knows the plans He has for us. He will cause all things to work together for good to those who love Him and are called to His service.[8] He planned these things before we were even born. All we have to do is live in simple obedience and dependence on Him.

Although we still need to apply basic common sense and wisdom to our circumstances, our actions need to be within the context of what God's Word says. We should have no plans or ambitions beyond pleasing God.

---

[7] Matthew 6:33
[8] Romans 8:28

9

THE ORCHESTRATOR

Recently some changes have happened in my life that have forced me to lean on the Lord more heavily than usual. To be honest, whilst I have not been doing anything bad, I think perhaps, the intensity of my relationship with the Lord has become a little weak and He has been trying to get my attention.

So now, once again, I must rely totally on Him for my finances—and I am not sure exactly what is going to happen in the future. I have been in this place before. One would think that with age and experience, I would be better equipped to handle it. With so-called "retirement" looming within the next ten years, I find myself wondering if I should make financial planning for the future a priority or if I should simply trust the Lord, as I have done for the past twenty-five years. Other stories in this book testify to the amazing love, grace, patience and provision of the Lord over the years, so we won't talk about that further here, but I wanted you to have a feel for the frame of mind I'm in as I write today.

When I was praying this morning, I was not actually complaining to the Lord, but I was reminding Him of my situation. I was telling him that although I am feeling a little fragile at the moment, I am willing to continue to walk in faith if that truly is what He wants me to do. I didn't actually ask Him for a sign, but He knew what was in my heart.

If there is one thing that always causes concern in life and ministry it's money, or rather the lack of it. There are so many people who would step out and give their lives and talents to the Lord if only they could be sure that the money was there to take care of their present and future needs. Many people have sought counsel from me concerning their desire to serve on the mission field. In almost every case, the stumbling block is uncertainty as to where the money will come from. I have to confess the same question is on my heart.

Almost immediately after I ended praying, the buzzer on our apartment door heralded the arrival of a registered letter. When I opened it, there was $2,000 Canadian, sent from some good Canadian friends living in the UK at that time. In the card they had written, "We hope this may be of some use. With our thanks and admiration for all you both do for God's Kingdom." Those were the words written by our friends, but those printed on the card were much more to the point: "Great things happen to those who get off their butts and go for it!" (These friends have a gloriously irreverent sense of humour which I love.)

There it was. No sooner had my prayers been uttered—even the prayer that was locked in my heart and not actually spoken—but the answer came in the form of finances and words of encouragement tinged with British humour just for good measure.

In this instance, the Lord provided both the finances that we needed *and* encouragement, a priceless combination. Does the Word of God not tell us that He will give us more than we ask or think?

But what about the timing? Am I saying God knew the prayer I was going to pray and orchestrated the timing of our friends sending the card and money from England even before I prayed? Absolutely! That's the way God works. He orchestrates things.

That is why, when we feel prompted by the Lord to do something—maybe call someone, share a word of encouragement or gentle admonishment, or perhaps give of our time and/or resources—we should obey. An act of obedience could be a small but vital part of some big symphony the Lord is orchestrating for someone else.

Let me give you another example of how the Lord, knowing the future, worked in a similar way. You're going to love this true story, so get comfy in your chair, freshen up your tea or coffee and get ready to be amazed and blessed.

In October, 1992, Ginny and I were driving back to the UK from Greece, where we had been presenting the drama, "Heaven's Gates and Hell's Flames." Our co-worker, Ann Forrest, was travelling with us. We were in our Toyota van which was hauling a large trailer full of the PA, lighting, drama equipment and costumes we needed for the drama.

We crossed the Adriatic Sea by ferry, from south western Greece to the south eastern Italian port of Bari, but as we drove from there, up the eastern coast of Italy, the gear box in our van literally disintegrated. Because this happened late on a Friday afternoon, we were unable to have the damage properly assessed until the following Monday—forcing us to spend the weekend in a small but beautiful medieval resort town right on the Adriatic coast of Italy.

Fortunately, we had American Express travel insurance that covered, what turned out to be, a very relaxing and enjoyable stay that weekend for all three of us. The insurance also covered our repatriation back to the UK and the broken vehicle and the trailer, but we had no coverage to pay for the repair to the van. When the full extent of the damage was assessed in England, the repair was going to cost £900 (English pounds), about $2,250 Canadian at that time, an amount we simply did not have.

Because the van was so essential to our ministry, in faith, we authorized the starting of the repairs, but we really did not know how we were going to pay for them.

Usually, upon returning from a long trip away, one of the first things I do, is open the pile of mail that has accumulated in our absence. Because cheques are the lifeblood of any ministry, I would always do an initial sort of the mail according to the appearance of the envelopes.

Bills were put in one pile, hand or typewritten envelopes in another, letters with stick-on address labels in a third (no one sends cheques in envelopes with stick-on labels) and finally, junk mail in a fourth pile.

Needless to say, junk mail gets opened last, and because of being busy and distracted by more important matters, the junk mail did not receive my attention until some seven days later, around the time that the repair on the van would be completed and we would have to pay the £900, which we did not have.

One of the last pieces of junk mail to be opened was a shabby-looking, medium sized, brown envelope with a barely legible scribbled handwritten return address on the front, indicating it had been sent from Birmingham, England. We don't actually know anyone in Birmingham, so you can imagine my surprise when, upon opening the envelope, I found tucked inside, £900 pounds cash in crisp new £10 and £20 notes.

I was shocked that anyone would send such a large amount of cash through the post. When I closely examined the return address on the envelope, I did not recognize immediately the name of the sender. Ginny, of course, knew who it was from right away, but she was puzzled, as it was someone who we understood lived in Canada. From an enclosed note, we learned that the sender—a lady who had never given to our ministry before (or since)—had gone to England to work on a six-month contract and had felt she should give her tithe to a ministry in the country where she had earned the money.

Her £900 gift was exactly what was needed to pay for the repair of our van. But here is the amazing part of the story: From the date on her letter and the postmark on the envelope, we saw that she had sent the money a full two weeks *before* our van had broken down in southern Italy. This lady had had no prior communication with us at all; she had simply responded to the prompting of the Lord.

Think about it! Even before we knew we were going to have a particular need, the Lord had already set into motion the mechanism to meet that need.

Isn't the Lord amazing! *"Before they call, I will answer"* (Isaiah 65:24).

To be honest, I do recall saying to the Lord at that time, "Why on earth did You go through all that trouble? Would it not have been easier for everyone if you had simply arranged that our van did not break down in the first place?"

No! No! God knows the lessons we need to learn and He always wants to demonstrate His love for us as a means of building up our faith.

If all this had not happened …

1. Ginny and I (with our co-worker Anne) would not have enjoyed an all-expenses-paid weekend in a beautiful Italian resort town on the Adriatic coast courtesy of American Express. We really needed that break.

2. The lady who was obedient to the prompting of the Lord in giving the £900 would not have had the thrill of knowing how the Lord had used her to be His channel of blessing to others.

3. And finally, you would not now be reading this incredible story of God's love, mercy and provision—a story which, we hope, has brought a smile to your face and encouraged your heart.

Isn't the Lord amazing!

Dear Reader: Whatever your need is at this time, please be assured that the Lord has already set in motion the solution. All you need to do is stay close to Him and be patient and obedient.

You can be sure He will not answer your need in the way that you think it should be done, but He is already at work orchestrating the circumstances for your good and for His glory.

All things *do* (eventually) work together for good to those who love the Lord and are called according to His purpose (Romans 8:28).

10

COME!

Dictionary.com defines the word "evangelism" as:
1. The practise of spreading the Christian Gospel.
2. Ardent or missionary zeal for a cause.

This second definition pertains to either the religion of Christianity or to any cause that an individual may deem worthy.

The same Dictionary.com defines "evangelical" as:

1. belonging to or designating the Christian churches that emphasize the teachings and authority of the Scriptures, especially of the New Testament, in opposition to the institutional authority of the church itself, and *that stress as paramount the tenet that salvation is achieved by personal conversion to faith in the atonement of Christ.*

2. designating Christians, especially of the late 1970s, eschewing the designation of fundamentalist but holding to a conservative interpretation of the Bible.

3. pertaining to certain movements in the Protestant churches in the 18th and 19th centuries that stressed the importance of personal experience of guilt for sin and of reconciliation to God through Christ.

4. marked by ardent or zealous enthusiasm for a cause.

It is interesting that this secular dictionary suggests that what was a prominent aspect of the Christian church in the late 1970s is no longer so today.

It has to be reluctantly admitted that despite some notable exceptions, many Christians today have lost that ardent, zealous, missionary enthusiasm for the cause of Christ.

We still *believe* in it, but we have become so comfortable in the social clubs that some of our churches have become, that we would rather pay others to go and do the work of evangelism than do it ourselves.

Consider this story:

THE LiFE-SAVING STATION

Lighthouse Storm

On a dangerous seacoast, where shipwrecks often occur, there was once a crude little life-saving station. The building was just a hut and there was only one boat, but the few devoted members kept a constant watch over the sea. With no thought for themselves, they went out day or night tirelessly searching for the lost.

Many lives were saved by this wonderful little station, so that it became famous. Some of those who were saved, and various others in the surrounding areas, wanted to become associated with the station and give of their time, money and effort for the support of its work. New boats were bought and new crews were trained. The little life-saving station grew.

Some of the new members of the life-saving station were unhappy that the building was so crude and so poorly equipped. They felt that a more comfortable place should be provided as the first refuge of those saved from the sea.

[9] *Lighthouse Storm by 1MAGINATE Digital Art / Drawings & Paintings / Landscapes & Scenery - Used by Permission*

So they replaced the emergency cots with beds and put better furniture in an enlarged building. Now the life-saving station became a popular gathering place for its members. They re-decorated it beautifully and furnished it as a sort of club.

Less of the members were now interested in going to sea on life-saving missions, so they hired life-boat crews to do this work. The mission of life-saving was still given lip-service, but most were too busy or lacked the necessary commitment to take part in the life-saving activities personally.

About this time, a large ship was wrecked off the coast and the hired crews brought in boat-loads of cold, wet, half-drowned people.

They were dirty and sick. Some of them had black skin and some spoke a strange language, so the beautiful new club was considerably messed up. So immediately, the property committee had a shower house built, outside the club, where victims of shipwreck could be cleaned up before coming inside.

At the next meeting, there was a split in the club membership. Most of the members wanted to stop the club's life-saving activities as being unpleasant and a hindrance to the normal life-pattern of the club.

But some members insisted that life-saving was their primary purpose and pointed out that they were still called a life-saving station; but they were finally voted down and told that if they wanted to save the life of all the various kinds of people who were shipwrecked in those waters, they could begin their own life-saving station down the coast.

They did.

As the years went by, the new station experienced the same changes that had occurred in the old. They evolved into a club; and yet another life-saving station was founded.

If you visit that seacoast today, you will find a number of exclusive clubs along that shore. Shipwrecks are still frequent in those waters, only now most of the people drown.

– Written in 1953 by Episcopal priest, Theodore Wedel

There really is nothing I can add to that.

Personally, I don't see evangelism as a legalistic ritual in which Christians participate to fulfill some sort of quota, to appease a strict God, to please a pastor, or even to make ourselves feel good.

If someone were to receive something that changed his or her life for the better, lifted the heavy burden of guilt and sin, and filled the person with joy, would he or she not want to share that with as many people as possible?

Becoming a Christian does, potentially, bring with it some benefits or "perks." Those benefits come as a consequence of surrendering our life to Christ. They should *never* be the reason for surrender.

If the desire for the benefits is the motivating factor of our desiring to be a Christian, we have started on the wrong foot.

Here is one last definition to help create the context for what I am about to write: The phrase is "conservative interpretation." According to thefreedictionary.com, conservative means:

    1. Favouring traditional views and values; tending to oppose change.
    2. Traditional or restrained in style: a conservative dark suit.
    3. Moderate; cautious: a conservative estimate.

Within Christianity, there are different views on the authority, inspiration and interpretation of the Bible.

The *authority* of the Bible refers to the importance of the Bible for decision-making; the question being this: "How much should Christians pay attention to what the Bible says in terms of how they live their lives?"

The *inspiration* of the Bible refers to whether the Bible is the complete Word of God, whether it is inspired by God, and what degree of exactness of wording is involved in the inspiration.

The *interpretation* of the Bible refers to one's conclusion as to whether, when reading the Bible, Christians should take everything it says at face value, or whether they should consider parts as being merely symbolic.

When discussing approaches to the Bible, we can divide Christians into three main schools of thought: fundamentalists, conservatives and liberals.

Fundamentalists believe the Bible to be the complete Word of God and that it should be followed at all times, for all issues. They believe it was written by humans who were told what to write, word for word, by God. They view it as being free from error and needing to be understood at face value. So, for instance, if the Bible says the world was created in six, twenty-four-hour days, then it was.

Conservatives believe the Bible is, first and foremost, a book about religion and morality. As such, it has absolute authority concerning moral issues but is not necessarily the final word concerning other areas, such as science. They believe the writers were inspired by God and that the Bible contains spiritual truths but that sometimes the personality of the writers are reflected in the writings. Conservatives believe these spiritual truths have to be understood within the context of the time the Bible was written and the people who wrote it. They believe the Bible answers "why" questions but not "how" questions.

Liberals believe that not everything in the Bible is relevant for today and that not everything it says is true at face value—or even actually happened. They consider the Bible to be a book of guidance but that other factors have to be taken in to account, such as their belief that the Bible was written by humans who may have experienced God and tried to put it into words but who made mistakes. When liberals interpret the Bible, they do so from the viewpoint of symbolism and poetry. They understand the truths to be spiritual, rather than literal. For example, they might say the miracles might teach us about Jesus' power but probably didn't actually happen. As such, liberals generally look for spiritual meaning in the Bible without taking it literally.

Personally, I have never been comfortable with societal pressures to label myself as belonging to any particular denomination. Rather, I prefer to call myself a full-gospel, fundamental conservative. Thus it was that Ginny and I were comfortable spending ten years of our lives—arguably the most exciting, productive, hard-working ten years of our lives—directing "Heaven's Gates and Hell's Flames" with no denominational barriers.

Using local church people to make up the cast, this drama presented nine mini-dramas, featuring ordinary people—such as secretaries, construction workers and teenagers—in recognizable scenarios such as family or work situations where they face unexpected death and suddenly find themselves at the gates of heaven, discovering whether they will go to heaven or hell.

The big question faced by the audience is this: who makes that decision? God? Or is the decision made by the people themselves, according to the choices they make in life?

Producing the drama for ten years, working closely in each church with thirty to fifty people from the full spectrum of cultures, ages and denominations (well over 15,000 people in total) was an unbelievable educational experience for us. Seeing tens of thousands of people respond to the invitation to surrender their life to Jesus was amazing.

It is that opportunity to receive salvation that I want to talk about here. In Christian circles, we call it the invitation or the altar call.

According to Dictionary.com, an "altar call" is "an evangelist preacher's invitation at the end of the sermon, asking people to come forward to acknowledge a conversion."

It is important to note the important distinction between the altar call or invitation, and the actual event of conversion. In responding to an altar call or invitation a person is *acknowledging* that the event of conversion has already taken place or that he or she is open to making that decision.

Because this has so often been presented to people incorrectly, their understanding of it has become flawed.

Back to Dictionary.com, we find the definition of conversion:
1. the act or process of converting; state of being converted.
2. change in character, form, or function.
3. spiritual change from sinfulness to righteousness.
4. change from one religion, political belief, viewpoint, et cetera, to another.
5. a change of attitude, emotion, or viewpoint from one of indifference, disbelief, or antagonism to one of acceptance, faith, or enthusiastic support, especially such a change in a person's religion.

So where does the conversion take place? At the front of a church? Standing before an evangelist in front of hundreds or even thousands of people?

No, conversion takes place in the heart of a person, wherever the person may be at whatever time.

My own conversion took place late at night in my bedroom. There were many circumstances leading to the moment, but right there I challenged God. "Okay God, if you *are* real, then I open my heart to you. Please come in."

At that time, with my frustration, my attitude was not really repentant, but God looked into my heart and knew I was sincere in seeking Him.

God will *always* find, and connect with, a heart that is truly seeking Him.

There was no one there except God and me. That night I felt nothing different, but the next morning I woke up and I *knew*—I just *knew*—that God had come into my heart.

I instantly stopped smoking, swearing and gambling.

Nobody told me to stop; I just knew!

A few days later, at a youth meeting attended by about twenty-five people, I gave a testimony as to what had happened in my heart. Soon after I gave further public testimony by obeying the scripture and being baptized.

That was the start of another story of my life of defeats and victories, ups and down, elation and despair. But every defeat, every down experience, every moment of despair—and every moment of incredible victory—has been a stepping stone to knowing God more intimately.

I am *still* on the journey! And God's patience is unbelievable.

His patience towards us does not give us license to sin, but it is inexhaustible to those whose hearts truly seek Him.

Before I move on to what I really want to say in this chapter, let me tease you with one more thought to ponder regarding invitations or altar calls.

Nowhere in the Bible did Jesus or His disciples lead anyone in a "sinner's prayer" and indicate that that prayer signified the point of conversion.

People were invited to follow Jesus. How were they supposed to do that? By taking up their crosses, laying down their lives, giving up their possessions and/or forsaking all others.

Goodness me! It would appear that, in biblical days, the cost of becoming a Christian was much greater than is apparently required of anyone these days. Just say the sinner's prayer and you're in. Right?

To satisfy the insatiable demand in our society for ease and instant gratification, have we marketed Christianity to suit today's expectations? In so doing, have we weakened it severely? Are we misleading people with regard to what they may face?

The question is worth pondering.

Among Jesus' last words to His disciples, before He was crucified, were these:

> *All authority has been given to Me in Heaven and on earth. Go, therefore, and make disciples of all the nations, baptizing them in the Name of the Father and the Son and the Holy Spirit, teaching them to observe all that I commanded you; and lo, I am with you always, even to the end of the age* (Matthew 28:18-20).

After He was crucified and rose again, just before His ascension to heaven, He spoke His last words to them:

> *It is not for you to know the times or dates the Father has set by His own authority. But you will receive power when the Holy Spirit comes on you; and you will be My witnesses in Jerusalem, and in Judea, and all Samaria and to the ends of the earth* (Acts 1:7-8).

The command is not to make converts but to make disciples.

So to interpret this simply:

1. Don't get bogged down and distracted by trying to figure out exactly when Jesus is going to return. We are not meant to know that.

2. Don't try to do anything in your own strength. God will give you His strength to enable you to do His work.

3. We are to be *His* witnesses, not *our* witnesses. It's all about Jesus. It's not about our ministry.

4. Where should we witness? Jesus was very specific:

Jerusalem	where we live.
Judea	the geographical area immediately surrounding where we live.
Samaria	by adding Samaria, this then encompassed what was known of the Northern and Southern Kingdom of Israel. In other words, wherever you have influence.
The ends of the Earth	that covers everywhere else.

5. To do what specifically?

"Go therefore"	That is pro-active, not reactive. Get *out* of the church rather than snuggling comfortably in it.
"and make disciples of all the nations"	We are to go beyond making converts to helping people become disciples.
"baptizing them in the Name of the Father and the Son and the Holy Spirit"	Although baptism is not a prerequisite for salvation, the willingness to obey scripture and be baptized is an indication of willingness to follow Christ.
	It is the responsibility of the church to teach this. If a person refuses to be baptized, that wilful refusal would call into question the validity of that person's conversion.

*"teaching them to observe all
that I commanded you;"*   It is one thing to *know* what is right but another thing altogether to *do* what is right.

As Jesus said, *"If you know these things, you are blessed if you do them"* (John 13:17).

It is not what you know that matters but what you do with what you know—how you actually live your life.

And finally these great words of encouragement from the Son of God: *"... and lo, I am with you always, even to the end of the age"* (Matthew 28:20).

As for me, I found myself, week after week, standing before hundreds—sometimes thousands—of people, inviting them to take that step of faith, to surrender their lives to Jesus and begin the process that would take them from being a converted believer to an effective disciple.

I took the burden of responsibility very seriously.

I knew I could not convert anyone, but I knew also, that if I did a bad job I could be responsible for someone not taking the opportunity, that day, to surrender to Jesus.

The drama "Heaven's Gates and Hell's Flames" was very hard-hitting in communicating the message that yes, there is a God to whom we are accountable. Jesus is real, and yes, there is a devil who is active in this world and who strives to keep people from believing in the existence of a loving God.

The drama was an effective demonstration of the fact that there is a heaven to gain and a hell to shun and that which determines a person's ultimate destination — heaven or hell—is not God but rather, the decision each individual makes whilst here on this earth.

The evangelist taking the altar call had to walk a very fine line in presenting the love of God (clarifying the fact that it is not God's will for anyone to go to hell) against the fact that hell is real. It was absolutely not our intention to scare people into heaven.

The following are three "Heaven's Gates and Hell's Flames" altar call incidences of many hundreds. I feel the Lord has laid these on my heart to share.

SCOTLAND

We were at a church in Scotland. As we were training the cast, we realized this church had some exceptional acting talent. In fact, they were so good that I was beginning to detect a slight attitude of over-confidence. Some of them seemed to be so sure of their own abilities that they didn't feel they really needed to be dependent on the Lord. They were all good people, but they needed to have their focus on the Lord recalibrated.

Over the years, I have noticed that the people with the most natural talent tend to be the least attuned to the need to pray or acknowledge the hand of the Lord in what they are doing. It comes too easy for them.

Even with minimal practice, pre-planning, preparation and prayer, such people can do a more-than-adequate presentation. I would often wonder how much more effective these gifted people could be if they humbled themselves before the Lord, took the time to properly prepare and submitted their talents to Him.

So it was on that Sunday afternoon, before the first performance Sunday night, instead of a final rehearsal, I called for a time of prayer. Several in the cast voiced their concerns about this, but that's what we did.

On Sunday night, the church was all fired-up. It was full to overflowing, with the church people and the cast having invited many friends and neighbours to attend.

The cast did a brilliant job with the drama—no technical hitches. Then came that critical moment when I stepped up to do the invitation (or take the altar call, whichever way you want to say it).

And I blew it!

I had not understood that my judgment of the self-sufficient cast should have been a hint to me as well. I could point to some mitigating circumstances to excuse my failure. I could try to say the devil was working hard to cause me to fail, but the fact is, I mentally lost my way.

I had done hundreds of altar calls before. I could practically do them in my sleep, but that night it seemed I couldn't put two coherent sentences together. The harder I tried, the worse I became. I waffled and talked for much too long.

If I recall correctly, I don't think one single person responded, for which I felt personally responsible.

When it was over, I wanted to run away and hide. The cast members and the people in the church were extremely disappointed. Everyone was deflated but no one more so than me.

The pastor asked me to join him in his office where he put a consoling arm around my shoulders and ... no, that is not what happened. What actually happened was that when the pastor had me alone in his office, he proceeded to give me a humiliating dressing down, pointing out all I had done wrong and all I needed to do to put it right.

It was beyond humiliating; I felt like I was being kicked while I was down—but everything the pastor said was true. I had to sit there and take it. There was no defence for me. Yes, there were a few extenuating situations at play, but I should have handled them better.

I have never before or since felt more deflated, humbled and inadequate.

My initial reaction was that I never wanted to take an altar call again, but the next night, shaking inside, my road to recovery began. This time I was far more focused and took much less time. Many people responded.

That incident has been etched in my mind's eye, never to be forgotten. It is ready to be recalled should I ever again slip into feeling I could do it in my own strength.

FRANCE

We were in Montpellier in the south of France one summer. It was excruciatingly hot, and the drama was being presented in a municipal building where there was no air-conditioning.

The "heaven" set, is created by hanging huge sheets of silver reflective Mylar from the ceiling and then covering everything else (that doesn't move) with this same silver Mylar.

If the lighting crew shines red light on it, hell is portrayed; whereas, if they shine white light on it—voilà—it's heaven.

The gates of heaven were two, five-foot long cases (used for transporting lights) covered in Mylar. They were stood on their ends with a three-foot arch joining them on top. The cases and arch were attached with masking tape to the Mylar hanging from the ceiling. The effect was extremely dramatic, especially when the stage lights,whether red or white, were beamed on to the stage. Yes, it looked very dramatic, but it was, in fact, rather delicate.

We could go any place—an old church, a new church, a prison or school gymnasium, an outdoor or indoor theatre—anywhere—and by covering the stage with Mylar, we had heaven and hell.

The twenty or so angels dressed in all-white gowns had to stand on stage on boxes or risers of varying heights. They had to stand there, looking angelic and not moving, for the entire performance. It was quite a feat of endurance.

On this hot summer night, we told the girls playing the angels that if they felt faint, they should leave the stage as soon as they could by unobtrusively slipping off to the side, preferably when the main stage lights were off and only a spotlight was illuminating two or three of the other actors. In this way, hopefully, their departure would go unnoticed.

Well, on the night in question one of the younger angels did begin to feel faint, which probably accounted for what she did next.

About midway through the drama, this young angel felt she needed to leave the stage, but instead of slipping off to the side as directed, she walked unsteadily towards heaven's gates while the full white lights were shining on the stage.

As the actors were trying to continue their scene, this girl started to walk through the pillars of heaven's gates, at which point, she fainted and grabbed at the pillars for support.

These pillars—lighting cases stood on end—were not designed to take any weight, and in a brief moment, the pillars, arch—indeed, all of heaven—came crashing down around the ears of all the other angels and with it, much of the Mylar curtain, which was ripped to shreds.

What would we do now?

This was a time for improvisation and thinking on our feet.

Making light of what had just happened—and using it as an illustration of the unplanned events of our lives—the invitation was given for those who wanted a closer walk with Jesus. Many responded.

The next night we had an even bigger crowd—and an even bigger response—as many people came back because they wanted to see the end of the drama.

Fortunately there were no more fainting angels.

MISSION TO LONDON

EARLS COURT, LONDON, ENGLAND

"Mission to London" is an event that has been running for twenty years. It is a six-day evangelistic effort organized and sponsored by a large group of churches in London. They pool their efforts into inviting big name evangelists from North America, the UK and around the world to speak throughout the six days and evenings.

The event is held in the 20,000-seat Earls Court in London where a variety of events, from Olympic sports to World Wide Wrestling events, have been hosted. Artists such as Pink Floyd, Celine Dion, Elton John, Take That, Oasis, David Bowie and The Spice Girls (to name just a few) have performed there.

In the late 1990s, we were asked to stage the drama "Heaven's Gates and Hell's Flames" on the penultimate Friday night of the mission, following Richard Roberts.

It was a huge undertaking because the stage was so large and because we had to make a special Mylar curtain that would comply with the British fire safety standards. These were stricter than the American safety standards met by our existing curtain.

It took several of us almost three full days in a large warehouse to lay out and piece together the new curtain that had to be about four stories high and almost as wide as a tennis court.

We could not hang the curtain in the Earls Court auditorium, or create the stage set, until after Benny Hinn had finished preaching on the Thursday night. With a special team of dedicated helpers, we started hanging the enormous curtain and setting our props at about 11:00 p.m. Thursday and worked through the night to be ready for the safety inspection that would take place at 8:00 a.m. Friday.

Needless to say, we were exhausted.

Sleep did not come easy during the day in the tiny hotel room that had been provided for Ginny and me in the busy heart of London.

That evening, I was going to be giving an altar call to 20,000 people, the largest crowd I had ever faced. During the afternoon, I spent my usual time alone with God, reading His Word and trying to clear my mind.

There are two opinions on how to take an altar call, and both have merit in their own way. One approach is to have a prepared, scripted and practiced presentation; the advantages of this being that the important points would not be forgotten and the speaker would be less inclined to ramble. The other approach involves going onstage (in this case, at the end of the drama) with nothing pre-planned, simply allowing the Holy Spirit to lead. Other than praying beforehand, this approach involves no preparation.

One could argue that both of these methods have both merits and flaws.

If an evangelist is working in just one country, in just one culture, it is relatively easy to tune in spiritually to that country, but as we were constantly working in different countries and different cultures, along with a reassuring structure to keep me disciplined, I needed the flexibility of allowing the Holy Spirit to speak to my heart. It was vital for me to be aware of the sensitivities of each new country and each unique situation. (I never wanted to repeat what happened in Scotland.)

Those were the thoughts uppermost in my mind as I contemplated that evening's presentation of the drama and my responsibility to make the altar call.

As I lay relaxing, soaking in a hot bath, a single word came into my mind. "Come." I closed my eyes to allow my mind to drift away, but the word was still there.

People who know me, know that I am a relatively pragmatic person not given to hearing voices or seeing visions. Nevertheless, over the years I have experienced a couple of occasions where I heard God speak to me. Each time, it was private, personal and as clear to me as anything I have ever heard—even though I heard it in my heart.

If you have never experienced God speaking to you, I could not possibly explain it, but if you have experienced it, then you know exactly what I am talking about. It is not something you blab about because people could justifiably think you are a little off your rocker.

So I towelled myself dry, got dressed and sat down to read to relax and clear my mind. But the word would not leave me. "Come."

Ginny was still over at the conference, so I had no one to talk to about what I was experiencing. After a while, I decided I would talk to God about it.

So I prayed, "Lord, this word is stuck in my mind. Are You trying to tell me something?"

And I heard, just as if it were an audible voice in the room, "Get out of the way, and just tell the people to come."

To be honest, I have debated with myself whether or not to share this incident in this book. But then I reasoned that if I didn't share it, it would be because I was more concerned with my own personal reputation than about what God has done through me.

I walked from my hotel to Earls Court and sought out David Forrest, a man whose opinion I value and whose discretion I trust. Dave is a friend who is a very experienced evangelist/pastor. As one of those who laboured tirelessly through the night to construct the stage set, he was more than familiar with the "Heaven's Gates and Hell's Flames" ministry.

I shared with him what I had been feeling and what I felt I was hearing from the Lord. In his inimitable way, Dave said, "If God had spoken to me like that, I sure would do as He says."

That Friday night, the "Mission To London" meetings started with a full capacity. After a time of worship, Richard Roberts (Oral Roberts' son) gave a rousing message. Then the lights dimmed as the opening music started for the drama. After briefly introducing it, I went backstage were I was lost in a world of my own thoughts, vacillating between fear and dread and a sense of inevitability. With my self-confidence still fragile after the Scotland debacle, I hid my struggle from my wife and friends. If I had this wrong, it would surely be the end for me.

When the drama came to its climatic end, I walked on to the vast stage and looked into the black void where, although I could not see them, I knew 20,000 people were looking expectantly at me.

In the bleed of the stage lights that illuminated the front row, I saw Richard Roberts, Benny Hinn, Morris Cerullo, Pastor Colin Dye (the pastor of Britain's largest Church, Kensington Temple London City Church) and other luminaries looking expectantly at me like the rest of the audience. This was it!

It is amazing how one can feel so alone amongst so many people. But then I reasoned that I was not alone; God was with me. I took a deep breath and said, "Normally, in these situations, I would say a few things to pull the threads of this drama together, but this afternoon I felt the Lord tell me to get out of the way and say only one word to you. So, from the Lord to you, I say, 'Come.'"

I closed my eyes, took one step back and waited. All I could hear was the thunder of my heartbeat pounding in my ears. I was tempted to peek to see what, if anything, was happening, but I dared not. Sweat was pouring from my forehead, causing my glasses to slip down my nose, but I made no move to push them up.

A voice inside me was niggling at me to say more, maybe repeat the word come, but I willed myself to stay quiet, to wait and trust God.

I have no idea how long the silence lasted, but I became aware of, rather than heard, a rustling that slowly got louder until it accelerated. It became the recognizable noise of feet, many feet, a great many feet. When I opened my eyes, I saw scores and then hundreds of people—some walking, others running—coming to stand in front of the stage.

It was a sea of humanity, every one responding to God's simple call to come. I remember vividly Richard Roberts looking around with a look of surprised incredulity on his face.

There had been no persuading, no cajoling, no threat of what would happen if a person did not respond. It was just God, absolutely not me.

I had arranged with Pastor Colin Dye that when people came forward, because his church was the lead church at the mission that year, I would hand the platform over to him at that point; so that is what I did.

I then left the stage and went back immediately to my little hotel room.

I had never made an altar call like that before, and I have never done so since.

This is what I learned from that experience:

1. First and foremost, we should always be diligent to do the very best we can in planning, preparation and rehearsing. There is no excuse—no matter how talented we may be—for slothfulness or throwing things together at the last moment. That is an insult to God.

2. If we involved prayerful consideration in our planning and preparation, then, if our hearts and motives have been right, it is likely we have heard from God and what we're doing—and how we're doing it—will line up with His will. The biggest mistake we as Christians make is having our own plans that we take to God for His stamp of approval. Such plans will take a lot of hard work and result in very little success. But if your plans originate from God, stay with the plan and the way you are doing things.

3. However, always be open to the possibility that maybe, just maybe, God may say, "Today I want you to do things a little differently. Trust me." If that happens, it is the exception—never the rule—but always leave room for the Holy Spirit to come and step in, in His own unique way.

4. Trust and honour those in leadership over you, and if you are a leader, don't be afraid to talk to someone who you recognise has greater experience than you.

5. Yes, it is a scary place to be, but living out on that edge is where we see God at work.

One of the disciplines I am learning in writing this book is to shut up when the Lord impresses upon me, "That's enough for now!"

FROM A VOLVO TO A BMW
VIA TWO TOYOTAS

We hear a lot about how God will supply for us. Writing how-to books about how we can get the Lord to provide whatever we want is an industry on its own.

God's provision is a delicate subject because there are certainly many scriptures which, when properly applied, most definitely indicate that if we are obedient to His Word, God will act—not according to our wants, but according to His will.

Consistent with all of this is the irrefutable fact that our desires have to line up with His will and our obedience plays a very important part in the process.

I make no attempt to provide you with a detailed biblical assertation on this subject, but rather, I share with you a true story of God in action.

By 1984, Ginny and I were well-established in our ministry in communist Eastern Europe, particularly in Poland and Romania.

During many visits to those countries, although we were detained and interrogated by the communist authorities on more than one occasion, we developed friendships with many wonderful people who were truly suffering for their faith.

At that time, a large church denomination had approached us to spearhead their work in Eastern Europe. After many interviews, it was decided that we would join them after we had fulfilled existing obligations we had made to various churches and pastors in Poland. Included in these obligations was an agreement to raise $30,000 to ship 10,000 Bibles into Poland, for which government permits in Poland had already been obtained.

Contrary to popular belief, it was not always necessary to smuggle Christian literature into Eastern Europe. Yes, it was usually necessary, but this was one of those exceptional occasions.

The Bibles were sitting in a warehouse in Sweden. They had not been sent into Poland because the original sponsors had failed to come up with the finances to pay for them.

So it was that after a brief, planned ministry trip to England, we were scheduled to return to Canada and the USA to raise the money for the Bibles—following which, we would join with the large denominational missionary organization.

I well remember that day, at the home of some friends in England, when we got the call from North America informing us that we were required to return immediately to start work with this missionary organization. I asked, "What about the commitments they agreed we could fulfill first?" The voice at the other end of the line informed us that the agreement had been changed.

Ginny and I knew immediately that we should not work with this organization. If they could arbitrarily make such a significant change to our agreement, this was not a good portent for the future.

A great deal of financial support for us had already gone into this organization and it became apparent that it would not be easy to get it back.

Nevertheless, there are times when one has to stand firmly by a principle and keep a promise. For the sake of peace and harmony in the Body of Christ, you just have to walk away from what you know is not right and trust the Lord.

This was such an occasion. So we returned to Canada, penniless and with no support base to speak of. All we knew was that we had to keep our word to the people in Poland to raise the $30,000, so that the 10,000 Bibles could be sent there. In those days of communism, who knew when such an opportunity would again present itself?

As human beings, it is normal to want to be in control of things, but when we are left in total dependence upon God and we know, for a certainty, He has called us to do something—but we have no idea how it is going to be accomplished—that is when the Lord acts and we begin to see amazing things happen.

We had already arranged a trip across Canada and the USA to visit with the friends and churches we knew over there. Whereas, before we had expected to make that trip under the auspices of the large organization, we now had to figure out how to do that ourselves, as we had no money and no vehicle.

Previous experience had taught us to simply move forward, trusting God. To paraphrase what our current pastor, Charles Price, has often said, "It is not important that you know where your journey will take you or how you are going to make the journey—as long as you know the One with whom you are making that journey."

After praying much, we felt we should go to all the churches across North America as had been arranged but that we should apply every love gift *entirely* towards the fund for the Bibles. We would trust God for the gas (for a vehicle that we did not yet have), for our food and for our accommodations.

It is interesting when you have a firm conviction that God wants you to do something. When you have nothing, it is relatively simple to believe Him for everything.

Very quickly, two totally unexpected and amazing things happened.

We were visiting two good friends, Kathy and Eddie Chu, who, because of their interest in our ministry, asked us what we were doing at that time. When we told Eddie about our intention to continue with the plan to raise the money for Bibles for Poland, he said he had a good car we could use, a car that was sturdy and could make the 10,000-mile (16,000-km) trip that we planned. It was a Volvo, ironically from the same country where the Bibles were sitting in a warehouse, waiting to go into Poland. (I don't suppose there is any spiritual significance to that, but it is interesting.)

While the availability of the car was helpful on one level, the reality remained that we did not have any money to buy it. Out of the blue, Eddie stunned us by saying, "Why don't you buy the car from me for one dollar? When you get back to Toronto, sell the car back to me for the same price.

I could not believe my ears. What an unbelievably generous and creative idea! This allowed us to be the legal owners of the car for all the necessary insurance purposes and for crossing back and forth from Canada to the USA. When it was all over, Eddie would get the car back, albeit a little worse for wear, but having served a worthwhile service for the Lord.

Although Kathy and Eddie were not called to go to the mission field themselves, they had the wisdom to be sensitive to whatever the Lord called them to do. They had a vitally important role to play in this story and they did not shirk from it.

The following Sunday, we were at our church. In the tone of a general, polite question, our Pastor, Dr. Paul Smith, asked what our current plans were. We told him what had happened, about our intentions and of the wonderful provision of the car.

Dr. Paul then asked us, "If you intend to apply all of the love offerings towards the cost of the Bibles, how do you intend to buy the gas you will need for the trip?"

Despite knowing how naive our response would sound, we said simply, "We are going to trust God to provide."

With a twinkle in his eyes, Dr. Paul reached into his pocket and pulled out his own personal credit card. Giving it to us, he said, "Use that to buy all the gas you need."

Shocked, we said, "But, Dr. Paul, we are going to be driving some 16,000 kilometres!"

"That's okay" was his reply. Smiling, he added, "Now that the Lord has provided you with a car and the means to buy the gasoline, I guess you had better get going!"

And so we did.

Across Canada via Winnipeg to Vancouver, down the west coast of the USA through Portland and down to Modesto. From there, we drove down to San Diego via Los Angeles, over to Phoenix and then up through Dodge City to Oklahoma City. Then we drove down to Dallas and on and on … mile after mile after mile. Ministering in churches of many different denominations along the way, we shared what the Lord was doing in communist Poland and about our opportunity to legally ship 10,000 Bibles to those precious people.

Sometimes we stayed in the homes of people in the churches; sometimes, hearing our story, people paid for us to stay in hotels (one of which was a wonderful four-night stay in an up-market Four Seasons Hotel in Arizona); sometimes we slept in the car; sometimes we ate with Christians in their homes or were taken out by the pastors for a meal, as was customary after ministering at a church.

Little by little, the offerings for the Bibles came in.

I will not bore you with the myriad of stories of the many things that happened, but I will share a funny incident that happened at a church in Rockwall, just north of Dallas.

After a morning service one Sunday, the pastor took us out for lunch along with several of his staff and family. It was one of those typical American restaurants that seemed to have everything on the menu; the portions were enormous. We were, after all, in Texas.

When ordering the food, the pastor said something to me that sort of clicked in my brain. In the generous manner for which North Americans are famous, this pastor, referring to the opulent menu, said, "Terry, you can have whatever is your heart's desire."

In the midst of all the animated, friendly chatter going on around me at the table, I felt myself retreating into a bubble as I considered just what was my heart's desire at that moment.

No one noticed what I ordered. I asked for four slices of white bread and butter and a large order of buffalo fries—the nearest thing in North America to English chips.

Picture the scene as the waitress arrived at the table with orders of steak and shrimp and other exotic Mexican dishes—and my plate of bread and butter with a side order of buffalo fries. The pastor (bless him) was horrified.

"Terry!" he exclaimed. "I said you could have whatever your heart desired. You could have had anything on the menu, and yet you ordered *that*?"

I explained to him that his offer had gotten me thinking. I knew everything was available to me, but that wasn't reason enough to order something extravagant. I had suddenly become homesick for England, so I ordered the ingredients to make a

Chip Buttie. (My English friends will be smiling right now, because they will know *exactly* what I am talking about.)

So, as the pastor and his entourage watched in disbelief, I carefully placed half of the bread and butter on my plate and then proceeded to lay the buffalo fries laterally onto the bread and butter, three deep. After applying a liberal coating of salt, I placed the other bread on top, cut the sandwich in half and then proceeded to inhale it with great gusto.

At that moment—deep in the heart of Texas—when I could have had the biggest, best steak in the world, my heart's desire was that with which I was most familiar.

The thing is, my early years were spent growing up in the north of England on a diet that consisted heavily of bread and butter (neither of which were available in low-fat forms) and fish and chips. For a snack, we would spread fat onto bread and sprinkle it with salt. Another of my favourites was Sugar Butties ... and yes, that was made exactly as it sounds. On Monday, we loved to eat "Bubble and Squeak," which was Sunday's leftovers fried.

I did like cooked vegetables, but I hated fruit, so how did I survive? Well, everywhere I went, I had to use "shank's pony"—I either walked or cycled. For many years, in order to get to school each day, I had to walk several miles, take two buses and a boat. Despite what would be called an almost suicide diet, my lifestyle was so full of exercise that I was very fit indeed. Life was simple and uncomplicated and I was very happy.

It is a good exercise for all of us to, from time to time, reflect not so much on what we want from life, but rather, what we need. If we can learn to be content with what we have instead of always striving for more, we will find the peace that otherwise seems so elusive.

Although my eating habits have improved greatly as I have come to understand my responsibility to take better care of this "temple" that the Lord has entrusted to me, my favourite food is still potatoes, hot or cold, in any form except raw. If any of you ever invite me to your home for a meal and serve me a Chip Buttie, I will be a very happy camper.

Before we leave Texas, I must share a little story about a Texas rancher meeting an English farmer.

When you think of Texas, you think of everything being bigger,. The egos of some Texans (not all by any means) do nothing to repudiate that image.

So it was, that the Texas rancher asked the English farmer the size of his farm back in England. The self-effacing English farmer replied, "Well, by English standards it's quite big: about fifty acres." To be courteous, he then asked the Texas rancher the size of his ranch.

The Texas rancher replied, with pride and a tinge of arrogance, "Well, you know, it would be hard to explain to you just how big my ranch is. Let me put it this way: if I were to get up in the morning before the sun comes up and get into my car and drive all day long from east to west, never stopping for anything, by the time the sun went down at night, I still would not have reached the other side of my ranch!"

"Really?" replied the English farmer. " I used to have a car like that."

It's all in your perspective, right?

Before returning to the journey, I must share another story of God's provision.

We had to carefully budget our money. One day we were in a Wendy's hamburger restaurant just outside Oklahoma City.

Before eating, Ginny and I briefly bowed our heads to say grace, thanking God for His provision, as we usually do. A few minutes later, an older gentleman who had been seated with his wife at the other side of the restaurant came over to us. With a typically polite Oklahoma drawl, he said, "My wife and I noticed you praying before you ate." He then asked, "Are you Christians?"

I answered that yes, we were. Upon hearing my English accent, he asked why I was so far from home.

I matter-of-factly told him about our raising money for Bibles for Poland, to which this gracious man said, "Then let me buy your meal."

When I told him we had already paid for it, he promptly gave us $200 toward the Bibles.

He was a total stranger—but a huge encouragement from the Lord.

So, back to our journey. Duly fortified, we travelled up through Tennessee, then Raleigh, North Carolina, Long Island, New York City and finally back to Toronto—a trip that took almost twelve weeks.

Along the way, we enjoyed wonderful fellowship with a wide variety of Christians in many different churches. They blessed us with their love and hospitality and we had the opportunity to minister to them through Ginny's singing and testimony and my preaching and sharing what God was doing in Poland.

The car faithfully brought us back to Toronto, having broken down only once when the alternator failed, a delay of just a few hours and minimal cost. However, Kathy and Eddie have since told us that the car pretty much "gave up the ghost" almost immediately after we returned it to them.

Before arriving at our home in Toronto, we called by our post office box to collect the mail that had accumulated during our absence. There were a few support cheques and when added to the love offerings we'd received, we realized the Lord had brought in just over the $30,000 needed for the Bibles for Poland—as well as taking care of all our needs during the twelve-week journey. God *is* faithful!

If you remember nothing else from this story, please remember that God can act only through people who are willing to trust Him and who acknowledge their complete dependence on Him. We must *never* take the credit for ourselves. *All* the glory goes to Him.

There we were, basking in the afterglow of having witnessed God do something marvellous, but we were still faced with the reality that we needed to get over to England and continue the ministry that the Lord had set before us, but we had only a very small support base and no vehicle over there. We did not even have the resources to get a cheap, pre-owned vehicle.

One day, as we were finalizing our move back to the UK, we received a telephone call from some good friends who prefer to remain anonymous.

The wife was a good friend to Ginny, but her husband was ill in hospital at the time. However, they had received a newsletter we had sent out asking people to pray for us regarding our need for a reliable vehicle in Europe.

We never sent out heavy-handed appeals promising all kinds of blessings from God if people gave to us, but we did feel that, where it was appropriate, we needed to let the people who cared for us know what our needs were.

It was in some ways irrelevant to us whether or not people responded. What mattered was that we were obedient to the Lord in letting the needs be known and then leaving it totally in His hands.

The newsletter simply laid out the options before us, none of which we had the financial wherewithal to purchase. The cheapest option was to buy a second-hand car. We knew, however, that that option might not be the best because the ongoing repair and maintenance would be high, and there would be occasions when the car would not be big enough.

The second option, slightly more expensive than the first, was to get a second-hand van; but it, too, would require considerable ongoing maintenance, especially as much of our travelling in Europe would be in the Eastern European countries that were still under the grip of communism and whose roads were awful.

The third option—and by far the most expensive initially—would be to buy a brand new van. It could be customized to seat nine and sleep four. This would be convenient when we found ourselves deep in Eastern Europe with no access to anywhere to sleep at night.

We had done our homework in researching many different makes of vans available in Europe—Ford, Renault, Mercedes, et cetera—before deciding that a Toyota would best meet our needs, but it was expensive.

We met with this couple at his bedside in the hospital and they informed us that they were going to donate the entire cost for the new Toyota van. We were amazed.

Van #1, trailer & Ginny

Van #2 & trailer on the road in Scotland

But should we have been? Is our God not faithful to supply the needs of those who trust and serve Him?

Over the years the Lord had used us many times to take money, medical supplies and Bibles, etc. into Eastern Europe. When people showered us with their understandable gratitude, we had learned to deflect that gratitude to the Lord.

To the Lord, we were thankful for this gift. To this couple, we were thankful for their obedience to the Lord in giving. It is very important to keep that perspective in mind.

The Lord called the husband home within a few years, and eventually, the Lord brought another wonderful Christian man into his wife's life.

Several years later, Ginny and I were in Florida, close to where Ginny's friend and new husband lived. They came to see the ministry in which we were currently involved, the evangelistic drama "Heaven's Gates and Hell's Flames."

I was tempted to use the word "coincidently" here, but there are no coincidences with God. By this time, the original Toyota had done over a half a million *miles*, pulling our equipment trailer on some of the worst roads you could imagine in Eastern Europe. So it was that the Lord prompted this couple to donate the finances required to purchase a badly needed, *new* Toyota van.

If you are thinking, "It must be nice to have wealthy friends," you have got it all wrong. In fact, when you have friends whom you know the Lord has blessed financially, you have to be very careful to *not* look upon them as a possible source of income. Our focus must rest securely on the Lord as our provider, the source of our supply.

You may be wondering where the story is going—especially considering the somewhat cryptic title. Well, we're nearly there. Fast forward to the year 2000, when the Lord called Ginny and me back to Canada.

During our last ten years in Europe, the Lord had used us to pioneer the drama "Heaven's Gates and Hell's Flames" all over Europe. In those ten years, we presented it in no less than thirty-three different countries, in twenty-three different languages. We used local churchgoers as actors and saw thousands make the decision to invite Jesus into their lives. Also during that time, we recruited, trained and mentored ten husband and wife teams in nine different countries to continue the work in Europe.

After ten years, however, we knew our work as pioneers was done. We were no longer needed in that capacity. We believe the goal for all missionaries should be to open up new mission fields for the gospel and then train others to continue the work as God moves the pioneering missionaries to new fields and challenges.

I have to be honest and say it was not easy to leave Europe. It was not easy to leave a work into which we had invested so much sweat and tears. It was wrenching. However, sometimes God has to pull us away from things to which we have grown too attached.

There is no doubt that by moving us out of that ministry, God created the space for other people to grow and develop into ministry that never would have happened had we stayed. It has been one of the greatest thrills of my life to see a couple very dear to us grow into a ministry and become so good at it that I can say—with deep humility—that they are way better at it than I ever was.

When we flew back to Toronto in March of 2000, we were met by Eddie and Kathy Chu, in whose basement we had briefly resided about twenty-five years before and who had sold us their Volvo for one dollar. We were going to stay with them again for a few months as we resituated ourselves in Canada and waited on the Lord for our next assignment.

As we walked to their waiting car at the Toronto airport, Eddie said, "Terry, I figured you would need a car to get around as you look for a permanent place to live, get your OHIP medical insurance sorted out and tend to all the other details of your return—so I bought a little car for you to use for as long as you need it. You can either give it back to me when you are finished or buy it from me.

Sitting there was a beautiful, gleaming gold, 1984 BMW 230 SL. While it was far from new, it was a *Beamer* and it was in excellent condition. I had to laugh at the amazing goodness of the Lord. Ginny and I had spent the last twenty-five years serving Him. We never had two pennies to rub together, and yet, during that time, He had supplied us with a Volvo, two brand new Toyota vans and finally a BMW.

To conclude, what can we learn from this story that spanned over a quarter of a century? Several things.

Although we look at time in small increments, God is not restricted by our perspective. When He promises to do something, He is not limited by our small thinking or by our impatience. He *will* keep His promises, but in *His* time.

While the only hero in this story is God Himself, He works through ordinary people who are willing to listen to Him and allow Him to work through them. That's when extraordinary things happen. It goes without saying that *all* the glory goes to God.

One of the constant challenges for me in writing this book has been keeping everyone's attention firmly focussed on God even though the stories are about my life. But that's what life is all about: journeying through our experiences while keeping our eyes fixed on God as the object of our hopes, plans and purposes.

The faithful servants in this story are Kathy and Eddie Chu and the couple who paid for the two Toyota vans. Ginny and I were the grateful recipients of God's provision, but if these people had not had hearts sensitive to the prompting of the Lord and had not been obedient to Him, the supernatural events of this story could not have happened.

Finally, I believe if we look at the events of our lives, we can often identify what I call "triggers," events that set in motion a series of other events.

It is important to note that these triggers are not self-serving actions and are most definitely not entered into with thoughts of possible personal gain.

So what was the trigger that started this twenty-five-year series of God's amazing provision of vehicles? I believe it all started with our decision to fulfill our promise to raise the $30,000 dollars for the 10,000 Bibles for Poland; even though, in doing so, we had to turn our backs on joining a large denominational missions organization. Staying true to our word set in motion the subsequent events.

I must add that we are in no way critical of large, denominational missions organizations; this was just what happened with us.

All the glory goes to God, but isn't it fun to be a Christian?

12

THE BIG PICTURE

When we are caught in the middle of a difficult situation—a personal trial, a difficulty, an unpleasant disagreement, a problem at work or at home, or even just an unexpected expense—we tend to view that situation in isolation. We seldom see it as being a part of a bigger picture.

In this true story, you will see how several disparate incidents, having no apparent relationship to each other, when viewed in hindsight, can be seen as being part of "the big picture."

Back in the mid 80s, in the early days of our ministry in Europe, we did a lot of concert/crusades, particularly in Poland, but also in the UK and other European countries.

My "superstar"

Often we would assemble a team of musicians and singers from Canada and the UK to form a band with backup singers to accompany Ginny. The Europeans did not like singers who used accompaniment tracks. They viewed them as being a North American, cheap alternative to the 'real thing;' which they considered to be a 'live' band with musicians and backup singers.

Small multi-national team in Portugal

Every time we put one of these tours together, we had to rent a suitable P.A. system with stage lighting, which added considerably to the budget.

One day, quite by chance, I discovered the church we were attending in the UK had £12,000 sitting in an account. One of the elders of the church, unofficially, suggested that if I were to present a suitable proposal to the church, *maybe* we could get access to that money as a loan to purchase our own P.A. and lighting system.

The idea was that we would save a considerable amount of money each year by not having to rent such equipment *and* we could generate income for the ministry by renting the equipment out to Christian conferences and festivals that proliferated across the UK each year.

So I asked my good friend and excellent P.A. guy, Chris Snook, to put together a budget of what P.A. and lighting equipment we could purchase for £12,000 if we had it—and to show how we could repay the church quickly through savings and hiring it out.

When presenting our proposal to the church, we discovered that the £12,000 was from the sale of some church property. One of the regulations of the charity was that the money could only be used for a similar purchase, another building or renovation to part of the existing church property.

So the church was unable to even consider loaning the money to us.

There was, of course, an initial disappointment; but then I started to think. It occurred to me that I had asked Chris to put together a wish list based on a set amount of money. This way of thinking put a limit on what we could buy. It was not actually based on what we needed.

Maybe God had other ideas. So I suggested to Chris that he take another look at the proposal and put together a budget, not being foolishly extravagant, for the type and calibre of equipment that we actually needed—without being restricted by cost considerations.

Chris did an excellent job of putting together a specific budget for it all. The amount needed was around $40,000 (approximately £24,000)—considerably more that the original £12,000 figure. For some reason, I did not feel we should send this information out to the people on our mailing list because, by-and-large, they would not understand why we needed a twenty-four-channel mixing desk, multiple main speakers and monitor speakers, power amplifiers, effects units, smoke machine, multiple microphones, 10,000+ watts of lights, playback decks, a multitude of cables, cases and a trailer to transport it all.

Of course, $40,000 was way beyond our means, so if anything was to come of this, it would need to be through the specific intervention and provision of the Lord.

I felt all I should do was carry the wish list/budget around with me and wait to present it to someone when the opportunity to do so felt right.

About six months later, such an opportunity arose!

That October, Ginny and I were making our semi-annual visit back to Canada to re-acquaint ourselves with our friends and those individuals and churches that supported us. As usual, Dr. Paul Smith, of our home church, The Peoples Church, invited us to his office for coffee and a casual chat.

Towards the end of our allotted meeting time with Dr. Paul, he suddenly asked, "Do you have any special needs at this time?" I immediately thought of the P.A. proposal that had been lying in my briefcase all those months.

Pulling out the proposal, I replied, "Well, since you asked, Dr. Paul, yes, we do have a special need at this time."

As he started to peruse the information, Dr. Paul asked, "What is the bottom line?"

I drew his attention to the last page.

Then it happened. Dr. Paul blew us away, saying, "Consider you have it. We will just have to work out how we can raise it for you."

As we walked out of his office, Ginny and I were stunned at how easily and quickly everything had happened. True, we still had to wait to hear back from Dr. Paul regarding how they were going to raise the $40,000, but he had given his word that we had it.

Dr. Paul spoke it in faith, and in faith we believed him.

What we did not know at that time was that—as can often be the case—God knew something about our future of which we were unaware and He was preparing us for that.

Within the next few days, we were called in to see Dr. Paul again. In that meeting, he told us that, to raise the money, he would like us to return to Toronto to attend The Peoples Church Annual Missions Conference the following April. He suggested we should invite a pastor from Eastern Europe, with whom we had been working, to accompany us to the conference.

They would feature the pastor and us in some of the missions meetings. The church would take up special offerings during the conference towards the goal of $40,000. Amazingly, they gave us the $40,000 before we left Canada that autumn, so we could get on with purchasing the equipment and using it in our ministry across Eastern and Western Europe.

PA & lighting equipment

To the conference the following April, we took two pastors from Eastern Europe. Initially, one of the Eastern European pastors said he would not be able to make the trip because he was in an embarrassing debt situation caused by a Canadian pastor who had visited him previously.

The previous year, the Canadian pastor in question had been visiting the East European pastor and noticed that his car was on its last legs. In an act of rash generosity, the Canadian pastor said his church would buy a new car for the Polish pastor, which, of course, seemed like an answer to prayer for the Polish pastor. The Canadian wanted the Polish pastor to get the car right away, whilst he was still there in Poland, probably because he thought if he could go back to Canada with a photograph of himself with the Polish pastor and the new car, it would be easier to raise the finances.

It should be noted that the size of the Canadian pastor's congregation was large enough to raise, in one offering, the $12,000 needed for the car. This Canadian pastor had a big heart but also a big persuasive personality whom the Polish pastor had known for years—and so the Polish pastor trusted him.

At the insistence of the Canadian, the Polish pastor, with full approval from his church elders, borrowed $6,000 from his church's funds and a further $6,000 from a Christian businessman who lived next door.

All of this was instigated by the charismatic Canadian, upon his absolute assurance that he would send the money over to Poland "as soon as he got back to Canada."

So the new car was bought. Amidst great fanfare, the keys were handed to the Polish pastor and the appropriate photographs were taken. Everyone was happy and rejoicing. A few days later, the Canadian pastor returned to Canada.

A wonderful story of God's provision. Right? Wrong!

The money from Canada never materialized.

The Polish pastor was a gentle man who would never have borrowed the money were it not for the insistence of the Canadian and the assurance the money would be sent from Canada within a week or two.

But nothing came! With the Polish communist economy being such as it was at that time, $12,000 was equivalent to about five years salary for the Polish pastor—an enormous amount.

After repeated attempts by the Polish pastor to get in contact with the Canadian pastor, the Canadian eventually confessed that all was not well at his church and he would not be sending the money—not ever, not even part of it.

This was devastating to the Polish pastor and his family.

Sadly, similar situations, in varying degrees, were not altogether unusual during those days, when Christians from the West would go into Eastern Europe and make all kinds of promises of financial assistance. Although the visitors were well-meaning at the time, many had not carefully considered the ramifications of their hasty generosity and were unable to fulfill the promises.

Ginny and I were victims of that sort of thing on several occasions. Fortunately, we never borrowed money against such uncertain promises.

It was into this delicate situation that we stepped when we invited this pastor to come to Canada, to participate in The Peoples Church Missions Conference.

Understandably, he questioned whether it would be appropriate for him to attend. He felt it would not look good to his parishioners for him to leave the country at this time. As a man now greatly in debt, he felt he needed to be at home, trying to figure out how he could get out from under the mountain of debt that weighed so heavily upon him, even though he had not been responsible for incurring it.

I, however, felt he *should* go to Canada. The church of the offending pastor was nowhere near Toronto, so a visit to Toronto would not be misinterpreted. The Polish pastor needed a break; he needed people to minister to him and to "love him up." He needed to be reassured in his faith and in the goodness of other Christians. As it was normal for any pastors invited to attend the missions conference to have all their travel and accommodation expense covered by the church, he would not be incurring any expense, either for himself or for his church.

So, somewhat hesitatingly, the pastor agreed to come on the proviso that I would not talk about his embarrassing situation to anyone at The Peoples Church; so I agreed.

Fast forward to the conference. The two Polish pastors were now in Canada, being blessed and being blessings to other people.

Being reunited with these two humble men, who had suffered grievously under communism, triggered a renewed sense of injustice in my mind and in my heart regarding the broken promises of someone who they should have been able to trust.

I woke up one morning and felt a sudden urge to telephone the pastor in question. I did not premeditate our conversation; you could call it "a prompting." I made the call straight away, before I could change my mind. It's important to note that no one—not the Polish pastor or even my wife—had any idea I was going to make the call.

Amazingly, despite being in different time zones, my call went straight through.

Initially, our conversation was very amicable, as this pastor knew me quite well. However, when I brought up the situation regarding the pastor in Poland, he became defensive, obtrusive and increasingly irritated. He was bordering on outright anger when he insisted he could not—and would not—be paying any of the $12,000 to the Polish pastor.

My appeals to his integrity as a pastor and his decency as a human being fell on deaf ears. I even asked whether he had considered taking out a personal loan to pay for even a part of the debt. After all, he was responsible for the heavy burden the Polish pastor now had to carry. But my words availed nothing. He did not deny his complicity in what had happened, but he showed no remorse whatsoever. As far as he was concerned, the matter was closed.

To be frank, his callousness got under my skin even more than his original recklessness in promising the money and pressing that Polish pastor to borrow against what turned out to be an empty promise.

As I said, I had not planned this call. Therefore, I had not thought of the possible outcomes—or my responses to them, so I was somewhat surprised at what I said next.

Quite calmly, I said that if I did not receive a cheque within the next two days from him or his church for $6,000 designated for the pastor in Poland, I would write immediately to the headquarters of the denomination where he held his credentials and inform them of the full story. Further, if they did not take any redemptive action, having tried to deal with the situation in-house, I would then feel compelled to take the story to the secular media.

Sometimes we are critical of large church organisations who try to sweep the misdemeanours of their clergy under a carpet, and yet, there remains a tendency to not be transparent with our own failings.

I am not suggesting we have to always "air our dirty washing in public," but in certain situations, we need not only to do the right thing but be seen doing it. The choice was his: do the right thing or suffer the consequences of his actions becoming public knowledge.

I did not feel I was violating any scriptures. I had gone to him personally. If he did not respond honourably, I would have gone to the authority to which he was answerable. If they had been unwilling to do the right thing, I would have taken it as far as necessary to see that justice was done for this innocent Polish pastor.

I had no axe to grind and nothing to gain personally. In fact, I knew my actions could possibly incur the wrath of some Christians; but I felt I should stand with, and for, my Polish brother, who was totally oblivious to the actions I was taking on his behalf.

Two days later, I received a personal cheque from that Canadian pastor for $6,000. I thank God for orchestrating the circumstances and for giving me the courage to speak up, graciously but firmly, to the offending pastor. I hoped that, in the midst of all this, he would have learned a lesson about the importance of keeping his word.

That very same evening, something else remarkable and unexpected happened.

After each meeting at the missions conference, people would go into the church gym, where displays by many of the missions agencies that The Peoples Church supported, were set up. This was an excellent opportunity for people to talk personally with the missionaries and representatives of the various agencies.

As I was casually walking around the gym, I came across a pastor whom I knew well, who had moved around Canada quite a lot during the course of his ministry.

He knew the two pastors from Poland and he had been thrilled to see them at the conference. He had been blessed by their ministry and encouraged by what they had shared of their work in Poland.

Suddenly, this pastor surprised me by asking if these pastors had any need that they were *not* talking about from the pulpit. From his experience and wisdom, he knew that often pastors found themselves faced with needs that were inappropriate to share in a public forum.

Should I tell him of this situation? I had promised I would not tell anyone at The Peoples Church about the debt on the car, but although we were physically *at* The Peoples Church, this pastor was not *of* The Peoples Church.

What should I say?

This pastor knew the Polish pastor in question and personally knew of his integrity, honesty and gentle spirit; so I decided, because he had asked, to tell this pastor about the car situation—and of what I had done that morning—but I left out the name of the offending pastor and any indication of where, in Canada, he lived.

Right there in the gym, to my utter surprise, this pastor then asked me, "Is the offending pastor … from … church in … city?" He had correctly named the pastor.

Quickly recovering from shock, I said, "I don't think it would be appropriate for me to say."

To which this pastor, who knew me very well, said, "Terry, I appreciate your discretion; so if I have not guessed correctly, would you please tell me?"

"Yes," I answered. "If you had not guessed correctly, I would have told you."

Apparently, this pastor was well aware of this man and that he was known for making big promises but not keeping them.

So, giving me his telephone number, he asked me to call him first thing the next morning, but gave no indication why I should call or what was in his mind or heart.

After duly calling him the next morning , I went over to his home, as invited. To my great surprise, he gave me a cheque for the other $6,000 needed to clear the debt for the Polish pastor. Just like that!

He had spoken to the board of his church, explained the situation, and they had unanimously agreed to this act of generosity.

The Lord had cleared the debt.

Sometimes we think, mistakenly, that when God works, money or solutions are just going to drop out of heaven, but that is not how it happens. God works through *people*, ordinary people who stay tuned to Him and are willing, sometimes courageously, to obey and act upon His promptings.

So how does our need to raise money for a P.A. system to spearhead an incredible ministry all over Europe, correlate with a pastor in Poland being $12,000 in debt through no fault of his own?

In the natural world, it doesn't, but in God's world, it does!

You see, about a year later, we were invited to go to Holland, specifically because of a ministry project over there that needed a P.A. and lighting system like the one the Lord had provided for us.

It was a drama ministry called "Heaven's Gates and Hell's Flames" about which, until that time, we knew absolutely nothing, but they needed to hire our equipment, as it was the first time ever that that drama was going to be presented in Europe.

We agreed to provide the equipment and help set it up, with the agreement that it would be operated by men from the "Heaven's Gates and Hell's Flames" ministry.

This was fine with me, as the project fell in the middle of the Word Cup of football (soccer) being played in Italy, so I would be able to watch the games each day and simply show up at the drama in the evening.

Rudy Krulik, the Director of Reality Outreach Ministries, the covering ministry for "Heaven's Gates and Hell's Flames" was very disciplined in his prayer life. He read God's Word and communed with Him faithfully every day. During his flight to Holland, he read a portion of Scripture, part of Jeremiah 12:5, "If you have raced with men on foot and they have worn you out, how can you compete with horses?"

These verses had no significance for Rudy, until he walked into the car park of the centre where we were all staying in Northern Holland and saw, on both sides of our equipment trailer, a large painting of galloping horses.

As for me, I was not interested in the drama—until I saw it. My first exposure to "Heaven's Gates and Hell's Flames" was that first night of the production in a large, old church in northern Holland. There were more people in the cast than there were in the audience. The acting was done by local people speaking the Dutch language. Although mostly non-actors, they communicated the message with dazzling clarity. Right there and then, in my mind's eye of faith, I saw that drama being performed all across Europe, in many different languages, always by the local Christians.

It was the P.A. and lighting equipment that brought us into contact with that ministry. Within ten years, by God's grace and provision, we saw thousands of people challenged to become Christians after seeing the drama "Heaven's Gates and Hell's Flames," as it was presented in no less that thirty-three different European countries in twenty-three different languages—always acted by local people. Ten husband and wife couples were recruited, trained and mentored in nine different countries; after which time, the Lord called Ginny and me back to Canada because He had other assignments for us, one of which was to care for Ginny's aging parents.

Remember how I said earlier that God knew something about our future that we didn't know and He was preparing us for that? Well, that is true of your life as well, no matter where you are or how old or young you may be.

We can never sit back and smugly say, "Well, that's it. I've done my bit. I can relax and take it easy now." No! There is no such thing as a retired Christian. A person can be a retired teacher, banker, accountant, office worker, nurse, factory worker, or whatever, and deservedly so—but never a retired Christian.

Large, multi-national team—cast & crew of "Heaven's Gates and Hell's Flames" in Poland

If you are still alive, and you would have to be to be reading this, God still has something you can do for Him and for His Kingdom.

Young people—be warned! Older people—wake up! God has not finished with you yet!

147

13

CROSSING THE IRON CURTAIN

On March 5, 1946, Winston Churchill, then the Prime Minister of Great Britain, gave his famous "Iron Curtain Speech"[10] to a crowd of 40,000 people at Westminster College in the small Missouri town of Fulton (population 7,000).

Imagine his imperious, aristocratic pose (more than compensating for his short, dumpy stature) as his compelling voice boomed forth over his audience.

> "It is my duty however, for I am sure you would wish me to state the facts as I see them to you, to place before you certain facts about the present position in Europe.

> "From Stettin in the Baltic to Trieste in the Adriatic, an iron curtain has descended across the Continent. Behind that line lie all the capitals of the ancient states of Central and Eastern Europe. Warsaw, Berlin, Prague, Vienna, Budapest, Belgrade, Bucharest and Sofia, all these famous cities and the populations around them lie in what I must call the Soviet sphere, and all are subject in one form or another, not only to Soviet influence but to a very high and, in many cases, increasing measure of control from Moscow.

> "The Russian-dominated Polish Government has been encouraged to make enormous and wrongful inroads upon Germany, and mass expulsions of millions of Germans on a scale grievous and undreamed-of are now taking place.

> "The Communist Parties, which were very small in all these Eastern States of Europe, have been raised to pre-eminence and power far beyond their numbers and are seeking everywhere to obtain totalitarian control. Police governments are prevailing in nearly every case, and there is no true democracy."

The first English use of the term "iron curtain," applied to the border of communist Russia, in the sense of "an impenetrable barrier," was derived from the safety curtain still used in theatres today, and was used in 1920 by Ethel Snowden in her book, *Through Bolshevik Russia*.

From 1945 until November 11, 1989, that guarded barrier blocked millions of people from crossing. They were imprisoned in their home countries. It was more than just a physical barrier. Even after that wall came down,—even today—crossing into or out of what we call "Eastern Europe" is still fraught with difficulty.

Terry stepping through the Berlin Wall

These are true stories of our crossing back and forth over that border and include the telling of an incident that, I hope, will bring a smile to your face.

As a contextual backdrop, it is important to establish a few facts about the Second World War of which some people may be unaware.

At the time of the Second World War, European politics saw Britain and France allied with Poland. This meant that if any of those three nations were attacked by some other outside force, the other two nations were obligated to go to the invaded nation's defence.

The war began on September 1, 1939, when Nazi Germany invaded Poland from the west, on a totally fabricated pretext. On the evening of August 31,1939, as tensions in Europe approached the breaking point, there was an unusual broadcast from a radio station in Gleiwitz, Germany. It was followed by a hate-filled diatribe by a Polish-speaking man who urged all Poles to take up arms and strike down any Germans who might resist.

When Gestapo officers arrived at the transmitter to investigate, they found the bullet-riddled body of one of the alleged Polish attackers. In the morning, there were reports of numerous other incidents of Polish aggression along the border. In response, Nazi leader, Adolf Hitler, used the incident to justify issuing his "final directive" to attack Poland, compelling the United Kingdom and France to declare war on Germany. Thus began World War Two, but it turns out that this incident at Gleiwitz, blamed as the final provocation for the terrible war that followed, was not quite what it seemed.

In August of 1939, Nazi forces had already been concentrating their soldiers and war-making machines along the Polish border in preparation for an all-out attack. In order to establish a pretence for invasion, Hitler enlisted the assistance of Commander Heinrich Himmler of the Nazi SS. The commander conceptualized, and set in motion, a collection of deceptions designed to make war seem inevitable; these were code-named "Operation Himmler." But the task of executing the initial subterfuge ultimately fell to another SS officer by the name of Alfred Naujocks.

On August 31, in the hours before the attack on Gleiwitz radio station, Alfred Naujocks lingered in the shadow of its 380-foot broadcasting tower with a group of Nazi storm troopers. The men were awaiting the arrival of "canned goods," a Nazi code word for expendable convicts. When one of these, an unconscious convict, was delivered by SS agents, his clothing was hastily changed into Polish clothing and he was dumped outside the entrance of the radio station. A doctor had administered a lethal injection before the prisoner was transported to the site, but it had yet to take full effect when he was riddled with pistol rounds on the ground outside the station.

With the more gruesome portion of their task behind them, Naujocks and his operatives entered Gleiwitz radio station at about 8:00 p.m., outfitted in Polish uniforms. The men seized control of the equipment, shut down the regular signal and powered up the emergency transmitter. The microphone was given to a Polish-speaking operative, who read a prepared speech about three minutes long, urging Poles to rise up and help in the invasion of Germany. At the end of the transmission, the officers fired their pistols repeatedly for the benefit of anyone who might be listening—and departed.

During the night, a handful of other such incidents were executed elsewhere along the border, using other "canned goods" from German prisons to create the illusion that Polish soldiers were attacking German troops. The following day, the bodies of the dead prisoners were presented to the press and to police as evidence of the Poles' organized aggression against the Nazis.

Now Hitler had his "justification" to invade Poland.

Soon after that, on September 17, the Soviet Union invaded Poland from the east. Both invaders acted in concert, upon the Ribbentrop-Molotov Treaty. The Soviet Union pulled back when the United States joined the military actions in December 1941 (when Germany declared war upon them and when they were assaulted by

Japan), and they joined the anti-Nazi alliance in the summer of 1941, when they were invaded by Germany. The allies of Poland, Great Britain and France, declared war on Germany on September 3, 1939.

It is very important to understand that:
- Britain and France fought the Second World War for the purpose of freeing Poland.
- The United States later joined the Second World War for the purpose of defeating Germany.

Those differing purposes would have a tragic impact on the final outcome of the war, not just for Poland, but for all of what we call Eastern Europe.

At the end of WWII, the entire nation of Poland was moved a hundred kilometres or so west to what was called the "Oder Neisse Line," on its new western border with East Germany. (Remember that the Iron Curtain dissected Germany down the middle.)

Overnight, towns that had been in eastern Poland, such as Lwow and Brest, now found themselves to be part of the western Soviet Union; and a large German city like Breslau, which had been in eastern Germany, now found itself to be in western Poland and renamed Wroclaw (phonetically pronounced "ver-os-wav." Say it quickly and you will impress any Polish friends you might have).

This kind of thing (borders being changed overnight) was happening all over Eastern Europe, as Russia and the Allies carved up Europe to satisfy their selfish political goals. The ordinary people, mostly uneducated, were thrown into confusion. That confusion bred insecurity; and that insecurity would cause the different ethnic groups, that had hitherto lived in uneasy harmony with each other, to turn on their former neighbours as they fought to claim territory to call their own. The need to have a place where they would belong was fierce.

Just look at the atrocities visited on former neighbours in what had been the country of Yugoslavia. While its communist, dictatorial President Tito ruled with an iron fist there was peace, but as soon as that iron fist was removed, long-suppressed ethnic animosities exploded like a volcano. Ethnic cleansing became bywords for brutal atrocities.

I know people in Poland who continue to live in fear that a politically and economically strong, reunited Germany could someday reclaim those cities in western Poland. As it is, many Germans refuse to call the city of Wroclaw by its Polish name and insist on calling it by its old German name of Breslau.

To give my North American readers a sense of what this could be like, imagine if you were born and brought up in San Antonio, Texas, and you are as American as apple pie, but you wake up one morning and are told, "This territory is no longer part of the USA. It has been returned to its former owner, Mexico. You are no longer American; you are now Mexican."

Does that sound ridiculous? Well, that is exactly what has happened to countless thousands of eastern Europeans, not only in the last 100 years, but even in recent history.

We may well have witnessed a Winter Olympic Games in Russia in 2014 or a European football tournament co-hosted by Poland and the Ukraine in 2012—all giving the impression of nations getting along peaceably with each other, but trust me when I say that, lurking not far from the surface in the minds and hearts of a myriad of ethnic groups that make up Europe, there are deep-seated animosities and territorial claims just waiting for certain regions to be restored to those they consider to be the rightful owners.

And if you think that sort of thing could not happen in a modern, enlightened Europe, then just look at what took place in Ukraine in 2014. Russia took back what they considered to be rightfully theirs by annexing Crimea.

There was a lot of sabre-rattling by the western powers, wringing their hands with political indignation—but was it stopped? Oh, a few wrists were slapped by placing sanctions on some of the oligarch businessmen (to whom losing a few million dollars made little difference in light of the billions they were making in their businesses), but Russia has successfully reclaimed Crimea and is still chipping away at other parts of Ukraine, unopposed by the West.

In my desire to communicate an understanding of the underlying tensions not generally broadcast on CNN or the BBC, I share a true story that is poignant but sad.

Ginny and I had the privilege to work for ten years for a ministry based out of Canada called "Reality Outreach Ministries." It was the organization that took the evangelistic drama "Heaven's Gates and Hell's Flames" literally around the world.

Ginny and I pioneered that ministry in all of Europe, seeing it performed in thirty-three European countries and in twenty-three languages.

One of the founders and the director of "Reality Outreach Ministries," was a Canadian of Polish descent by the name of Rudy Krulik. Rudy is a very special person. He is a real man of God, a tough negotiator (with a passion for soul-winning ... and ice hockey) and he is fiercely proud of his Polish heritage. Why not? Rudy would proudly regale us with stories of how, in the Second World War, his father would stay one step ahead of the Nazis and the Russians and other dangerous partisans, until finally, he ended up in Canada, where Rudy was born.

One day Rudy found his father's birth certificate, but he couldn't read it because it was in Polish. We sent the birth certificate to Czarek and Jola, a couple who worked for us in Poland, and asked them if they could identify exactly where in Poland, Rudy's father was born so Rudy could visit his deceased father's birthplace.

What Czarek and Jola discovered was that, although the village in which Rudy's father was born was a Polish community, at the time of Rudy's father's birth, that village was officially situated in Romania. Technically speaking, Rudy's father was a Polish-speaking Romanian.

This kind of situation has been, and still is, the reality for some people in that part of Europe.

GOING IN

Whether it's justifiable to knowingly break the laws of a sovereign nation for the sake of the gospel is a question that always generates lively discussion amongst Christians, especially those who are involved in ministries in what we call "difficult countries."

For the purpose of this story, let's define "a difficult country" as one that is openly against Christianity, one that passes laws against Christian practices and allows for—if not encourages—the persecution of Christians.

There are some people who go to work in such countries in some professional capacity but with the surreptitious intention of sharing their Christian faith with those with whom they come into contact, perhaps even starting a Bible study and/or discussion group in their own home.

Such people may not be breaking any actual laws, but they are walking a dangerous fine line and courageously taking considerable risks. However, I am not talking about such people in those situations.

I am talking about people who engage in smuggling Christian literature, money or other items into countries where it is against the law to do so. Do Christians have some moral or ethical right to break the laws of such a country, if those laws impede Christian activity?

Many of us are familiar with the work of Andrew van der Bijl, a Dutchman known in English-speaking countries as Brother Andrew. He was a Christian missionary famous for his exploits smuggling Bibles to communist countries at the height of the Cold War, a feat that earned him the nickname of God's Smuggler.

During the Cold War, although communist countries did not specifically forbid its citizens to actually posses a Bible, they did explicitly forbid the importation of Bibles or any other Christian literature that they saw as being subversive propaganda against their communist ideals.

Looking for an answer to whether a Christian should always obey the laws of the land, my research led me to an interesting article on the following web site: *www.gotquestions.org*

> "Romans 13:1-7 states, 'Everyone must submit himself to the governing authorities, for there is no authority except that which God has established. The authorities that exist have been established by God. Consequently, he who rebels against the authority is rebelling against what God has instituted, and those who do so will bring judgment on themselves. For rulers hold no terror for those who do right, but for those who do wrong. Do you want to be free from fear of the one in authority? Then do what is right and he will commend you. For he is God's servant to do you good. But if you do wrong, be afraid, for he does not bear the sword for nothing. He is God's servant, an agent of wrath to bring punishment on the wrongdoer. Therefore, it is necessary to submit to the authorities, not only because of possible*

punishment but also because of conscience. This is also why you pay taxes, for the authorities are God's servants, who give their full time to governing. Give everyone what you owe him: If you owe taxes, pay taxes; if revenue, then revenue; if respect, then respect; if honour, then honour.'

"This passage makes it abundantly clear that we are to obey the government God places over us. God created government to establish order, punish evil and promote justice (Genesis 9:6; 1 Corinthians 14:33; Romans 12:8). We are to obey the government in everything—paying taxes, obeying rules and laws and showing respect. If we do not, we are ultimately showing disrespect towards God, for He is the One who placed that government over us. When the apostle Paul wrote to the Romans, he was under the government of Rome during the reign of Nero, perhaps the most evil of all the Roman emperors. Paul still recognized the Roman government's rule over him. How can we do any less?

"The next question is, 'Is there a time when we can, or should, intentionally disobey the laws of the land?" The answer to that question may be found in Acts 5:27-29: *'Having brought the apostles, they made them appear before the Sanhedrin to be questioned by the high priest. 'We gave you strict orders not to teach in this Name,' he said, 'Yet you have filled Jerusalem with your teaching and are determined to make us guilty of this man's blood.' Peter and the other apostles replied: 'We must obey God rather than men!'* From this, it is clear that as long as the law of the land does not contradict the law of God, we are bound to obey the law of the land. As soon as the law of the land contradicts God's command, we are to disobey the law of the land and obey God's law. However, even in that instance, we are to accept the government's authority over us. This is demonstrated by the fact that Peter and John did not protest being flogged, but instead rejoiced that they suffered for obeying God (Acts 5:40-42)."

In all our years of working behind the Iron Curtain, Ginny and I operated by the same principle as outlined above. This will help you to understand our feelings concerning the following incident.

THE INCIDENT

It was August, 1986. Ginny and I were waiting at the Frankfurt International Airport in Germany for a team of nine pastors from Pittsburgh, PA. We were taking them to Poland so they could meet with believers there and see for themselves how the church in Poland was faring.

The Chernobyl disaster, a catastrophic nuclear accident, had taken place at the Chernobyl Nuclear Power Plant a few months earlier on April 26, 1986. The plant was under the direct jurisdiction of the central authorities of the Soviet Union. The explosion and fire released large quantities of radioactive particles into the atmosphere, which spread over much of the western USSR and Europe.

The Chernobyl disaster was, at the time, the worst nuclear power plant accident in history, in terms of cost and resulting deaths. The battle to contain the contamination, and avert a greater catastrophe, ultimately involved over 500,000 workers and cost an estimated $18 billion, bankrupting the Soviet Union. Crops and animal and dairy products in several neighbouring countries, such as Poland, were severely contaminated.

Although thirty-one people died during the actual accident, it is estimated that over 4,000 people died soon after from related illnesses. Out of an estimated 50,000 people who got cancer from the nuclear fall-out, it is conservatively estimated that over 25,000 will die prematurely. Long-term effects, such as cancers and deformities, are still being studied.

There had been a brief discussion amongst these pastors as to whether or not we should continue with the already planned visit to Poland, but we had unanimously agreed that we should go ahead.

When the nine pastors came through the arrivals hall with their luggage, I saw they also had about twenty medium size, sealed boxes with them. I was told by the pastor who had arranged for all the others to come on the trip that the boxes contained packages of dried milk.

Apparently, they had heard on the news that because of the nuclear contamination of dairy products in Poland, there was a severe shortage of milk for babies. As an act of compassion and kindness, they had brought these twenty boxes with them from the USA.

I explained that we might not be allowed to take the milk into Poland because we did not have a permit to do so. I said, however, that we could try.

I had, on many occasions during the planning of this venture, clearly explained to the lead pastor and his church that we did not get involved in smuggling things into Poland. If we took money for the pastors, we declared it at the border as the regulations required. As it was possible to get official permits to import Bibles and other Christian literature into that country, we did not participate in that kind of activity.

Several years earlier, Ginny and I had raised the money to ship 10,000 Bibles into Poland. On another occasion, we had taken an entire Braille Bible, which consisted of twenty-seven large books, into the country. We had also taken three electronic typewriters, two new photocopying machines and a large quantity of paper and ink into Poland for a translation project.

Getting permits for such things would often take some time and required patience, but it could be done. The government of Poland, although still communist controlled at that time, allowed it. Smuggling of such items was not necessary, although we knew of some people who, foolishly, continued to do so.

Presenting a new electric typewriter to a pastor in Poland

So, on that bright and sunny morning, tired from their overnight flight from the USA (and our drive down from England), we loaded the boxes of dried milk on to the roof rack on the rented Volkswagon van and squeezed in with our luggage. Fortunately, there was not too much as it was all men (who tend to travel light) and Ginny, who, as an experienced missionary, had learned to travel light as well.

We headed east towards the West German-East German border, which we crossed relatively easily, though it took about four hours. A few hours later, by late afternoon, we arrived at the East German-Polish border, at a town called Gorlitz (Polish name: Zgorzelec).

I had warned everyone that at these border crossings, we should remain quiet— no animated conversation or laughter and definitely, no singing. We should be extremely respectful to the border guards and officials, but answer only the questions asked and not elaborate or try to engage them in conversation at all. Absolutely no cameras should be visible as they would be immediately confiscated, never to be seen again.

After arriving at the border, and after the usual long wait in the line-up of vehicles waiting to go through the Passport and Customs Control we had to surrender our passports and then exit the vehicle and line up outside while our faces were checked against the passport photos.

At the same time, border guards with dogs, which sniffed each of us "intimately," searched through the vehicle. Other border guards, with mirrors on long poles that looked like gigantic dental tools, checked the underside of the vehicle and the wheel arches. They were very thorough.

And then came the border guard who was obviously in charge.

She was about 5'5" tall (or short, depending on your perspective) with blond hair pulled back severely from her face into a tight bun. Her face was pasty and even her excessive make-up could not completely cover the evidence of childhood measles or chicken pox. Her red lipstick was almost comical. Her uniform was immaculate but probably two sizes too small. The other thing she wore was a practised scowl that never broke. She reminded me of a stylized KGB operative from an old James Bond film.

To this lady I had to, of course, show the utmost respect.

She started by demanding in broken English, "Who is the chief?" I stepped forward, after which she addressed only me, as if the other people in our group did not exist. All the while, there were five or six other border guards watching us, with their semiautomatic guns held loosely at the ready. It was their way to intimidate.

Her questions were fired at me in rapid succession and I was ready for them, as I had heard them so many times before at this, and other, communist border crossings.

"Where have you come from?"

"Who do you represent?"

"Where are you going?"

"What is the purpose of your visit?"

"Where did you get your visa to enter Poland?"

"Who is your contact in Poland?"

"Where are you staying?"

"How much money do you have with you?"

"Do you have any guns or ammunition with you?"

"Do you have any pornography?"

"Do you have any Bibles or other religious literature?"

The questions were fired at me quickly, not necessarily in that order, and repeated ad hoc, to try and catch me with any inconsistencies in my answers.

Perhaps a little disappointed that I had not failed the first test, she pointed to the boxes on the roof rack, demanding to know what was in them.

I explained the situation and why the pastors had brought them from the States.

I said I realized we did not have a permit for the dried milk, but we had not had time to get one and hoped they could let us take them through anyway, for humanitarian reasons.

She surprised me by not immediately rejecting our request, but she did randomly select five of the boxes and ordered that they be brought down and placed on the ground in front of her. She then ordered me to open each of the boxes to reveal the contents. At no time touching the boxes herself, she insisted that I do it. So I opened each box in turn and, sure enough, each had large, flat, sealed plastic packets filled with dried baby milk.

She then ordered me to remove the packets of dried baby milk. Under an initial layer of baby milk, each box was filled with *Bibles*, about thirty in each box.

She ordered all the remaining boxes to be brought from the van. When opened, each one was the same: one layer of dried milk and then more Bibles.

My heart sank. I went though a plethora of emotions:

- Extreme anger at the arrogant stupidity of the pastors

- Concern for the local Polish pastor whose name appeared on our visas, that he and his family would be imprisoned for complicity in breaking the law by smuggling Bibles

- Concern for the damage that would incur to his church in Poland
- Anxiety from thoughts of my wife and I almost certainly being imprisoned for smuggling

- Dejection and anxiety regarding the certain end of our ministry.

With one soldier on either side of me, and two behind, I was marched into a nearby building, down some stairs, along a long, badly-lit corridor and into an equally badly-lit room. I was seated at a table under a single, low-wattage light.

I sensed the lady border guard had been about to let us resume our journey—and take the dried baby milk with us—but now, her demeanour was totally different, and why not? In her mind, and in the minds of all the other watching soldiers, the boxes of Bibles were the irrefutable evidence that I had lied. Protestations of innocence were to be expected, so were meaningless.

Growing up, I recalled my father telling me never to lie. He told me if I lied I would have to remember what the lie was and I would eventually get caught. On the other hand, if I told the truth, it would not matter how many times I was asked; the same truth would always come out. So I decided I could not concern myself with the possible ramifications there could be for the American pastors; I was going to tell the truth. What else could I do?

There was no physical abuse or threats, but for three hours, in the damp and musty bowels of that building, they hammered constantly about why I had lied.

From me, they got exactly the same explanation time and time again. The truth!

Ginny and the pastors had been ordered back into the van, so she conducted a prayer meeting on my behalf—while suppressing the rage she, too, felt towards these pastors.

What happened next? All I can say is that, after about three hours, the border officer abruptly seemed to lose interest in me. They confiscated all the dried milk and Bibles, gave us back our passports and sent us on our way into Poland with a very stern warning.

You have to know that it just doesn't happen like that; it should *not* have happened like that. We deserved to be arrested and pay the consequences, but I believe *prayer* changed the outcome.

As we drove away in the van, there was no sense of victory, or even relief. I made sure of that, by maintaining a stoic silence for about an hour before pulling over into the entrance to a field, way out in the countryside.

Seven of these pastors I had never met before that morning. I had met only the pastor who had gathered this group together and his assistant pastor, but I made the reasonable assumption they were all culpable.

So, in measured tones, I told them *exactly* what I thought about their actions in lying to me, deceiving me and putting the lives of the sponsoring Polish pastor and his family in danger—as well as Ginny's and mine—and, for that matter, their own lives.

It was a subdued van of people who continued the drive to Bielsko-Biala in southern Poland, to the homes of Christians with whom we would stay for a week.

To this day, I have never told my pastor friend in Poland what happened that day.

Interestingly, in the next twenty-four hours, each of the seven pastors, who were new to me, came to apologize for what had happened, to assure me that they had had no idea the boxes contained the hidden Bibles and that they would never have agreed to do such a thing.

It had been the responsibility of only the lead pastor and his assistant, despite the fact that, as we organized the details of the trip, I had *clearly* explained—several times—that we did not smuggle Bibles, and there was no need to do so in Poland at that time.

The rest of the visit went well. The pastors made personal connections with local pastors and churches that led to reciprocal help and fellowship links that have lasted down through the years.

And there was another unexpected silver lining. Individually, all seven innocent pastors told Ginny and I they wanted Ginny to sing and me to share about the church in Poland in their churches in the Pittsburgh area. They all promised a good offering towards our work in Eastern Europe. Would that be a 'guilt' offering?

Within the year, we had visited each of the seven churches, and the pastors had been true to their word with generous love-offerings.

In addition to that, four of the churches decided to support Ginny and me for several years from their missions fund. One church supported us faithfully for ten years, until the pastor moved to another church.

And the pastor who lied and organized the smuggling? His vibrant church of 600+ disintegrated within eighteen months.

I don't want to sound flippant in saying this, but sometimes God does work in mysterious ways.

COMING OUT

There have been so many incredible stories of our comings and goings across the borders into communist Eastern Europe.

- From West Germany into East Germany, driving to West Berlin, a 'free' city right in the middle of East Germany, encased in a barbaric wall

- Driving across East Germany to Poland

- Driving From Poland across Belarus to Russia, and down from Moscow to the Black Sea area

- Driving from Poland through the Czech Republic and Slovakia to Hungary— all of which were communist states

- Driving many times across the entire length of Ukraine and Crimea, when it was still part of Ukraine

- Driving from the UK, crossing the English Channel, and then down through Belgium, France, Germany, Switzerland, Austria and Hungary to communist Romania and then all the way across Romania to the Black Sea resort of Constanta to work with a little Baptist church there

- After presenting the drama "Heaven's Gates and Hell's Flames" in Greece, driving back home up through Macedonia, Albania, Montenegro, Bosnia Herzegovina, Croatia and Slovenia before going through Austria and the Czech Republic to Poland and then on through East and West Germany, Holland and Belgium and back across the English Channel to England.

Phew! I feel tired just writing about it ... and those were just our journeys involving countries that, at the time, were staunchly communist. Added to those are all the rest of Europe, from Iceland in the north to Gibraltar in the south, all of the Iberian Peninsula (Spain and Portugal) and all of the Scandinavian countries as well as the other Baltic communist states. And let's not forget Bulgaria and Moldova and all the countries that constitute Great Britain: England, Scotland, Northern Ireland and Wales—and, of course, Eire.

I could fill the pages of an entire book about crisscrossing all of Europe, both by road and by sea multiple times; about crossing the English Channel, the Bay of Biscay, the North Sea, the Irish Sea, the Aegean Sea, the Adriatic Sea, the Baltic Sea, the North Atlantic Ocean and the Norwegian Sea. I wish I could say these were pleasant sea crossings, but I can't, not with a high percentage of the passengers in vomit mode.

I would be remiss in not sharing an incident that happened when we were finally on terra firma and needed to drive back from southern Russia to Poland and then on to England.

While I've made it clear that I don't think Christians should knowingly break the laws of sovereign nations, there is a tantalizing "but ..." that hangs within arms reach and tempts me to say, "Well ... maybe."

We had been in the southern Russian city of Krasnodar (not too far from Sochi, where the 2014 Winter Olympic Games were held) presenting the drama "Heaven's Gates and Hell's Flames" to packed audiences in the Krasnodar Academic Drama Theatre.

Krasnodar is now a thriving city in the homeland of the famous—or infamous—Cossacks. The Cossacks have been described as "... a caste of warriors, who have guarded the borders of the Russian empire for centuries and who, recently, have played a key role in the Russian occupation of the Crimea."[11]

---

[11] Simon Shuster, Time magazine, March 12, 2014

When we were there, there was no inkling of the ethnic upheavals we see today; but that is the nature of that whole geographical area we call "Eastern Europe." When the heavy hand of Soviet communist repression that has kept the peace in that region for decades (albeit by force and fear) is removed, what emerges is a cataclysmic explosion of deep-seated, centuries-old ethnic animosities.

Sorry! I digress! Getting back to *this* story …

Several years prior to the "adventure" with the nine pastors, I had been invited to have tea with a consular officer of a certain Eastern European nation at his consulate in Toronto.

The consulate had a large file on me because of the many visits we had made to their country, mostly for humanitarian reasons. They had called this meeting to discuss some similar upcoming projects we were proposing.

During the course of our conversation, the officer gave me some off-the-record, unofficial advice as to how to deal with difficult, deliberately uncooperative, border officials.

He told me that almost all the border guards were looking for kickbacks. These were bribes in the form of either US dollars or (at that time) western instant coffee. He advised me to never offer such a bribe because most often, the guard would take the bribe and then arrest the person for giving it. The guard would get a feather in his cap for catching a westerner in this illegal activity.

However, when dealing with "bent" border officials, there was a way to exert pressure on them to combat their dishonesty.

Apparently, in the communist system, every official was afraid of two things: one being the official who was immediately *above* him or her in seniority, who could seriously impair promotion prospects; and the other being the official immediately *below* him or her, who was after his or her job and just waiting for them to mess up.

Understanding that climate was essential, so that if one encountered the almost inevitable belligerent border official, one way to deal with that person would be to demand to speak to his or her superior officer. When used in the right situation, it worked. It really did!

Our plan was to drive in our trusty Toyota Hi-Ace van pulling our four-wheel trailer containing our PA system, stage lighting, props and costumes from Krasnodar, Russia, up the Crimean Peninsula, through the Ukraine to Poland, where we would drop off our Polish co-workers, Czarek and Jola, and then continue across northern Europe, back home to the UK.

We were on a tight schedule because we had ourselves and the van booked on a ferry to cross the English Channel. It was at the time of year when the ferries were fully booked months in advance.

Early in the morning, heading west, we reached the Russian-Ukrainian border post, and that is where our troubles began. The building was very run-down and unkempt. The guards and officials were similarly slovenly, bored and disinterested, working at a snail's pace to deliberately antagonize everyone who wanted only to get on with their journey.

After waiting a long time for our turn in line, the border official finally told us—with a smirk on his face—that we could not drive across Ukraine that day because they had run out of the transit visas that one had to purchase for that purpose. We would have to drive north and go around the top of Ukraine, through Belarus, a detour that would add eight to ten hours onto our journey.

Were we encountering bureaucratic incompetence or was a bribe being sought here? Well, mindful of the advice previously given to me, I was not going to fall into that trap, but neither was I going to be meekly cowed. So I said, "Fine—as you wish! I demand to speak to your superior officer," in my best show of British indignation. When I received no response either way, I stalked out of the office to the van and equipment trailer, to where Ginny was waiting with Czarek and Jola.

I told them what had happened and said, 'Come on we're going."

"But how can we if we have no transit visa?"

I replied that if the border officials *really* had no transit visas, then it was a case of gross bureaucratic incompetence. I let them know it was more likely that we were being hit up for a bribe.

Either way, I was not going to drive an extra eight to ten hours and miss our ferry booking to England. We would drive across Ukraine to the Ukrainian-Polish border, where I would happily buy our transit visa—after the fact. And yes, we would probably have to pay a little "over-the-odds" for it, but the detour delay was unacceptable.

Czarek and Jola, because they were born and brought up under communism in Poland, were worried. As we drove away from the border post, they worriedly watched the road behind us, convinced that, at any moment, a Ukrainian police car would pursue us—but nothing happened. No one seemed interested. We had successfully called the border guard's bluff.

After a long and tiring drive, we approached the village of Shehyni, which straddles the Ukranian-Polish border in western Ukraine. Here we faced a completely different, but no less intimidating, situation.

Just outside the village, we had to pull in behind a long line of traffic that snaked eastward. It stretched so far we could not even see the village, let alone the actual border, situated on the far western edge of the village.

We didn't think anything of it, as long lines of trucks, cars, coaches, vans and buses were completely normal at eastern European border checkpoints. But after awhile, we saw something unsettling that we had not seen before.

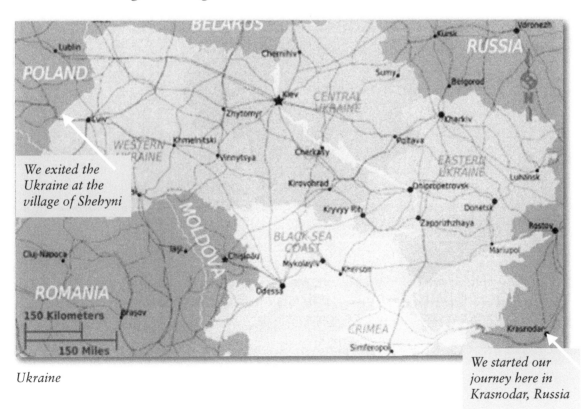

We exited the Ukraine at the village of Shehyni

We started our journey here in Krasnodar, Russia

Ukraine

167

Sauntering along beside the line of traffic were two unkempt men with cigarettes hanging on their lips, as if attached by invisible threads. Their clothes were dirty, as was their hair, and their scruffy beards looked about a week old. However, the most startling things were the AK47 Kalashnikov automatic assault rifles casually slung over their shoulders and bandoliers of spare ammunition crisscrossing their chests. These men looked dangerous ... and they walked directly over to our vehicle.

I was amused to see that it took them awhile before they realized the steering wheel was on the right side of our van, as it is on all British vehicles, but I did not let that show on my face.

As one of them started to look—with way too much interest—at our trailer (which, as I said, contained all our sound and lighting equipment, props, costumes and stage make-up), the other man started to jabber aggressively at me, but I could not understand him.

Fortunately, Czarek, beside me in the van, could understand.

We knew this was the line of vehicles waiting to be cleared at the border checkpoint, but this man informed us that he would send us to the front of the line if we paid him $300 US. Otherwise, we could end up waiting three days or more before we cleared though—yes, three days!

Czarek informed me that these men had no official standing, but they were from the local Russian Mafia and that in this part of the world, this kind of thing was quite normal.

I have to be honest. I was tired. I was fed up with all this corruption and bribery and was in no mood to kowtow to people who preyed on the innocent by creating situations of fear. I wanted to get home to England and I did *not* want to face the consequences of missing the cross-channel ferry.

From the registration plates on our vehicle and the fact that the steering wheel was on the right side, it was obvious that our vehicle was from Britain. I was convinced these men would not risk an international incident by firing upon us; after all, what they were doing was totally illegal.

I had Czarek get in the back of the van with his wife, Jola, and Ginny joined me in the front. I then pulled out of the long line of static traffic and drove towards the village at a steady, but unthreatening, speed. As we neared the village, we saw there was a group of six or eight more of these Mafia men, all with AK47s, who had constructed a makeshift barrier, but that the barrier did not block the entire road.

As we approached the men and the barrier, still at the steady, unthreatening speed, Ginny and I leaned out of our respective windows, waving our British passports and shouting loudly, "We are British! We are British!" repeatedly. When they realized we were not going to stop, the men jumped out of the way, enabling us to drive past their inadequate barrier and proceed on through the village, which seemed to be deserted.

When we reached the western edge of the village, we encountered the Polish customs checkpoint. One might think we would have encountered the Ukrainian exit checkpoint first, but that's not how it worked at these checkpoints.

Let me try to explain. When travelling from east to west, if one were to check out of Ukraine and then discovered Poland would not accept you, you would then be caught in the no-man's land between the two countries. So it's mandatory to confirm that the country you are travelling to will accept you *before* leaving the country you're travelling from.

Amazingly, after safely and quickly clearing through the Polish checkpoint, as we drove the hundred yards toward the Ukrainian exit checkpoint, we were accosted again—by the *original* two men who had first tried to extort money from us. They still wanted their money! Again, we refused to pay. At which time, they angrily gave up.

Czarek and Jola were more than relieved when they arrived home in Olenica, Poland—as were Ginny and I when, a day later, we reached our home in Waterlooville, England.

A FUNNY INCIDENT

... THEY SHALL NOT PASS

To fully appreciate this incident, it's necessary to understand that British people feel very strongly about respecting the integrity of a queue, or "line-up," as many would call it.

Whether it be at a bank, in a store, queuing to get into a movie theatre, or just to get on a bus, we would never think of jumping the line, and we would take a very dim view of anyone who did. It seems to offend some instinctive sense of decency in us. I have heard it said, "You can insult an Englishman's mother, but whatever you do, don't push in front of him in a queue." Tuck that thought in the back of your mind as I share an incident that occurred one summer night at the westbound border between Russian and Belarus.

Our Russian husband-and-wife team, Lara and Vova, who presented the drama "Heaven's Gates and Hell's Flames" in Russia, had a canary-yellow, Ford mini-bus, which was constantly breaking down, due to inadequate and incompetent maintenance performed in Russia. The problem was exacerbated with the fact that it was very difficult to get replacement parts for it in that country.

As I had to be in Moscow to speak at a conference, and we wanted to bring Lara and Vova to the UK for more training, we decided I would drive back with them from Moscow in their van, which then could be gone over 'with a fine tooth comb' by an excellent, trusted mechanic in England. Our hope was to get it properly fixed and made road worthy, once and for all.

So, early one summer morning, we left Moscow and drove west, reaching the border with Belarus at about 4:00 p.m. There, we joined the inevitable, long line of vehicles waiting to get through the border.

After a couple of hours of waiting, we had barely moved forward. Leaving Lara and Vova at the van, I walked towards the border checkpoint to see what was causing the lack of forward movement of the queue. I had no means of measuring it, but it seemed to be maybe a couple of kilometres before I discovered the problem.

Back at the van, we had noticed some cars had driven down along the outside of the line. We had assumed they were turning off, somewhere down the road, to go to a different destination; but I discovered there was no turn off and there was no other destination. This road led only to the border checkpoint. The cars we had observed, had been driving past the rest of the vehicles that were waiting patiently in line and, when they reached the front, they would merge into the front of the line.

Two thoughts came to my mind: why would anyone have the selfish audacity to do such a thing, and why would the people in the line—people who had waited patiently—let other people force their way into the front of the line?

Either way, I decided I was going to do something to stop it. Some people might ask, "Why bother?" Others might say, "Don't get involved!" But it offended that British part of me that said to do such a thing was just not right.

It was about 7:00 p.m. when I got back to the van, a pleasant summer evening still with plenty of light. I planted myself in the middle of the road (it was only one-car width wide) and proceeded to stop any, and all, cars that tried to drive down the road passing us. I knew their intent, and they were *not* going to get away with it.

Not being able to speak Russian or Polish, and not being physically-imposing, I employed the only other asset I had, that being the British-bulldog-they-shall-not-pass determination. And *nobody* got by! I am sure Sir Winston Churchill would have been proud of me.

There was a lot of shouting ... and I mean a *lot* of shouting. Many drivers revved their car engines at me in a threatening manner. On two or three occasions, I had to literally jump up on the front fender of a car whose driver was trying to intimidate me with the threat of running me down ... *but no one got by*. I made them all turn around and join the back of the line, as all decent people should do.

To begin with, Lara and Vova disowned me by slinking down in the van, pretending they didn't know me, but then, as a crowd gathered to enjoy the entertainment, they got out to enjoy the spectacle of this crazy Englishman stopping all the cars. Our line of vehicles started to creep slowly toward the border crossing.

At one time, four soldiers walked up from the border crossing to see what all the fuss was about. When they reached the "scene of the crime," they just stood there, smoking and laughing, but did absolutely nothing to stop me.

The forward motion of the line was slow, but it was steady. Then, as the summer light quickly faded, I found myself operating in the dark with few street lights, most of which did not work. Now, as cars tried to get by me, I was confronted only with headlights, which added an eerie sensation to the whole proceedings—but still *they did not pass*.

But then a car came down the road with a "Taxi" sign on its roof. (Did you know that the two most internationally recognised words all over the world are "Taxi" and "Coca Cola"?) Of course, the taxi driver got out of his car and started to shout at me. As he did so, I noticed, because of the car's interior light, that his three passengers were wearing military uniforms.

Quick as a flash, I deduced they must be border control officials and the taxi must be taking them to work, so I stepped back and magnanimously let them through—

but I had to jump quickly back into the middle of the road to prevent another car from sneaking through.

Inevitably, the driver of this second car got out and started yelling at me. I was puzzled when the taxi driver stopped his car and he, too, got out to yell at me.

Picture the scene:

- It's dark and this drama is unfolding under the dancing lights of the cars and onlookers with their flashlights.

- I am the "piggy-in-the-middle," stoically shooing on the taxi driver, trying to get him to move along ...

- ... whilst, at the same time, defiantly stopping the other car from following the taxi.

- For some reason, the watching crowd were laughing and shouting. Apparently they knew something that I did not.

- And then I saw it! It was then I looked down and saw, to my horror, the tow rope between the taxi and the following car.

Have you ever wanted the ground to open up and swallow you?

When the crowd saw that I had seen the tow rope, they laughed and cheered all the more. In order to extract myself from this impromptu vignette with some dignity, I, with a degree of aloof aplomb, motioned for the following car to move on with the taxi—not that he could have done otherwise.

Lara, Vova, Ginny and I have laughed many times since about what happened, but Lara said something interesting. She said that observing that incident taught her a lot about the British character, and why we had, at one time, had the greatest empire the world has ever seen. Her words—not mine.

Where is the dividing line between pig-headed stubbornness and consistent determination? Only in Britain, you say? Pity.

ALBANiAN PRAiSE!

On January 24, 1997, thousands of Albanians took to the streets in the southern city of Lushnje. Their country was nearing political meltdown. Protestors stole over 500,000 rifles and other arms from government depots. This triggered the same thing happening all across the nation.

Now deadly weapons were in the hands of children, teenagers and undisciplined men, many of whom were excessively drunk on cheap alcohol and on the feeling of power that comes from having a gun in one's hand.

It was into this cauldron of dangerous civil unrest that I flew a few weeks after the incident. I went to join our Romanian drama team. They had driven from Romania, across Serbia, down to the city of Laç in northwestern Albania. The official population of Laç was 23,400; however, the accuracy of official population statistics is questionable.

After presenting "Heaven's Gates and Hell's Flames" several times at Kensington Temple, in London, England, our contact person connected us to a small church in Albania, which had the courage and vision to want to see this drama presented in their country, performed in the Albanian language.

After arranging a date, civil unrest erupted. We would have been inclined to delay going until a time when it might have been safer for us, but the local Christians were full of faith and hope. This was a big event for them and they did not want to delay it, in case it just never happened. So—truth be known—we piggy-backed on their faith. If they were willing to proceed, we did not feel we could disappoint them.

We proceeded to train a small group of enthusiastic, local Christians to act in the drama, but we had no idea if anyone would come to see it.

The theatre booked for the performances had not been used for over ten years. It was decrepit and ramshackled. The auditorium floor ascended in layers, as do normal theatre floors, but there were no fixed seats, just a crazy collection of loose chairs.

About an hour before the first performance was to begin, we heard repeated gunfire from outside, but as this was a frequent occurrence at that time, we did not think too much about it. But then someone rushed into the theatre to tell us there was a huge crowd of people trying to get into the theatre, and they were not displaying any sort of decent patience. They were trying not only to force the front doors open, but they were also trying to force their way in via the emergency exit that led directly into the auditorium.

The local pastor called for help from the police, but they turned him down flatly. Because the people had more guns than they, the police were not going to put their own lives at risk.

As we were pondering whether or not we should cancel the drama for the sake of our safety, the decision was taken out of our hands when the emergency exit doors crashed open inwards and a sea of dishevelled humanity poured into the auditorium. Our audience had arrived and the show had to go on.

Everyone was shouting boisterously and fighting amongst themselves. Many were obviously very drunk. Some were affecting threatening poses with the guns they carried.

The fact that the seats were not fixed only added to the pandemonium, as the unruly crowd started falling and fighting over the chairs, some actually throwing them at each other. I have never in my life—before or since—experienced such a scene of undisciplined mayhem.

At no time did this crowd ever fully quiet down, but some of the scenes in the drama did seem to be getting though to some of the crowd, particularly to those who were not drunk.

When it came to the altar call, with the local pastor translating, I did my best (against a backdrop of catcalls and whistles) to invite those who wanted to become Christians—or who were sincere about wanting to know more—to come to the front ....

In retrospect, that was probably a mistake. Several hundred people surged forward, knocking over other people and loose chairs, resulting in fights and more mayhem.

It was bizarre!

We managed to return safely to the pastor's little home where we were staying, all squeezed together. We were a little shell-shocked and needed a good night's sleep. We arranged to meet the next morning to discuss what needed to be done differently. Because we could not count on any help from the police and the theatre's security was nonexistent, we knew we had no control over people flooding into the theatre. We needed to come up with an idea to at least calm them down.

One of the sixteen-year-old Albanian girls in the church made a suggestion that I thought was brave but ill-advised. She offered to sing some worship songs with two younger female friends at the beginning of the presentation. I fully appreciate the value and function of praise in the church, but I could not see that it would calm about 800 baying, drunken men, who were just out to have some fun at the expense of other people.

There was no PA system for these girls to use and they had just one inexpensive acoustic guitar. Even if they were very good, I couldn't see them quietening such a rowdy crowd, but having no better suggestion, I acquiesced.

Sure enough, the next evening the theatre was, if anything, more packed than the night before, with the same guns in evidence and the same jostling and fighting amongst the audience.

When the girls walked onto the stage, the decibel level of noise increased with the wolf whistles and jeers the crowd threw at them. In the face of such an onslaught, I felt sure they would break down and run off the stage in tears.

But they didn't. They just stood there and sang.

Standing against the wall of the auditorium to one side, where I had a clear view of both the stage and the audience, I watched as these girls doggedly carried on singing, even though they could not be heard over the sheer pandemonium of laughter, jeers and catcalls. I was almost willing them to leave the stage in order to spare them further embarrassment; but they carried on singing their simple songs of worship to God.

What happened next I would not have believed had I not seen it with my own eyes. Slowly but surely, the crowd quieted down. As those precious, courageous girls continued to worship in their simple way, the presence of the Holy Spirit unobtrusively slipped into that place and took control. There was no other rational explanation for what I witnessed.

I found myself, in my heart, thanking God for the courage and simple faith of those girls and, at the same time, asking Him to forgive me for my lack of faith.

After the drama was performed, we came again to the altar call: the invitation to meet with people who wanted prayer, or who wanted to give their lives to Jesus, or who simply wanted to know more about how to become a Christian.

Earlier that day we had come up with an idea that was totally different—radical if you like—but we felt it stood a chance to avoid the chaotic scenes that had transpired the night before. We called it "The Reverse Altar Call."

After giving the usual recap of what they had just seen, plus a closing prayer, I explained we would like to talk to and pray with those who felt God had touched their hearts that night. Rather than asking people to come forward, we asked those who wanted to be ministered to, to remain in their seats. We asked everyone else to quietly leave the auditorium.

It worked like a dream. We brought the girls back on stage to sing some more as people were leaving. Then, in an atmosphere of peace and calm, we were able to minister to all those who had stayed in their seats.

There was a wild spirit abroad in the nation of Albania at that time, but we witnessed the power of the Holy Spirit at work in a way we had never seen before.

TWO TANTALIZING TITLES

ESCAPE FROM UKRAINE
& ESCAPE FROM POLAND

Part One—Escape from Ukraine

During my ten years as director for "Reality Outreach Ministries, Europe" ("Heaven's Gates and Hell's Flames"), I was invited often to speak at conferences all over the UK and Europe. This involved visits to many places like Volgograd, (formerly Stalingrad) Russia; Reykjavik, Iceland; Pori, Finland; Krasnodar, Russia; Gibraltar; Lisbon, Portugal; Sofia, Bulgaria; and many more to either troubleshoot or speak to pastors and churches that wanted to host the drama. All were visited as a result of invitations by the local churches.

One such visit was to Kiev, the capital of Ukraine. I had booked the return flight from London to Kiev via Warsaw, Poland, so I could meet with our Polish team for important discussions.

I had a British Airways round trip ticket, but they shared some routes with LOT, the Polish national airline, so I was not surprised that my connecting flight from Warsaw to Kiev, Ukraine, was on LOT.

Over the course of a few days, I had some successful meetings with American missionaries based in Kiev and also with some local Ukrainian pastors.

To get to the airport on my day of departure, rather than subject me to an inefficient taxi service that would price gouge me, one of the pastors said he would arrange for one of the men from his church to collect me at my hotel to drive me to the airport.

As I strictly adhere to a personal policy of arriving at least one hour prior to the time my flight ticket says to check in at the airport, I arranged for the driver to collect me at the hotel at 8:00 a.m. Because I don't like to be rushed, I make sure I have checked in with my luggage long before the main rush of passengers arrives.

It was a bitterly cold morning with several months of snow having accumulated on the ground.

By 9:00 a.m. there was still no sign of the driver. It was not until around nine-thirty, that he breezed into the hotel as if nothing was wrong.

When I challenged him as to why he was late he just smiled, shrugged his shoulders and said, "No problem," in Ukrainian.

When I pressed him for an answer he said, through someone at the hotel who could translate, that he had decided that 8:00 was too early and there would be plenty of time to get to the airport if he picked me up at 9:30.

It was not his call to make, but he was one of those infuriatingly effervescent people who did not stop smiling and whose response to everything was "no problem."

Before the day was over, I would grow extremely tired of those words. His arriving at the hotel late was my first inkling that this was not going to be a good day.

On the way to the airport, every few miles the driver would pull over to the side of the road, get out, gather some snow and stuff hands-full of it into the radiator of his car to try to keep it from overheating.

He would smile and say, "No problem."

Amazingly, we arrived at the airport right around the time I was due to check in, but we could not find my flight on the departure board. There was no such flight to Warsaw listed under either British Airways or LOT Polish Airlines.

Because this portion of my ticket was in Ukrainian, I had to seek out someone at the information desk who could translate it for me. This was when I discovered that, although my flight out from England had been on British Airways and the flight from Poland to Kiev had been on LOT Polish Airways, my return to Warsaw was on neither of these carriers. It was, in fact, on Ukrainian National Airlines.

I was relieved that we at least had the necessary information to board the flight. So now it was my turn to say (to the lady at the information desk), "No problem," and ask,"Can you please direct me to the boarding gate."

To which she replied, "I am sorry sir, you are at the wrong airport. This is Kiev Boryspil Airport. Ukraine National Airlines flies out of Kiev Zhuliany Airport."

I had no idea there were two airports servicing Kiev. Is it not a reasonable assumption that when you book a round trip ticket, you will be flying out of the same airport you fly into? Apparently not!

Back to my trusty driver with the ever-smiling face and indomitable spirit. I showed him the portion of the ticket concerning this leg of the flight. He said (you guessed it), "No problem."

Those familiar with the English comedy "Faulty Towers" (British slapstick comedy at its best, starring John Cleese) will appreciate the fact that communicating with this driver was like trying to communicate with Manuel, a character on the show. For those who know who I am talking about, I see the smiles on your faces.

When we finally arrived at Kiev Zhuliany Airport, after many stops to fill the car's radiator with snow, it was already twenty minutes after my flight was due to have taken off. But that fact did not seem to deter my driver. After all, his life's mantra was "no problem."

Arriving at this airport was like stepping into a scene from an old 1930s black and white film. It was composed of a few decrepit, single-story buildings and old pre-war Nissan huts made of tin or corrugated iron. They were scattered around with no apparent sense of purpose. It was in front of one of these buildings that my driver screeched to a halt.

This incident took place very nearly twenty years ago. In researching for accuracy in this story, I came upon the following description of this Kiev Zhuliany Airport by an anonymous flyer. "Avoid this place! The most disorganized and chaotic place I ever came across. The custom officers believe they have a God-given right to create their own rules and simply rob the travellers by using their official position. A lot of disrespect and shocking behaviour, especially from teenage custom officers. What a way to represent the country. Shame on you."

As I had already paid the driver at the start of my odyssey with him, without looking back, I ran into the nearest building and staggered inside on that bitter cold day with no idea what the tattered, Ukrainian sign over the door said. The plane had either gone already or was at least taxiing down the runway by now.

Inside, a few customs officials were standing around smoking. They looked up at me with practised disinterest and indifference. But for some reason, one of the customs ladies came over to look at my ticket.

She was cheery-faced with red cheeks that shone through her badly applied, cheap make-up. Her uniform no doubt fit her ten or twenty years prior, but now the bulges were most unflattering. Her hair was greasy and pulled back into a severe bun. Her breath would have knocked anyone over at ten paces.

But this customs lady became my angel. As soon as she saw my ticket, it was as though she made it her life's mission, no matter what, to get me on that plane, which apparently had not yet taken off.

Not quite.

She grabbed my heavy suitcase and literally threw it on the conveyor belt to take it through the security camera. She then grabbed my arm and forcibly ran me through that room, much to the amusement of onlookers, through the next room and into a third room that had a single door leading outside.

In this third room, I retrieved my suitcase, whereupon the customs lady threw me out the door into the bitter cold—and there it stood, my nightmare!

I am not sure how old the plane was, but it looked like something out of a "Raiders of the Lost Ark" film. It had just two propellers, one on each wing. They were making an awful noise as the rear end of the plane slowly turned around to line up with the runway.

I didn't have time to think. My "angel" was repeatedly shouting something at me in Ukrainian as she gesticulated urgently towards the plane. As it slowly accelerated, I ran toward an opening I noticed near the tail, out of which an arm was urgently beckoning me.

Trust me, I am not exaggerating any of this. This *is* just as it happened.

I was younger and fitter then, so as the plane accelerated slowly, I was able to narrow the distance between myself and the rear opening. As I drew alongside the opening, still running, I swung my suitcase with all my might and it sailed up through the opening, whereupon a pair of strong arms reached out and grabbed me, pulling me off my feet and through the opening—literally just before the plane reached the optimum speed to take off.

It really hurt my stomach and knees as I was hauled, unceremoniously, over the lip of the opening and into the plane, but I had made it. Phew!

I then looked up to find myself staring into the face of a goat. I kid you not (excuse the pun). It was a nonchalant, live goat, looking about as happy to see me as I was to see it. It was tethered to the door of the plane's only washroom. Welcome to Ukrainian National Airlines.

I squeezed down the aisle of the small plane to find my seat, which surprisingly was vacant, but the space in front of my seat was filled with a large package wrapped with plastic and string. No one offered to move it and so, as the plane was full, I awkwardly positioned myself in the seat with one leg stretched out into the aisle and my other leg tucked under my chin.

Most of the people who passed me on their way to the washroom either didn't see my leg in the aisle or deliberately kicked me—or fell over the leg, uttering what I assume were Ukrainian or Polish expletives. Happily, I could not understand what they said. So, having learned from my Ukrainian driver earlier that day, I smiled and, like a good Canadian, said, "Sorry."

I tell you the truth when I tell you the lady sitting next to me by the window had a live chicken in her lap. Its wings were bound, but it made a lot of noise, fussing as it struggled against its unnatural surroundings.

The plane made so much noise that I could hardly hear myself think. It leaked water and condensation. My seat belt was broken and the pilot seemed to seek every air pocket in the skies over Ukraine and Poland as we were mercilessly buffeted up and down.

The in-flight refreshment was a small cup of lukewarm water in a grubby plastic cup, not that it mattered because the turbulence conspired to ensure that the water ended up all over my clothes rather than in my mouth. That might have been a blessing in disguise.

When, several hours later, the plane creaked to its final stop on the tarmac at Warsaw Airport, I was never so happy, relieved and grateful to step out onto terra firma. I vowed never again to fly in Eastern Europe.

To be fair to Ukrainian National Airlines, they have almost certainly improved since those days. And they *did* have an angel who ensured that I didn't miss my flight.

Part Two—Escape from Poland

More than thirty years ago, the Soviet Union shocked the world by shooting down a 747 airliner. Korean Air Lines Flight 007 had strayed over Soviet territory. Cold War tensions in 1983 had fuelled Soviet suspicions that the 747 was spying. Two hundred and sixty-nine passengers and crew died. It was a Cold War tragedy that still seems surreal.

The tragedy had far-reaching ramifications on the relationship between communist-controlled Eastern Europe and the rest of the world. The idea that Soviet fighter jets would shoot down a Boeing 747 airliner was shocking. The tragedy is now largely forgotten.

On a sultry August night in 1983, at New York's JFK airport, Alice Ephraimson-Abt, a brilliant, twenty-three-year-old, blue-eyed blonde was about to board Korean Air Lines Flight 007 for Seoul, South Korea. For one last time, she held her father, New Jersey businessman Hans Ephraimson-Abt, before saying goodbye. "There were hugs and I-love-yous," her father, now ninety-one, told CNN.

Alice, who was excited about heading to Beijing to teach English and study, could have been a diplomat, a contributor to peace, her father said. "Her death was a great loss to her generation."

The implication of this tragedy reverberated far beyond the lives lost. It sparked global outrage, conspiracy theories and great political tensions between the nations controlled by Moscow and the rest of the free world. It joined a list of disturbing developments that made 1983 one of the scariest years of the Cold War. Not since 1962's Cuban Missile Crisis had the world teetered so close to the unthinkable.

And we were caught in the middle of that tragic incident.

Our ministry in Poland had been having a great effect as we used gospel concerts to bridge the gap between West and East and to share God's love in a non-threatening way. In 1983, the Polish authorities wanted to present Ginny with a special medal in recognition of the work we had been doing presenting gospel concerts to raise money for children who suffered because of their parents' alcoholism or drug addiction.

A week before Flight 007 was shot down, we left England with a team of musicians and singers from Canada and the UK and drove into Poland to do some more gospel concerts in the theatres and cultural houses that every Polish city seems to have in abundance. Driving through Belgium on our way, our coach broke down and had to be replaced by two vehicles: one with hard wooden seats for our people and a van for all our P.A. and stage lighting equipment.

E-mail was not universally available back then, but our team members wanted to connect with family members back home to reassure them that they had arrived in Poland safely, so we relied on being able to use the telephone.

Everything was fine for a few days, but then, with no explanation, we found we could neither make telephone calls out of Poland nor receive calls in. We had no idea why, and our local Polish friends could not tell us because they did not know either. Apparently all of Eastern Europe was in a total news blackout. We were totally cut off.

The first we had any inkling of what was happening was when we were touring a salt mine. When we were deep underground, our guide pulled me aside to say he listened to "Voice of America," a clandestine radio broadcast in Eastern Europe that was illegal for East Europeans to listen to. Being caught doing so would result in a long prison sentence.

From this person, we learned about the Korean plane being shot down and that the USSR had imposed a total clampdown on any news entering or leaving the communist bloc countries.

But even the communists could not enforce a complete blockade of news. A few days later, we had confirmation when a pastor friend in Poland received a phone call from a pastor friend in Sweden. Sweden was a neutral country, not subject to the blockade.

Well, we did the only thing we could do and continued with the gospel concert tour, singing to packed audiences wherever we went. It seemed that our presence with our Polish brothers and sisters gave them encouragement that we were "standing with them" during this difficult time.

As we approached the last concert in the city of Opole, to my shame, I had no idea that Ginny had been growing increasingly ill. After the final curtain call following the concert, she collapsed. A doctor quickly diagnosed her as having severe food poisoning and said she needed to be hospitalized immediately.

That was bad enough, but what was even worse was that our visas expired the next day. (We had expected to drive home after this last concert.) The authorities insisted that I could not stay on in Poland when the rest of our team drove home.

Ginny was much too ill to be moved and had to stay in the hospital, but I had to leave Poland and leave my wife behind, suffering from a life-threatening sickness. The authorities did not give me any choice. They would absolutely not allow me to stay with Ginny, but neither would they allow Ginny to travel. Yes, I was responsible for the team that had come with us from Canada and the USA, but what about my wife?

In our first year of marriage, Ginny had been diagnosed with cancer in her colon and given just four months to live. On that occasion, I'd had to trust Ginny into God's hands. I had to literally give her back to God ... and He had miraculously healed her. So now, here I was again, having to give Ginny back to God. I left Poland with no certainty that I would ever see her again.

(Now over to Ginny)

Everything happened so fast; my body was so sick. I had to say good-bye to Terry and I had no idea what to keep with me at the hospital. I was left behind with all the American money we had and one small carry-on knapsack that contained a nightdress, socks, underwear, my passport, purse, a pen and my Bible. I was too weak and sick to take anything more.

After I was admitted to the hospital, a doctor gave me some medicine and I was told to drink lots of liquids—but what liquids were safe to drink in Poland at that time? There was no staff to care for me between the doctor's occasional visits on his weekly rounds and, to make matters worse, he couldn't speak English nor I Polish.

The local Polish patients had family members who had accompanied them to the hospital and brought food for them and cared for their loved ones.

Well, my family was gone.

The pastor with whom we were working eventually took me out of the hospital to the apartment home of a young lady and her very old father. They were members of his church. The girl worked during the day and so I was left with her father. While she could speak some broken English, he could not speak one word. So here we were, the three of us, in this tiny, cramped apartment. Night after night, day after day, I was left to fend for myself.

Terry had been forced to leave me, and although the Polish pastor was doing all he could, I still felt very much alone with God.

The girl gave me her bedroom, which was very simple with a small cot for a bed. The old man stayed away from me, in their lounge, where he slept at night. He did not want to catch whatever I had contracted.

Day after day, I suffered. I spent most of the time in the bathroom, being sick from both ends. I found an old metal pail, for which I was so thankful at the time. After being sick for hours, I would have to try and clean myself up and clean the toilet and pail. I would then almost crawl down the long hallway, back to the cot to try to rest and regain some energy.

Each day the pastor would come and see me. With him, he brought a communist leader who had loved the music we performed at the concerts in Poland and who had actually been sitting on the front row of the concert on that fateful evening when I passed out behind the stage curtain after our last song. He apologized that he couldn't do anything more, but on each visit, he would bring me little Polish souvenirs to cheer me up. With the money Terry left for me, the pastor would go to the black market each day and try and get some fresh juice and fruit, hoping it would give me back my strength.

Everything I tried to eat or drink would go right through me and make me even sicker. In the first week, I lost fifteen pounds. I could see fear in the pastor's face as he saw my health and strength deteriorating each day. He said, "You really need to get back to England and get medical help, but communication by phone is not working and so it is impossible."

Even the communist leader was trying everything to get me out of Poland, but he could not. East Europe was totally cut off from the West.

Whilst I was left alone all day and evening, I would read my Bible and pray for my dear Terry and the musical team, who were travelling back to England in the old truck and trailer. I prayed that they would have no problems at the borders and get home without incident.

I knew I was never really alone. God was with me and He would never, ever leave me. I would continue to trust in His protection. I knew that even if these were to be my last days on earth, I would still praise Him. I would think of all the beautiful songs He had given me to sing to Him. This comforted me, as I knew He was always with me and that with Him, *all things were possible.*

Near the end of the week, the pastor came in with a huge smile from ear to ear. He said, "Ginny, a miracle has happened and I have great news. I received a phone call from my Swedish friend today and told him all about you. He has arranged for a flight for you tomorrow out of Poland. The sympathetic communist leader has prepared special letters so you won't be troubled at the airport. But he said you have to be well enough to fly, and so you must not act like you are sick."

Well, just the thought of being reunited with Terry made me so happy and gave me strength to do my very best.

I was still terribly sick all evening and through the night. But then, in the wee hours of the morning, the pastor came and assisted me out of the apartment block. With no elevators in the buildings, I had to walk down many flights to get to the ground floor and then, in that fragile state, I had to endure a five-hour drive to Warsaw.

The pastor's wife had prepared some cooked rice , which they tried to feed to me all the way to the airport, but I could hold down only a few grains of rice and then would lose it. Many, many times along the bumpy roads, they had to stop so I could be sick at the side of the road. I didn't care about privacy or dignity. I just wanted to reach that airport and go home.

When we got to the airport, the pastor said, "Ginny, don't let them know how sick you are. You have to look well." So I went to the airport washroom and tried to put on my best happy-healthy Ginny face and prayed, "Oh God, please help me."

Then came the line up to show my passport and the special letter to the authorities. Waiting for them to go through my bag on the long table seemed to take forever. I kept looking back at the pastor, who I knew was praying for me. I kept praying, asking God to help me stand there without wavering.

Have you ever seen the movie *Shining Through* where Melanie Griffith is so ill and, with the help of Michael Douglas, has to look okay to get through the communist lines and pass the scrutiny of the communist border guards? Well, that was me—

except that in the movie, she fainted from her illness and was carried across the lines. I believe I was carried by angels, as I didn't fall down … and I was able to fake it to the authorities that I was just fine.

When I got on the airplane I was so relieved, but then realized that the plane was divided into two sections; right side for smokers and left side for non-smokers … so not only was I still feeling horrible, but I had to endure the smoke.

However, I was very happy to be in an aisle seat, where I could make a fast escape to the washroom. Shortly after taking off, a small meal was delivered and, needing to act normal, I had a few bites. Needless to say, I headed quickly for the bathroom and stayed in there almost the whole flight back to England.

When the plane landed in London, I was so weak I didn't think I could stand up to walk. Nevertheless, I managed to get into the airport terminal building and go through customs. I had no idea who was meeting my plane, as I knew Terry was still travelling with the group by road and boat back to England.

After I passed through customs, I heard two familiar voices calling my name. Our English pastor and another friend ran towards me and caught me as I fell into their arms. They laid me out in the backseat of their car with a blanket and drove me back to Portsmouth to stay with some dear friends who nursed me back to health.

A Christian doctor friend came to their house to check me out and said I was totally dehydrated and must drink a large pitcher of water every hour. He examined the medicine that had been given to me in the Polish hospital and said it was twenty years out of date and had been doing nothing for me. He gave me some new medicine and said that if they had not gotten me back to England, I could well have died from the severe food poisoning.

God saved me from cancer back in 1980 and here He saved me again, almost ten years later.

I was so glad to be reunited with my darling husband. There were times, during the ordeal, when I hadn't been sure if I would ever lay eyes on Terry again.

God was so faithful. He gave me the strength to do the final concert of our tour in Portsmouth.

God brought me back safely to England. It was not yet my time to be with Him.

WEEDS IN GOD'S GARDEN

As a boy, I hated gardens and gardening because my dad made me do it to earn my pocket money. Even as an adult, I never took a liking to it.

I remember one day, after several hours of back-breaking work pulling weeds, I was shocked when my father got extremely angry with me. Apparently, the "weeds" I had pulled were actually perfectly good plants that were not yet fully grown. What can I say? They all looked the same to me!

So how do we tell the difference between good plants that have not yet grown and weeds that can choke and destroy? Sometimes they have to grow side by side in the garden, until the difference become apparent.

For many years, Ginny and I have been privileged to help two ministries in Romania that seek to help Gypsies, especially Gypsy children.

Through this work we have gained a new perspective on the heart of God and on His garden, in which He placed us to do His work.

The world in which we live is God's garden. In it He has planted many nations of many diverse colours.

Some nations are planted in fertile soil with an abundance of natural resources. These flourish with not only enough to meet their own needs but a great overflow that would enable them to meet the needs of other poorer nations—if only they would share their abundance.

Some of the poor parts of the garden receive much more attention than other, equally poor, parts of the garden, but from the gardener's point of view, how satisfying can the garden be if small parts look barren and impoverished, even though most of it looks beautiful?

The Gypsy nation is a very small part of God's garden but, with no garden of their own, they are hated and reviled wherever they try to find rest and solace. Whatever negative things have been said about them may be true to some degree, but as part of God's garden they have equal importance to every other part.

What is needed—what I am sure is God's will—is that some of God's people need to go to that desolate part of God's garden and help the Gypsies—loving them, introducing them to the love of Jesus and patiently teaching them all they need to know—to be integrated into society.

When tending that part of the garden, the aim should be not to save the Gypsies from being Gypsies, but rather, to help them become the kind of Gypsies God

With a Gypsy family

always intended them to be. When that happens, I am sure *that* part of God's garden will be one of the most colourful and joyous parts.

May we, as God's gardeners on earth, never cease to take care of *all* of God's garden, those nations that instinctively we don't like, the old and infirm and those with physical and mental disabilities. May we not overlook those small, rough parts. If parts of a garden are neglected, weeds will grow and eventually pollute and infect the entire garden. Once they get in and take root, it is hard to get them out.

It is too easy to blame the Gypsies for being Gypsies, or blame the infirm for their infirmities. We forget that they were all created by God just are we are, so God has a purpose for them too!

When we look at other people, may we see them through the eyes of God. Only through being equally tended, can the entire garden look the way God intended.

For we are fellow workmen (joint promoters, laborers together) *with and for God; you are God's garden and vineyard and field under cultivation* (1 Corinthians 3:9).

If I find myself growing in God's garden, though I be the tiniest plant in all the bed, yet it is such a mercy to be in the garden at all—I who was a wild rank weed out in the wilderness before—that I will not doubt but that He will water me when I need it, and that He will tend and care for me till I shall come to perfection.[12]

Can you find Terry?

---

[12] C. H. Spurgeon—one of England's best known 18th Century Baptist preachers

CANCER!

GINNY'S HEALING

TERRY'S PERSPECTIVE

From a husband's point of view ...

One Thursday, in 1980, after just one year of marriage, Ginny heard the words from her doctor that no one wants to hear: "Ginny, you have cancer in your colon. You have only four or five months to live. We have made an appointment for you to see a bowel specialist."

Such news leaves one numb. It takes awhile before the realization comes that life must somehow go on, however long that life may be.

On the following day, Friday, David Mainse, host of the national, daily Christian television program *100 Huntley Street* asked for all the viewers across the nation to pray for Ginny. She was well-known to them because of her regular appearances on the program.

Word spread quickly. On Saturday we had a call from some people in England. News had spread so fast that they had already had prayer for Ginny at their Friday night prayer meeting. Out of that prayer time, a word from the Lord for Ginny had come forth. As our friends had recorded it, they were able to play it over the telephone for us. It was a word of encouragement for Ginny. The person speaking it believed God was going to send His healing power through her colon. It was very encouraging but gave us nothing to cling to in terms of specifics.

When, on Sunday, the announcement was made at The Peoples Church that Ginny had been diagnosed with cancer, the visiting preacher suddenly turned to her (she was on the platform because she would be presenting the special music) and said, "Ginny, read Psalm 91:14-16. I trust these words will be a comfort to you." He suggested it was okay to insert her gender into the verses so they would read as follows: "Because she loves me," says the Lord, "I will rescue her; I will protect her, for she acknowledges My name. She will call on Me, and I will answer her; I will be with her in trouble, I will deliver her and honour her. With long life I will satisfy her and show her My salvation."

That was nice; nothing earth-shattering, but it was comforting to a degree. To be honest, I did not think about those verses too much until, very soon after, they came thundering back into our life.

On the Monday morning, we thought about what had happened since we had received the devastating news on Thursday. We felt that if God wanted to heal Ginny supernaturally, we needed confirmation from His Word, the Bible, so we held hands and prayed, "Lord, if this is Your will, please confirm it through Your Word." Within one hour, we heard from God.

I know that can sound very pompous, but it is absolutely true. Let me explain. Ginny and I had ministered a lot in Northern Ireland, where we had developed many friendships. Two in particular were with a wonderful, northern Irish pastor and his wife who, at that time, were pastoring a church in Orangeville, in Ontario, Canada.

Within an hour of our prayer that Monday morning, we received a telephone call from these friends to say they had a letter addressed to us, sent via them from Northern Ireland. It had been in their possession for six weeks, but they had lost track of where we were until they heard about Ginny from David Maine's request for prayer on *100 Huntley Street*. They wondered whether this unopened letter might contain some important news for us, and so (as we were in the middle of a postal strike), they drove it down immediately to Scarborough where we were living with Ginny's parents at the time and delivered it personally.

The letter was, of course, still sealed. No one had tampered with it. The postmark and the date confirmed it had been written and sent over six weeks previously. It was from a lady in Northern Ireland in whose home Ginny and I had stayed for a week or so some nine months earlier.

The woman wrote at length about her family and all the good things happening in her church. Suddenly, the tone of her letter changed as she wrote: "As for you Ginny, Jesus alone is your healer. He wants to heal all thirty-six feet of your colon. He wants to make it brand new. Yea, I am the Lord that healeth thee. Read Psalm 91:14-16." And there the letter ended abruptly.

We were stunned. This letter was sent from Northern Ireland over six weeks prior to us receiving it. Our minds were filled with questions. How could the woman have known Ginny was in need of healing —when we knew less than a week ago ourselves? How could she have known that the colon was the source of her illness? We seriously had been considering its total removal. How could she declare that the Lord wanted to make it "brand new"? Was the Lord saying *He* would heal Ginny without the help of someone else? And how could this lady, writing over six weeks previous to us receiving the letter, have known that six weeks after directing Ginny to read Psalm 91:14-16, a visiting preacher to a church halfway around the world would feel compelled to point Ginny's attention to those very same verses? Was this all just a series of amazing coincidence—or was God trying to speak to us?

It certainly seemed that this was a direct answer to our prayer that morning!

When Ginny saw the specialist the next day, he recommended she should have her entire colon removed, in the hope that the cancer had not already spread to other organs in her body. Apparently, cancer spreads from the colon faster than from other parts of the body. To remove it was a last ditch measure in the hope that it had not already started its journey through the rest of Ginny's body.

Our initial reaction was yes, Ginny should have the operation as soon as possible ... but what about the phone call from England? What about the letter from Northern Ireland? What about the immediate answer to our prayer on Monday morning?

We always pray anyway, but situations like this cause people to intensify their prayers and we were no exceptions. The emerging circumstances caused us to spend even more time talking to God.

We knew that many people were praying for Ginny. At that time, we had three main circles of friends: our church in Toronto, our friends from work and our dear friends and church in the UK, which was not only my home, but a place where we had ministered several times. Our church in Toronto, The Peoples Church, was a vibrant but conservative congregation. Because we worked at the *100 Huntley*

Street television studio, which was multi-denominational, our circle of friends there was more charismatic and varied.

Everyone cared for Ginny and wanted the best for her, but without going into great detail, there were conflicting opinions as to what we should do and what the focus of our prayers should be. To put it simply, there were those who felt Ginny should have the operation as soon as possible and that we should trust God to heal her through the doctor, while others felt we should trust God for supernatural healing and assured us that God wanted to heal her in this way.

We respected both viewpoints, but it was Ginny who had the cancer, not the other people. We needed to know what *God* had to say about it.

Initially, we were not thinking of anything but taking the pragmatic advice of the expert, the cancer specialist. We were living with Ginny's parents at the time, and all around us there was the normal turmoil of a busy Italian family. When we retreated into the sanctuary of our bedroom, however, all we felt was a strange peace. We had no specific direction from God, but the strange, comforting peace was undeniable—no matter how it defied understanding and logic, given the severity and urgency of the situation.

For me, the turmoil was doubled. As Ginny's husband, I was experiencing a struggle that I could discuss with no one, particularly not with Ginny. She had enough to deal with. It involved the fact that while I appreciated everyone praying for my wife, it seemed no one was praying for me.

As I saw it, Ginny was in a win/win situation. Either she was healed—in which case, she would have a wonderful testimony to share—or she would die and go to Heaven, the place where we all long to be.

As for me, I could end up losing the love of my life to whom I had been married for barely one year. If that sounds selfish, being in the same situation might temper anyone's possible judgement on me.

I questioned the Lord about my struggle and His response was very direct. My recollection of it is as vivid now as it was the day I first received it.

His answer came in the form of several challenging questions He spoke directly into my heart.

Terry, who do you love the most, Ginny or Me?

If I decide to take Ginny to be with Me in heaven, will you accept that?

If I decide to take Ginny away from you, will you still love Me?

If I decide to take Ginny away from you, will you accept that as being My will for Ginny?

Will you accept that as being part of My will for you?

Will you still trust Me for your future?

I responded, "Lord, how can I answer those questions with anything but yes? But Lord, this is not fair!"

Who decides what is fair, you or Me? Remember, Ginny does not belong to you; she belongs to Me. She is My gift to you, but you have her for only as long as I decide.

Are you willing to give her back to Me? Cherish every moment you are together.

The Lord showed me that if He decided to take Ginny, then yes, I would miss her terribly. Yes, I would weep, probably inconsolably. These emotions are natural and understandable. But I needed to remember that my life was also in His Hands.

Somehow Romans 8:28 would come to pass. *"And we know that all things work together for good to them that love God, to them who are the called according to His purpose"* (KJV).

That encounter with God gave my life, and especially my marriage, a perspective that remains to this day. Every morning when I wake up and see Ginny breathing gently beside me I say, "Thank You, Lord, for another day." (I have tears in my eyes as I write.)

A song Ginny will be singing on her new recording was written by singer/songwriter Laura Story. The words are flooding my mind and heart right now. Perhaps they would minister to you, too, whatever the circumstances of your life may be.

The song is called "Blessings" and begins with a list of the kind of blessings we all pray for—things like peace, protection, healing, prosperity and relief from suffering.

But the writer pauses to ask whether the better blessings could come through rain drops and tears. She questions whether the trials of life could be God's mercies in disguise, helping us to know Him in a deeper way—the greatest blessing of all. We pray for wisdom and to hear God's voice. We struggle with doubt and the inability to feel the presence of God. But He hears our desperate pleas. The songwriter leaves us with the poignant discovery that the greatest disappointments and aches of life may be the greatest blessings, the very things that draw us closer to God. Such awesome words. If you have been there, or if you are there now, you will know what I mean.

I didn't know it then, but God was preparing Ginny and me to live lives that had been tested for genuine faith. We needed to experience, firsthand, that which we said we believed. Our testimonies would be proven through the fire of our experience.

The contents of the letter from Northern Ireland were not greeted by everyone in a positive light, especially when followed by the comments of the colon specialist, who, with a somewhat flippant attitude, said, "I'll see you again when you decide to have the operation."

As we began to feel more and more that God did not want Ginny to have her colon removed, there were people whose love for Ginny and whose desire not to lose her were blinded by the seriousness of the circumstances. In their opinion, what was needed was sensible decision-making, not irresponsible risk-taking.

Again I found myself in a no-win situation. In their eyes, I was either directly influencing Ginny to make the wrong decision—or I was *not* influencing her *away* from a wrong decision. I even received a thinly veiled threat that if Ginny died as a result of all this, I would soon follow her.

And so the turmoil continued to swirl around us as we were caught in this vortex of well-meaning people. When we retreated into our sanctuary (the bedroom) however, we again experienced God's unusual peace.

We were in need of good counsel, but many of the people whom we trusted had already declared themselves on one side or the other of this dilemma. Was it possible to find an unbiased voice in all the clamour? We needed to speak to someone whom we trusted, someone with impeccably sound well-balanced biblical knowledge, someone who knew us but who was not so close that he or she would not be brutally honest with us. Did such a person actually exist?

A name came instantly to both of our minds. It was the name of one of the most well-respected, well-liked men we knew. Rev. Hudson Hilsden, at that time the pastor of Scarborough Gospel Temple,[13] was recognized as someone with the highest degree of integrity and compassion.

We called Pastor Hilsden on the Thursday, one week after we had heard the devastating news. He was about to go off on a family holiday in his RV but kindly said he would delay for a hour or so to meet with us. When we met at his church office the next day, he said he would not make any decision for us but that he would gladly listen to what we had to say.

And that's what he did. He listened! He sat there looking intently at us with a neutral expression that contained just a hint of that enigmatic, inscrutable smile that was never far from his lips. He listened as we poured out all that had happened and all we were feeling.

When we had finished, he said, "As I have listened to you talking, one thing has come through very clearly to me, and that is the peace you both obviously have."

We answered that yes, when we were together alone with God, we felt His peace very strongly, but when we were with other people—despite their great love for us—that peace was drowned out by the clamour of their understandable concerns.

To that Pastor Hilsden said, "The decision as whether to have, or not to have, the operation can be only yours, but let me say this: In my experience, the most telling and powerful confirmation that any course of action you are considering to take is right with God or not is whether or not you have His peace. I do not want you to tell me what decision you have made, but it is obvious to me, by the calm peace that surrounds you both, that you have already made a decision."

With that, Pastor Hilsden prayed with and for us and then departed for his holiday.

We were reminded of Philippians 4:4-7, which, for obvious reasons, has come to mean a lot to us.

> *Rejoice in the Lord always. I will say it again: Rejoice! Let your gentleness be evident to all. The Lord is near. Do not be anxious about anything, but in every situation, by prayer and petition, with thanksgiving, present your*

---

[13] Now known as Global Kingdom Ministries

requests to God. And the peace of God, which transcends all understanding,
will guard your hearts and your minds in Christ Jesus (Philippians 4:4-7).

The sequence is all-important.

1. We rejoice in the Lord at all times.	Whether those times be good or bad. And perhaps we need to rejoice especially in the bad times.
2. We keep our cool.	Let people around us see that trusting in God brings peace. It is not our peace but rather, God's peace. God is always close to us.
3. Don't worry about anything.	You don't get to choose what things you will or will not worry about. Let go of it *all*. Give it *all* to God. Let Him worry about it.
4. In every situation pray with thanksgiving.	We are very good at praying complaining prayers to God. We have a lot of practise with that. We are also good at praying asking God for things that *we* want. But no—if we pray with thanksgiving all the focus of our prayers are taken away from *us* and are on *Him* as we consider all the wonderful things He has done for us.

And then, ah yes, and then that mysterious and elusive peace of God is no longer mysterious and elusive. Then we experience the peace of God that transcends all understanding. Get that? It transcends all understanding. It's illogical. There is no rational explanation for it. We can't buy it, it can't be bargained for and we can't earn it. But there it is—God's peace.

What does God's peace do? It stands on guard—alert, defending and protecting.

And where does it stand on guard? Around our hearts that can be so easily broken. And around our minds that can be so easily swayed, influenced and corrupted.

Can you picture the wonderful image of God's peace, standing on guard around your heart and your mind?

We knew we had God's peace to not have the operation but to let God alone be Ginny's healer, to allow Him to make her colon "brand new."

Whenever we needed our faith to be reinforced, God was there. For instance, my hairdresser, a girl from Southampton, England, had heard about Ginny's situation and called one day. She was a great person, a great hairdresser and a great friend, but she came from a mixed bag of familial beliefs and couldn't understand our faith. She challenged me on the wisdom of Ginny not having the operation.

Just before she called, I had been reading from the book of James, chapter one, and so was able to share with her that the decision was easy because in verses two to seven, it says:

> *Consider it pure joy, my brothers and sisters, whenever you face trials of many kinds, because you know that the testing of your faith produces perseverance. Let perseverance finish its work so that you may be mature and complete, not lacking anything. If any of you lacks wisdom, you should ask God, who gives generously to all without finding fault, and it will be given to you. But when you ask, you must believe and not doubt, because the one who doubts is like a wave of the sea, blown and tossed by the wind. That person should not expect to receive anything from the Lord. Such a person is double-minded and unstable in all they do (James 1:2-7).*

We had not been presumptuous. We had not tried to bend God to our will. We had not jumped to quick, easy, or currently popular solutions. We had been open to what God wanted, to the point of having to blank out the desires of other people. They were, of course, entitled to their opinions, but this matter was between us and God, not us and them. We did not want to be counted among those people who are continually blown and tossed by the wind of popular opinion. While God still loves them, He can't use them.

In many unusual and unexpected ways, God made His will known to us. Now it was up to us whether to listen to Him and act on what He said or ignore Him and never be able to make a difficult decision again.

So, over the objections of some people, the die was cast. There was no looking back.

This was a pivotal experience and a pivotal decision. Now God knew He could trust us with bigger decisions and bigger situations.

Ginny used to sing a song that talked about not knowing what the future holds, but knowing who holds the future.

All of this happened just before Ginny and I were due to fly out to Frankfurt, Germany, to work with Youth for Christ Germany for two months. We were then to go to Sweden for three weeks. On our way, we were scheduled to go to a week-long conference in the UK. The Youth for Christ Germany had arranged for Ginny to sing at sixty concerts in two months. We would be gone from Canada for over four months.

The colon specialist, upon receiving the news that Ginny was declining the operation, had said he would see us again when we changed our minds.

Ginny's Polish doctor (a lady who loved her and whom Ginny loved back) said bon voyage by saying she would come back to Canada in a coffin. Yes, she really said that.

The cortisone medication Ginny had been taking had caused her body to balloon a little and when she washed her hair, it came out in tufts. She felt, and I totally supported her in this, that because of the specific words she had received from God, when we arrived in Europe, she should stop taking all of the medicines that caused unpleasant side effects. We prayed that she would have a thin body and fat hair. Seriously, we did.

With the words of the doctors ringing in our ears, we flew off to Europe. While we had the verbal blessing of Ginny's parents, we knew in their hearts they did not expect to see their daughter alive again.

That whole time in Europe was amazing. If I were to write about it, it would fill a whole book of its own. Ginny never missed a single concert—and those sixty concerts were spread over three countries.

By the time we arrived back in Canada some three months later, Ginny was the picture of good health. When she went to see her doctor, she kept touching Ginny's face and kissing her because she was so thrilled to see her, and to see her looking so well.

The story of Ginny's healing deserves not a single chapter, but a whole book. But for now, let me say this: When Ginny was originally diagnosed with cancer in her colon, it was after many years of suffering from severe ulcerated colitis. X-rays showed her colon to be badly scarred from its ravages over time. Several years later, after Ginny and I had moved to England to base our ministry there, Ginny felt it would be sensible to put herself under the precautionary care of a local bowel specialist in the UK. This would also serve as a source for a second opinion regarding her health. After being told of her past history, the UK doctor suggested that Ginny should have a colonoscopy and x-rays of her colon—just to be thorough in his doctoring. Ginny had no reason to say no to this request, but we had no idea of what the tests would reveal.

Are you ready for this?

The tests revealed that Ginny's colon was *perfect*. There was *no* scar tissue to be seen anywhere. Remember "... and I will make her colon brand new. Yea, I am the Lord that healeth thee."

I had given Ginny back to God, and He had given her back to me. Now, together, we were ready to move forward into His unknown.

It is now over thirty-five years later and Ginny is still with us, in great health—still singing, still smiling her radiant smile.

All the glory goes to God!

18

TERRY'S HEALING FROM SYSTEMIC SCLEROSIS SCLERODERMA

About a year after Ginny's cancer scare, our doctor, that same Polish lady, told me she thought our family was cursed as, after having had a skin biopsy, I was diagnosed with a rare disease, systemic sclerosis scleroderma, for which there is no cure. It is not always fatal, but it can be ... slowly.

I was suddenly thrust into a process of learning about this invader, this thing called scleroderma. I discovered it is an autoimmune disease (meaning that the immune system causes damage to some of the body's own cells). In systemic sclerosis, it damages the connective tissue cells, so is classed as a connective tissue disease. Although it is not known what triggers the destructive process, there may be an inherited tendency to develop it, or it may be triggered by certain germs (viruses), drugs, or chemicals.

I learned that scleroderma means hard skin. Anyone with it has areas of hardening of the skin. In one type of the disease, systemic sclerosis, one can also get hardening of some of the internal organs. This stops them working normally.

It was overwhelming to learn of the number of possible symptoms and problems that might develop. It was impossible to tell what I could eventually develop because the extent of the disease can vary greatly from person to person. Consequently, regular monitoring of blood pressure, blood and urine tests and tests for lung function were critical. Any unexplained symptoms needed to be reported promptly to a doctor.

The possibilities seemed endless. I learned that the skin can become tight and possibly produce ulcers or nodules. There may be problems with teeth if the mouth cannot be opened wide enough to brush them properly. Reduced saliva production can cause dryness of the mouth. There may be bleeding from the gut, blockage (obstruction) or incontinence of the bowels. Men may experience impotence. Heart complications may occur if the heart muscle is affected by scar tissue. The thyroid gland can become underactive. Depression and thinning of the bones (osteoporosis) are common. Blood pressure can become high and kidneys may become less efficient.

Sometimes kidney problems get worse quickly and the blood pressure becomes very high, necessitating urgent medical care. Headaches, blurred vision, seizures, breathlessness, leg and foot swelling and reduced urine production are all warning signs of crisis. People with leathery, disfigured faces and/or leathery disfigured hands may be in an advanced stage of this disease.

Once the diagnosis was confirmed, I was sent to the Women's College Hospital in downtown Toronto. I assumed it was to meet with another skin specialist, but when I arrived, I discovered that I was a sort of guinea pig. Apparently no less than nine dermatologists had flown in from across Canada to see my condition. It was that rare.

I remember sitting there, stripped to the waist, as one by one these men and two women prodded a three-inch, uneven circle of skin high on my left arm. The skin was shiny and hard, the colour of old, well-worn leather. It didn't hurt or itch or give me any discomfort at all. It was just there!

So they measured it, took photographs of it and talked amongst themselves about it as I sat there, feeling like a horse in a fair whose teeth were being checked for evidence of health.

When the doctors left the room, I waited until a nurse finally informed me I could go home.

"Is that it?" I asked.

"Yes, thank you, Mr. Bridle."

"Is no one else going to see me, or will there be another appointment?"

The nurse replied kindly, "Mr. Bridle, the condition you have is incurable so there is no need for a further appointment. Just be sure to inform your doctor as it grows so we can keep an eye on how fast it spreads."

"How fast will it spread?" I asked, concerned.

She responded, "It is a very rare condition, and the speed with which it spreads varies widely. Just keep on eye on it."

With that she bid me goodbye and left the room. So that was it!

Although it gave me no pain nor caused any restriction in my activities, I had a gnawing consciousness of a creeping parasite that would slowly but surely take over my body.

At that time, I was still working at *100 Huntley Street*. It was a time of transition before actually moving to Europe with Ginny to work with Youth For Christ International as evangelists-at-large. During this particular week, there was a world-renown preacher/teacher from the UK who was at the studio to give daily inspirational/devotional talks to the staff. He was very good.

Several of my friends suggested I should ask this man to pray that God would heal me of this skin condition. It did not seem to be an unreasonable thing to do. After all, it was incurable.

So I plucked up the courage to speak to him and this is how the conversation went:

"I wonder if you would be so kind as to pray for me, please."

"Certainly, what can I pray about?"

"Well, I have this incurable skin condition that I would like to be healed of."

"Why do you want me to pray for you?"

Fumbling a little over my answer, I replied, "Well, I thought that—you know—God would listen to you."

"And you don't think God listens to you?'

"Yes, of course, but ...."

"Have you asked the elders of your church to pray for you?"

Fumbling even more and beginning to feel a little silly, I answered hesitatingly, "Well, actually, no, I haven't." I supposed he was referring to what scripture says in James 5:14-16:

> *Is anyone among you sick? Let them call the elders of the church to pray over them and anoint them with oil in the name of the Lord. And the prayer offered in faith will make the sick person well; the Lord will raise them up. If they have sinned, they will be forgiven. Therefore confess your sins to each other and pray for each other so that you may be healed. The prayer of a righteous person is powerful and effective* (James 5:14-16).

"Why not?" he asked.

"I've never seen the elders of our church pray for the sick, so I don't think they do that sort of thing."

"Let me ask you this: If you do believe in praying for sickness to be healed, evidenced by you being here now asking me, why do you attend a church that does *not* believe in praying for the sick?"

This was getting to be way too complicated. All I had wanted was for him to pray for me, not subject me to a theological interrogation.

So I decided to do what this man had challenged me to do. I called The Peoples Church and asked if they ever prayed for the sick. To my surprise, they said yes, they do, but they don't make a big public demonstration of it. Would I like to be prayed for?

I was given an appointment at 11:00 a.m. the following Tuesday. The senior pastor, Dr. Paul Smith, was out of town that day, but I was greeted by Dr. George D'Sena, Pastor Don Jost, Dr. David Williams, plus a couple of other elders. Sitting in the office of Pastor Jost, we chatted amicably over coffee and biscuits as I explained to them my condition.

And then, seating me in a chair in the middle of the room, these men anointed my forehead with oil and, individually and collectively, with the laying on of hands, they prayed that the Lord would heal me of this condition.

What happened next? Nothing of a dramatic or demonstrative nature. Thanking the men for their time, I left the office and got on with my day and my life.

But do you know what? Gradually, over the next few weeks, the "incurable" systemic sclerosis scleroderma began to slowly but surely decrease in size. Within a year, it was totally gone.

This bears repeating:

> *Is anyone among you sick? Let them call the elders of the church to pray over them and anoint them with oil in the name of the Lord. And the prayer offered in faith will make the sick person well.... The prayer of a righteous person is powerful and effective* (James 5:14-16).

Now, thirty-five years later (at the time of this writing), there has been no sign of a recurrence of that condition.

The only reminder of what tried to overtake me is that whenever I have physically overdone it or am extremely stressed, I may feel a small, pricking sensation at exactly the place on my left arm where the systemic sclerosis scleroderma was.

To me, it is my personal warning system, telling me to slow down.

There is no theology in that, by the way, it just happens.

From my understanding of the Scriptures, after many years of experience in the practical application of God's Word in many usual and unusual scenarios of life, I have gleaned some vital understanding.

- We must never, ever doubt the ability of God to heal today.

- We must always understand that it is God's prerogative to decide who He will or will not heal.

- We must never demand that God heal either us or someone else. To demand anything from God is at least disrespectful of Him, if not downright dangerous.

- It is perfectly okay to ask for healing.

- It is perfectly okay to let Him know that you want it.

- It is perfectly okay to let Him know why you want it.

- Never put your will before God's will.

- If you truly want to be like Jesus, then emulate Jesus in the garden of Gethsemane where, although He adamantly did not want to go to the cross and pleaded with His Father to be spared that fate, He submitted to His Father's will, saying, "Not My will, but Thy will be done."

- If God chooses to heal, it is His prerogative as to how and when He does so.

I personally have several health issues at the moment, especially an incurable degenerative back problem that could see me permanently in a wheelchair in five to ten years time. I believe 100 percent that God can heal me. I have, however, stopped asking Him to heal my back because we don't need to continually pester Him, as if we can somehow change His mind. As I continually seek to know His heart, I am comforted to know that He knows *my* heart. To live without pain would be wonderful, but to live knowing I am in the will of God is even better.

My prayer now is this: Lord, I know you know my heart. All I ask of You is that for whatever You have for me to do, You will please give me the strength and resources to do it. Please enable me to do it with joy and thanksgiving. Let there be *nothing* of myself, but *all* of You. May my life bring the greatest glory to Your Name. It's all Yours to do with as You will.

Amen.

19

EAT YOUR FRUIT...
IT'S GOOD FOR YOU

When you were growing up, did your parents ever make you eat something you didn't like? As you looked sullenly at the food on your plate, did they ever sternly say, "Eat it!" and follow with some dire threat if you didn't?

In my case, despite the threats, I would stubbornly and defiantly reply, "I don't like it!" And so the battle lines were drawn.

My parents would dig in with "Eat it anyway!"

Usually, at this point, my parents would employ that tired old emotional blackmail tactic of reminding me that there were many children in the world who were hungry and would be glad to eat what was on my plate, to which I would ungratefully reply, "Then let them eat it!"

For that disrespectful, callous comment, I would be rewarded with a sharp clip around my ear that would sting for some time. In those days, for a parent to administer an immediate reminder of who was the boss was not only permissible, but acceptable.

I was a regular recipient of such reminders and I have to say that it did me no harm. Such brushes with authority usually hurt my pride far more than anything else. Indeed, I had a *very* healthy respect for my parents' authority —and all subsequent authority figures in my life.

What usually followed was a tantrum, some tears, maybe some shouting and table-thumping, but eventually, I would force the food down, making a distorted face as if I were eating something the cat had dragged in from the garden. I was convinced I had the worst parents in the world.

I sense you may be smiling because you have been there, either as the child and/or as the parent.

But what was all this drama really about? Was that particular food so important, so distasteful, to warrant such a fuss?

Back then we didn't have all the nutritional information and the sometimes conflicting consumer reports that confuse us today. In "the good old days," our food was naturally grown and had fewer of today's additives that make products look better and extend their shelf life for the financial benefit of the producers.

Just how clever were my parents back then? When I grew up—and it pains me to say that was over fifty years ago—the mantra was "Have a good breakfast and eat three meals a day." We drank plenty of water because Coca-Cola (and the plethora of sugar-loaded soft drinks we have today) had either not yet been invented or because television was very rare. At any rate, the BBC did not show commercials. Thusly, we were not inundated by enticing advertisements and were happily unaware of the onslaught of marketing that was about to threaten our well-being.

Today's experts have "discovered" that breakfast is the most important meal of the day. We're told that, for sensible weight control, we need a good night's sleep. Eating several small, nutritious meals each day and drinking lots of water is touted as a radical new discovery. Strange, isn't it? My parents knew all that over half a century ago.

As for regular exercise? My dad did not even own a car until I was nineteen—and no, he did not let me drive it.

In my teens, I played for three different football teams, each of which required training during the week and had games each weekend. I went everywhere by "shank's pony" (walking), by running (when I was late, which was often) and by cycling. For my first job at the age of sixteen, I cycled thirty miles each day to and from work. It was no big deal. That was the way it was.

Television did not enter my life until I was about eight. Computers were a science fiction dream and to "play" was assumed to mean engaging in physical activity. It was a different world back then.

In those days, I could eat as much fish and malt vinegar soaked chips (powdered with salt); roast beef, potatoes and Yorkshire pudding; English-style breakfast with fried bread, baked beans and toast; dripping (dried fat) spread on bread with salt added; "bubble and squeak" (fried roast left over from Sunday); and my favourite, bread thickly spread with real butter ... all to my heart's content. How did I survive all that? I burned it all off with my normal, daily lifestyle.

But back to the conflict at the dinner table. My parents loved me. They knew, instinctively, that for me to be healthy and achieve my potential, warding off any potential diseases, I needed to eat the right food at the right times.

Of course, my belligerent attitude at the dinner table revealed another element that had to be dealt with—and that was rebellion. If my parents were to lose that battle, it would hardly have mattered how well I ate or exercised. I simply would not have turned out to be the person they hoped I would be. Wow! Who would have thought the dinner table could be such an important, strategic battlefield?

Why have I been thinking about these things?

Recently I went through one of those "uninspired" periods in my Christian experience. I was not backsliding or sinning more than usual, but I was feeling "dry." My quiet times with God had become, at best, sporadic, and my prayer times lacked enthusiasm.

I decided I needed to revitalize the time I spent with God at the beginning of each day: the time I would talk to Him in prayer and the time He would speak to me through His Word, the Bible.

My usual routine had been to get up around 5:00 and watch the early news and sports whilst eating breakfast. Then, if I had time, I would spend some "quiet time" with God. To make a change, I decided to put my quiet time first, before eating breakfast or watching the morning news. I would start each day by putting God first.

I then—quite unexpectedly—discovered something of great importance. Like many people, I was accustomed to using an inspirational booklet written by some respected author to guide me in my devotions. One day when reading a designated portion of Scripture that made absolutely no sense to me, I wondered what on earth good this was doing for me—and then it hit me.

I realized that this was not about me. The important thing was not that I understood the part of God's Word that I was reading. No, the important thing was that I was being obedient in reading it. This was part of putting my faith into action. Suddenly, reading the Bible took on a whole new meaning for me.

Now, whenever I read the Scripture portion for the day, I do so with a smile in my heart, knowing that it does not matter if I understand it or not. By reading it, I know I am pleasing God. If I don't understand it, I know He will unfold the understanding to me when I need it. This revelation led to a revolution in my personal life.

Unfortunately, many Christians read their Bibles—which should be their primary source of spiritual nourishment—the same way as they eat food. Well, that is not quite true because many like to eat food way more than they like to read the Bible, but there is a justifiable parallel.

When we eat, we gravitate towards foods that look and taste good (hence the additives). Having broken free of the restrictions imposed by our parents, we do not force ourselves to eat anything just because it is good for us. So we satisfy the lust of our eyes (it looks good) and the lust of our flesh (it tastes good)—and we treat our Bible reading in exactly the same way. This was a revelation to me and the revelation led to a revolution in my personal life.

We all have our favourite Scriptures, some of which we have memorized and can repeat by rote. Sometimes we highlight our favourite passages in the Bible, adding colour to the otherwise bland black and white pages (unless you have a red-letter Bible).

We have our basic diet that we get from our regular home church, but every now and then, we like to "eat out" somewhere different. In North America, the wide diversity of theologies, available on television, enable us to try different spiritual food in the comfort of our own homes, where no one can see us indulging in things of which they might not approve. On the surface, this seems reasonable and healthy, but in practice, it can lead to an unhealthy mixture of spiritual indigestion and confusion.

Most of us only want to feed on "the good stuff" in the Bible—the promises for health, wealth and a good time. After all, we need to stay positive, right?

Just as our bodies need a balanced diet, for healthy spiritual growth, we need to understand that the *whole* of God's Word is essential for our instruction, guidance, discipline and balance.

May I suggest that you try reading those parts of the Bible that you have *not* highlighted rather than extracting your favourite sound bytes of Scripture. Read entire chapters so you understand the context.

If you don't understand what you are reading, don't get bent out of shape or frustrated. It's okay! For you to be just reading God's Word pleases Him. He will give the understanding that you need exactly when you need it. Just be patient.

This is a part of what it means to trust God and to recognize your dependence on Him. If you can grasp the simplicity of this truth, it will liberate you.

So, why did I call this chapter "Eat Your Fruit ... It's Good for You"?

Well, you see, I don't like fruit! I like all the fruit flavours and juices (as long as there are no "bits" in it), but I cringe at what, for me, is the unpleasant texture in my mouth. It's not an allergic reaction; I just don't like it. Why? Well, I guess my parents never made me eat it. I may well have won that battle, but ultimately, I am the loser.

So, *eat your fruit; it's good for you!*

ARE YOU LISTENING?

Have you ever had the frustrating experience of talking to someone and you just know they are not listening?

They may well be looking at you, nodding politely in the right places and appearing to hear your words. They are *hearing*—but not *listening*. Their minds are elsewhere, perhaps formulating what they are going to say. Often—if you give them half a chance—they jump right in with what they want to say. Some people are far more adept at this than others.

They have perfected the art of actually appearing interested in what you are saying while compiling and composing their own thoughts. They put their minds in pause mode and then, at the appropriate break in conversation, they release the pause button. Subsequently, what comes out bears little relation to what you have said.

The worst experience I had in this regard was during an interview on a television show in Canada. Let me set the scene for you.

It was a live-to-air television show. There was, therefore, no chance to edit anything or tidy up any mistakes.

There were three cameras being used. One was out in front for general wide shots; one was behind me, over my right shoulder, to get frontal shots of the interviewer; and the third camera was in a similar position, behind the interviewer, to get frontal shots of me.

When the interviewer asked a question, the little red light on top of the camera facing me came on to indicate that the television audience would be viewing and hearing me as I answered the question.

The trouble was the interviewer, having asked me the question, was then not listening to me at all. He wasn't even looking at me. As I was speaking to him, he was rummaging through his papers, talking quietly off-camera to the floor director and paying absolutely no attention to me or to what I was saying.

Knowing the camera was still on me and that the television audience had no idea of what was really happening, I had to continue to answer his question, pretending there was a person there who was interested in what I was saying.

Part of my mind was employed in answering the question, while the other part of my brain was screaming, "Listen to me when I am talking to you!"

You have probably said those words yourself many times, especially to your own kids, but you may well also have wanted to say them to some adults, both in social and in business situations.

So, what's my point?

Well, good communication is the glue that holds civilized society together, whether that be friend to friend, spouse to spouse, parent to child, employer to employee, politician to politician or world leader to world leader. From the smallest level to the highest level, the principles of good communication are exactly the same.

It involves talking *and* listening. What is the use of a two-way walkie-talkie device if one is not switched on?

Despite the fact that we have two ears and just one mouth, we seem to employ our mouths far more than our ears. A few thoughts ...

- If all you do is talk, you will never learn anything.

- If all you do is talk, you will never get to know someone.

- If all you do is talk, you will never understand someone else in order to be able to empathize or help them.

- If all you do is talk, you may have a lot of acquaintances but very few friends.

- Be patient.

- Learn to listen.

- Disengage your tongue.

- Be genuinely interested in the other person.

- Turn off your transmit button and listen to what is being said.

- Allow that which you are hearing to be absorbed into your mind where you can assimilate it, judge it, sort it out and understand it in context.

If you make these thoughts your own, you will really start to learn. You will be able to understand people and their situations. You will be able to actually formulate answers that can help.

And the best part is this: Although you may not talk as much, when you do, people will be far more inclined to listen.

One could probably write a whole book on the subject. (In fact, I'm sure someone already has.) But let me end with this: When you indulge in the awesome privilege of prayer—that mechanism that allows us to talk to God directly, not through some intermediary—may I suggest you set aside your "shopping list" for a while in order to listen? You never know; God may actually be trying to say something to you.

Yes, believe it or not, God actually wants to talk to *you*.

Think about it!

21

IT'S JUST A LOCAL CALL

Anyone who knows me knows I love a good joke—and I think this is a good one.

One day, the president of America was being visited in the White House by a dictator from a country that had a very poor record of human rights.

While sitting in the oval office, the dictator commented on the two telephones on the president's desk; one was white and the other red. He asked the president what those phones were for.

The president told the dictator that the white phone was for calling heaven, while the red phone was for calling hell; so the dictator asked if the president ever used those phones.

The president answered that he used the white phone—the line to heaven—every day, but he never used the red phone—the line to hell.

The dictator was curious about this and asked the president why he did not use the red phone—the line to hell.

The president was a bit evasive and said, "Well, for one thing, it is very expensive to call hell."

"How much does it cost to call hell?" asked the dictator.

"It costs $10,000 a minute," answered the president.

So, when the dictator got back to his country, he ordered a white phone, a line to heaven—and a red phone, a line to hell—to be installed immediately in his private office.

When the work was done, the dictator sat behind his desk and looked at the phones. His curiosity got the better of him; he just had to try the red phone—the line to hell. So he picked up the receiver and this is the conversation that followed:

Operator: Yes? What can I do for you?

Dictator: Is this hell?

Operator: No, but I can place the call for you. Would you like me to do that?

Dictator: Yes, and make it quick.

Operator: Okay, sir. That will cost ten cents a minute.

Dictator (surprised): Only ten cents a minute? The president of America said it costs $10,000 a minute to call hell.

Operator: Yes sir, that is correct. From America it is $10,000 a minute, but from your phone, it is just a local call.[14]

There is perhaps a kernel of wisdom in this joke, in that calling God—that thing we call "prayer"—does not even cost ten cents a minute. It is, in fact, totally free, and yes, it is most definitely a local call.

Although the call is free to us now, the price was paid over 2,000 years ago, when Jesus Christ was crucified. We are told, when that happened, the veil in the temple, the large curtain that kept people from entering God's presence, was torn from top to bottom. God was saying, "You can now come and talk to Me personally. You do not need a mediator. When you speak to Me, I will listen."

Older church traditions said we could speak to God only through some other holy person. Even today, some pontificate a subtle suggestion that if we send our prayer requests to some special celebrity person, God will somehow listen to them more than He will to us.

Not true!

---

[14] Author unknown

There is nothing intrinsically wrong with our praying together or for other people. It can be very comforting and builds bonds of friendship. It should not, however, lead us away from the most important thing: our personal relationship with God through Jesus Christ. Personal relationships need regular communication; otherwise, they will stagnate.

Satan is very clever and subtle in the ways that he seeks to deceive us. If there is one thing he hates, it's this: We can go directly to God and talk to him Him personally, like the close friend and Father He is.

If Satan can convince us it isn't that simple, he can greatly weaken our relationship with God. He can also weaken our potential effectiveness, often the means through which God accomplishes His wonderful plans for the world.

May I respectively say that the church is full of good people who may well work very hard for Him and give generously of their resources but who rarely talk to God. It's like a marriage where the husband is a good provider, but where the actual relationship between the husband and wife is, at best, stagnant or, at worst, almost nonexistent.

When I was a young teenager, to get to school, I had to make a one-and-a-half hour journey on two buses and a boat. This took me past an old Methodist church that had, outside, what they used to call a "wayside pulpit." Every few weeks, there was some saying on it, intended to challenge or encourage the passing traveller.

The one I most vividly recall, to such an extent that here I am sharing it with you some 50 years later, said this: "Seven prayerless days makes one weak." Think about it! There is no spelling error and it is every bit as true today as it was fifty years ago.

Make no mistake; talking to God is just a local call. It's free and you can make it at any time, from any place. *Nothing* is too trivial for God, Who really is interested in absolutely every aspect of your life.

You do not have to be in any special place or in any special physical posture.

Personally, I have my most meaningful chats with God whilst I am walking or driving my car—and I most certainly do not have my eyes closed during those times!

Yes, there are other times when I will respectfully bow my head and close my eyes as a means of cutting out the distractions around me, but my physical posture or location does not make me more or less worthy nor does it, in any way, affect whether or not God is listening to me—or to you.

He is *always* there, *always* ready to listen.

I have heard it said that God is as close as a simple prayer, and whilst I understand the comforting sentiment behind that comment, it is perhaps a little misleading, even inaccurate.

You see, God is *always* there with you; wherever you are, whatever you are doing, God is there with you. It is not like, when you start to pray, God comes scurrying over to where you are to listen. Born again Christians need never pray, "Dear Lord, please be with us." God is *always* with us.

Christ is in and with us all the time. When we sleep, He doesn't.

When we wake up in the morning, He is there.

Wherever we go, He has gone there ahead of us.

And remember this (and I don't want to appear to be sacrilegious here): When we start to talk to God, it brings a smile to His face.

You see, we should never ritualize what is essentially a very personal and intimate privilege.

As with any relationship, it will thrive through regular communication. So make it a normal part of your life to talk to God every day, not because you feel you *have* to and most certainly not in any ritualistic way.

We should never forget what an awesome privilege it is, to be able to talk directly with God, nor should we forget the awful price Jesus paid to make that possible. Let's take the mystique out of what we call "prayer." He is, and always should be revered as our Lord but He allows us to call Him "Abba," which is translated as "Daddy."

There are many other books on this subject written by authors far more capable and accomplished than I, but let me just say that all conversation is a two-way process, and the primary means that God talks to us is through His Word, so I hope the following will be helpful.

Remember you do not need to go through an operator; your call will not go to some call centre in a foreign country. It's a direct, local call. And God loves you personally so much that He is *always* listening.

Now here are some really good numbers to call when you need them.

EMERGENCY TELEPHONE NUMBERS

(More effective than 911)

When ...

You are sad, phone John 14.

You have sinned, phone Psalm 51.

You are facing danger, phone Psalm 91.

People have failed you, phone Psalm 27.

It feels as though God is far from you, phone Psalm 139.

Your faith needs stimulation, phone Hebrews 11.

You are alone and scared, phone Psalm 23.

You are worried, phone Matthew 8:19-34.

You are hurt and critical, phone 1 Corinthians 13.

You wonder about Christianity, phone 2 Corinthians 5:15-18.

You feel like an outcast, phone Romans 8:31-39.

You are seeking peace, phone Matthew 11:25-30.

It feels as if the world is bigger than God, phone Psalm 90.

You need Christ like insurance, phone Romans 8:1-30.

You are leaving home for a trip, phone Psalm 121.

You are praying for yourself, phone Psalm 87.

You require courage for a task, phone Joshua 1.

Inflation and investments are hogging your thoughts, phone Mark 10:17-31.

You are depressed, phone Psalm 27.

Your bank account is empty, phone Psalm 37.

You lose faith in mankind, phone 1 Corinthians 13.

It looks like people are unfriendly, phone John 15.

You are losing hope, phone Psalm 126.

You feel the world is small compared to you, phone Psalm 19.

You want to bear fruit, phone John 15.

You want the apostle Paul's secret for happiness, phone Colossians 3:12-17.

You have a big opportunity or discovery, phone Isaiah 55.

You need to get along with other people, phone Romans 12.

ALTERNATE NUMBERS

For dealing with fear, call Psalm 47.

For security, call Psalm 121:3.

For assurance, call Mark 8:35.

For reassurance, call Psalm 145:18.

All these numbers can be phoned directly.

No operator assistance is necessary.

All calls are *free*.

All lines to heaven are available twenty-four hours a day.

Feed your faith and doubt will starve to death.

Let me end this chapter with this: For ten years Ginny and I were involved in a wonderful drama ministry in Europe. Drama has always been a medium I enjoy.

The following is a fictitious dramatization of what it could be like when someone prays the Lord's Prayer but does not really know why he is doing it or what he is saying.

I share it with you here in the hope that it will put a smile on your face. I hope, too, that it will challenge you and perhaps, revitalize your view of the most famous of prayers, one so many of us know by rote; sadly, to the extent that its words may have lost their meaning for us.

THE LORD'S PRAYER

Rather cleverly done. I did not write this and, unfortunately, cannot find out who did. It is very good, but I admit to tweaking it a bit.

Legend: ❏ The prayer ❏ The young man's words ❏ God's response

Our Father who art in heaven ...

Yes?

Don't interrupt me. I'm praying.

But ... you called Me!

Called You? No, I didn't call You. I'm praying.

Our Father who art in heaven ...

There ... you did it again!

Did what?

You called Me. You said, "Our Father who art in heaven." Well, here I am. What's on your mind?

But I didn't mean anything by it. I was, You know, just saying my prayers for the day. I always say the Lord's Prayer. It makes me feel good—kind of like fulfilling a duty.

Well, all right. Go on.

Okay. Hallowed be thy Name ...

Hold it right there. What do you mean by that?

By what? By "Hallowed be thy Name?" It means ... it means ... good grief—I don't know what it means. How in the world should I know? It's just a part of the prayer. By the way, what does it mean?

It means, "honoured, holy, wonderful."

Hey, that makes sense. I never thought about what "hallowed" meant before. Thanks. I'll carry on now with the prayer.

Thy kingdom come. Thy will be done on earth as it is in heaven.

Do you really mean that?

Sure, why not?

So what are you doing about it?

Doing? Why, nothing, I guess. I just think it would be kind of neat if You got control of everything down here like You have up there. We're in a mess down here, You know. Everything seems to be out of control.

Yes, I know, but have I got control of you?

Well, I go to church ...

That isn't what I asked you. What about your bad temper? You've really got a problem there, you know. And then there's the way you spend our money—all on yourself. And what about the kind of books you read and the television and movies you watch?

Now hold on just a minute! Stop picking on me! I'm just as good as most of the rest of those people at church.

Excuse me? I thought you were praying for My will to be done. If that is to happen, it will have to start with the ones who are praying for it—like you, for example.

Oh, all right. I guess I do have some hang-ups. Now that you mention it, I could probably name some others.

So could I.

I haven't thought about it very much until now, but I really would like to cut out some of those things. I would like to, You know, be really free.

Good. Now we're getting somewhere. We'll work together, you and Me. I'm proud of you.

Look, Lord, if you don't mind, I need to finish up here. This is taking a lot longer than it usually does.

Give us this day, our daily bread.

You need to cut out the bread. You're overweight as it is.

Hey, wait a minute! What is this? Here am I, doing my religious duty, and all of a sudden You break in and remind me of all my hang-ups.

Praying can be a dangerous thing. You just might get what you ask for. Remember, you called Me—and here I am. It's too late to stop now. Keep praying.

Pause ...

Well ... go on.

I'm scared to.

Scared? Of what?

I know what You'll say.

Try Me.

Forgive us our sins as we forgive those who sin against us.

What about Ann?

See? I knew it! I knew you would bring her up. Lord, she's told lies about me and spread stories. She never paid back the money she owes me. I've sworn to get even with her.

But, your prayer .... What about your prayer?

I didn't ... mean it.

Well, at least you're honest. But it's quite a load carrying around all that bitterness and resentment, isn't it?

Yes, but I'll feel better as soon as I get even with her. Boy, have I got some plans for her. She'll wish she had never been born!

No, getting even with her will not make you feel any better. In fact, you'll feel worse. Revenge isn't sweet. You know how unhappy you are? Well, I can change that.

You can? How?

Forgive Ann. Then I'll forgive you and the hate and the sin will be Ann's problem, not yours. You will have settled the problem as far as you are concerned.

Oh ... You know, You're right. You always are. And more than I want revenge, I want to be right with You ... (sigh). All right ... all right ... I forgive her.

There now. Wonderful! How do you feel?

Hmmmm ... Well, not bad. Not bad at all. In fact, I feel pretty great. You know, I don't think I'll go to bed uptight tonight. I haven't been getting much rest, You know.

Yes, I know. But you're not through with your prayer, are you? Go on.

Oh, all right. And lead us not into temptation, but deliver us from evil.

Good! Good! I'll do that. Just don't put yourself in a place where you can be tempted.

What do you mean by that?

You know what I mean. You are not being careful about what you watch on television and at the movies.

Yeah, I know. But the television programs are good and so are the movies. Are you saying I should just stop watching them altogether?

No, I'm not saying that; but whenever you're watching something, why don't you ask yourself how I would feel if I were sitting there with you— because I am, you know.

You're kidding!

No, I'm not kidding.

(Embarrassed pause)

Go ahead. Finish your prayer.

For Thine is the kingdom and the power and the glory forever. Amen.

Do you know what would bring Me glory, what would really make Me happy?

No, but I'd like to know. I really do want to please You. I've got to admit I've really made a mess of things. Please forgive me. I want to truly follow You. I can see now how great that would be. So, tell me ... how do I make You happy?

You just did.

22

THE NEW ARRIVAL

For several years Ginny and I have been involved with a wonderful organization called "Seeds International," which is dedicated to helping new Christians through those critical and delicate early years. We are still working to help Gypsy and orphaned children in Romania.

As I often think in terms of modern day parables, I wrote the following drama. It is intended to be funny and poignant whilst conveying a certain message.

If you like it, feel free to use it.

THE NEW ARRIVAL

(A Drama by Terry Bridle)

Setting	– A room in a home
Characters	– New Grandmother (GM)
	– New Grandfather (GF)—Bob (with a beard or moustache)
	– Son—Jeremy
	– Daughter—Jessica
Props required	– Table
	– Two chairs
	– Baby wrapped in blanket
	– Coffee mugs

Sound effects	– Baby gurgling
	– Baby crying softly
	– Baby wailing
Lighting effects	– Lights slowly dim at the end.

A young married couple have just had their first child. The scene is at their home, where the proud new grandparents are waiting for the couple to come home from the hospital with the new baby.

It will be the first time for them to see the baby.

The new grandmother (GM) is worriedly pacing back and forth; GF is sitting relaxed at the table.

1. New GF (firmly): **If you carry on like that, dear, you're going to wear a hole in the carpet. Just sit down and relax.**

2. New GM (agitated): **Relax? How can I relax at a time like this? This is our first grandchild.**

3. New GF (soothingly): **Yes, dear, I know. But everything is alright. The delivery was quick and the baby was born perfect, so there is nothing to worry about.**

4. New GM (calming down a little): **Yes, I know. I just wish we could have been at the hospital.**

5. New GF (perhaps a little sarcastically): **Well, we couldn't ... and amazingly, everything went well—even with you not being there ... (slight pause) ... so just sit down and relax. They should be here any time now.**

6. New GM (sitting down, calming down in a thoughtful and reflective mood): **You know, I am still amazed at the miracle of bringing a new child into the world. I can hardly believe our kids are now parents, too. It means so much to me. Does it affect you too, dear?**

7. New GF (a little cynically): **Oh, yes! It affects me a lot. I have just realized that now I am married to a grandmother.**

   (GM playfully slaps grandfather's hand or arm.)

('Feel' the audience. If there is laughter, let it happen before continuing.)

8. New GM: **Well, we certainly prayed a lot for this baby. I thought it was never going to happen, but the Lord faithfully came through and answered all our prayers.**

9. New GF: **Yes, He sure did! And I'm proud of the kids too.** (Looking around) **They have really fixed this place up nice. The baby's room is so bright and cheerful. I wouldn't mind sleeping in there myself.**

10. New GM: **Not with your snoring. You'd cause all the baby toys to rattle.**

11. New GF (indignantly): **I don't snore.**

12. New GM (firmly): **You do!**

13. New GF (indignant and a little louder): **I don't!**

(Son and daughter carrying the new baby walk in, unnoticed.)

14. New GM (laughing—not angry): **Oh, yes, you do.**

15. New GF (annoyed): **No, I do not!**

16. Son (laughing): **Hi there! Are you two still arguing over Dad's snoring?**

17. New GM (with shock and delighted surprise): **You're here!**
(running over to the baby as GF walks over) **Oh, look at the baby. She is so beautiful. Can I hold her?**

18. Daughter (smiling and handing the baby over to GM): **Of course you can.**
(GF goes over to look at the baby.)
(Son and daughter hug each other, as they watch the delight of the grandparents.)

19. New GM (doting over the baby as only a grandmother can): **Oh! She is so beautiful. Look at those tiny little hands; they're so perfect. Her eyes are just like yours Jessica ... and she has Jeremy's nose ... and look Bob, when she smiles, her mouth is just like yours.**

20. New GF (with cynical humour): **Oh really? Has she got a beard too?**
(''Feel'' the audience. If there is laughter, pause)
I don't know how you girls always manage to see so much in a baby. To me, they all look the same, all pink and wrinkled.
(taking the baby from his wife)
But I must admit this little bundle of joy is the most beautiful baby in the whole world.

21. New GM (looking at her watch): **Oh dear! We really do need to get going.**
(GF hands baby back to daughter)
We'll get back as soon as we can—probably in a couple of hours.
(GM and GF walk towards the door—GM in front of GF)

22. Daughter (sitting down nestling the baby): **Don't hurry; we'll be okay.**

23. Son (just before GF and GM disappear): **Oh, Dad!**
(GF and GM turn to listen)
Mom's right. You do snore, real bad.
(GM pulls GF out with her before he can say anything in response.)

24. Son (laughing, goes to sit with his wife)
Well, here we are. Can you believe it?

25. Daughter: **It is a bit hard to believe. We prayed so much for this baby. We really scrimped and saved ... and then all the hard work you did to prepare the baby's room ... but it's all been worth it!**

26. Son: **Yes, it certainly has been. God has been so good in answering our prayers.**
(a slight reflective pause ... then in a 'let's get on with it' business-like manner)
Well, I guess we had better show the baby the ropes ...

27. Daughter: **Okay!**
(stands and carries the baby to stage left—showing it an imaginary room)
This is your bedroom. Daddy has done a lot of work to make it a beautiful place for you to sleep.
(walking over to another imaginary room)
Here is the bathroom. This is where you wash and shower and keep yourself clean. There is always plenty of hot water and clean towels. Feel free to use it as often as you want.

28. (walking over to another imaginary room)

    Over here is the kitchen. This is where you will find all the food you will ever need. Just help yourself to whatever you want. Okay?

    (walks back over to the table and carefully lays the baby on it)

29. Son (to his wife): **Well, I think that's about all we can do for now. There is everything here that the baby needs. I can't think of anything we have forgotten. Can you?**

30. Daughter: **No, I guess we had better be going.**

    (as they walk out, speaking to the baby ...)

    Take care, Sweetie. Call us if you need any help. 'Bye.

31. Lights dim on the baby as the sound of gurgling, then crying, then wailing is heard. Lights out.

As the baby continues to cry, the director, minister or speaker (someone cast for the "wrap up") walks onstage and comments on the fact that responsible people would not go to the trouble of praying for, preparing for, conceiving and giving birth to a baby only to then leave it on its own, and yet, that is exactly what happens in some churches, where those who are newly born again are concerned.

Nice buildings and good programs are not what new babies in Christ need. They need *mature Christians* who are willing to take the time to help them understand their new lives, grow properly and hold their hands as they learn to walk their new pathway.

They *will* make mistakes—lots of them, but they need to be loved patiently and unconditionally by those who brought them into the new life in Christ, just like real babies.

23

ARE YOU PRAYING
FOR YOUR WIFE?

At first glance, that may seem to be a reasonable question, but that is not so, in light of the time and place the question was first asked of me.

I was confronted with this question by a very gracious pastor in England by the name of Hoddy Jones.

Imagine the scenario: I was in my early 20s, with absolutely no thoughts of marriage. At that time, Pastor Jones had recently left the police force and still had the aura of "an English copper" about him—a mixture of smiling charm effortlessly mixed with steely you-really-don't-want-to-mess-with-me undertones. (How do they do that? Wearing that silly "bobby helmet" and no gun, they have the uncanny ability to fill you with comfort, confidence and fear—all at the same time.)

Anyway, back to my story. It was at a youth meeting held in Pastor Jones' home, when he suddenly turned to me and asked, "Terry, are you praying for your wife?"

I remember looking at him, startled, and not just a little confused. You see, Hoddy not only knew very well that I was not married, but he also had three daughters, none of whom was married at the time. Each of these daughters was beautiful physically, unaffectedly friendly and, it seemed, always laughing. To cap it off, they were all really on fire for the Lord.

Yes, of course I fancied them, each one in turn, but to be honest, I also felt somewhat intimidated by them—especially by the fact that they were obviously closer to the Lord than I was. But surely their father was not trying to act as matchmaker between me and one of his girls.

Well, as it happens, I had no such luck, but Hoddy's questions and subsequent comments were profound (although, at the time, I thought he was a little bit nuts). He asked me a few simple questions.

"Terry, do you want to get married someday?"

"Yes, of course, but not soon."

"Do you believe that God has a plan for your life?"

"Yes, I just wish I knew what it is."

"All in good time Terry; all in good time. Now, in this plan God has for you, do you think there is a wife in there somewhere?"

"I never thought of it, but yes, I guess so."

"Okay, Terry. Because God loves you and has a plan for your life, is it not reasonable to consider that He has a wife picked out—just for you?"

My first thought was "poor girl." This is beginning to sound like a conspiracy. Does she not have any say in all this?'

Hoddy explained that she—whoever "she" was—had as much free will in the matter as everyone does. The key question was this: Are you willing to allow God to guide you in this important decision?

This was all getting a little too heavy for me, so I was relieved when Hoddy brought us back to the original question. "So, Terry, this girl whom the Lord has made for you, whoever she is, wherever she is—are you praying for her?"

In making a hasty retreat, I think I mumbled something like, "No, but if I think of it, I will."

In the months and years that followed, I occasionally thought about Hoddy's question. At first, I dismissed it as an eccentricity of someone who was too heavenly-minded to be of much earthly good, but later, I realized there was logic to what he had said. So, often feeling a little foolish (and *never* out loud where others could hear), I would occasionally ask the Lord to be with and protect whomever He was preparing to be my wife.

Fast forward now several years to January of 1978, when I emigrated to Canada. I was flush with the excitement of a great new job, earning tons of money and happy to be "a good Christian"—but I had no thoughts of marriage.

On June 2 of that same year, I met Ginny. Talk about not being able to wipe the smile off my face! I remember calling England and telling a friend that my face ached because I was smiling all the time. Five days after meeting Ginny, I proposed to her. I knew she was the girl I had been praying for.

To my surprise and delight, she said yes. Apparently, years before, she had complied a list of what she wanted her husband to be like—and I fit the bill. We were married six months later.

Ginny

Now, in June 2014, that was thirty-six years ago. Today we are in the midst of an exciting life serving the Lord together, and our love for each other grows stronger and deeper every day.

Interestingly, during the years prior to my meeting Ginny—while I was praying for this girl whom I didn't even know—she got engaged three times, but it never worked out. I wonder why!

Hoddy is with the Lord now, but I am thankful for his wisdom and for having the courage to challenge me to pray for my wife.

I still pray for her—every day.

Thanks, Hoddy!

THE COFFEE STORY

This absolutely true, unembellished story has taken on almost legendary status since its occurrence and my sharing it with people. My friends would never forgive me if I did not include it in this book.

To give this story some context, you have to understand that I seem to disappear when I am in a restaurant. My wife laughs at my lamentable attempts to attract the attention of a waiter or waitress. They seem to studiously ignore me, even when I am trying to pay the bill.

Not so my brother, Doug. He is good-looking, slim, always immaculately dressed (even in jeans and a T-shirt) and has a confident air, born out of his many years of business success. Unlike me, he can attract waitresses like bees to a honey-pot.

As for me, I was once graciously described in a newspaper article in England as "portly." I do admit that my wife thinks I am handsome, but then *she would,* wouldn't she? I cannot remember the last time I ever wore a tie. "Comfortably casual" would best describe the way I dress now. The problem is that while I may be comfortable in myself, I am *invisible* to waiters and waitresses.

Because this makes me laugh, I will digress a little to share the one and only incident, to my knowledge, when my brother did *not* have success at attracting a waitress.

When my parents and brother emigrated to Canada, I declined to accompany them. (My reasons are contained elsewhere in this book.) After being in Canada for a year or so, Doug returned to England to visit some of his friends.

One evening, he and I went to a typical English fish and chips café. (We tend to call them *cafés*, as the word *restaurant* is usually used for establishments of a higher grade.) So we were sitting in this fish and chips café, trying to attract the attention of a young, gum-chewing, bored-looking waitress. My brother (who had, in recent years, become accustomed to the excellent service one usually receives in Canadian eating establishments) was becoming increasingly annoyed with being ignored. Finally, as the waitress was walking by, he gently grabbed her by the arm and, in mock courtesy, asked, "Excuse me, madam, are we in any immediate danger of being served?"

Other than causing some giggles from people eating at tables close to us, the question made no difference whatsoever to the service we received. Needless to say, that waitress did not receive any tip at all.

Well, I guess you had to be there, so let's get back to me and my frustrating attempts to get a cup of coffee.

I was flying from Orlando back to Toronto, and my flight made a stop in Pittsburgh. It wasn't the best route, but because the reason for the flight was a family emergency, it was the only one I could get on short notice.

To set the scene: the plane was one with a centre aisle and six seats on either side. There was a first class section at the front which, in flight, was separated by a curtain across the aisle. I was seated in the cheap seats, about three-quarters of the way towards the back of the plane, in a right-hand aisle seat.

Seated to my right were two boisterous American guys, with three of their friends immediately behind us. They had obviously had a great holiday in Florida and, in celebration mode right to the end, had had a few drinks before boarding the plane. They were not obnoxious, just rather loud, opinionated and, for a Brit like me, too friendly. After all, I didn't know them from Adam, so it was way too soon to be calling them my buddies. Apparently, with our American cousins, one can qualify as a buddy very quickly and easily. This is a little disconcerting for those of us brought up in the British culture where it takes a little longer to earn friendship.

I hope you have now got a visual fix on the scene because it will help you to appreciate what happened next.

At the onset of the flight, the American on my right tried to engage me in friendly conversation. When he discovered I was "a Brit," he and his friends tried to befriend me by trotting out a load of jokes, mostly anti-British, but I gamely went along with them. They meant no harm, but they were a little worse for wear; not drunk enough to be asked to leave the plane but drunk enough to be irritating.

The in-flight meal was served, the hostesses working their way from the front of the plane to the back. Then came the coffee, served again from the front to the back. When the hostess reached our row, she served the two men sitting to my right, but that emptied her coffee jug. She politely said she would be right back with a full jug of coffee.

So I waited—and waited—but she never returned.

The guy sitting next to me said, "Hey, man! What about your coffee?"

To which I replied, "Not to worry, I only want one cup of coffee and she'll be back to serve the customary second cup. I can wait until then."

Sure enough, a few minutes later, we saw a different hostess working her way from the front of the plane, serving people who wanted a second cup of coffee. I waited patiently. Amazingly, when she reached the row in front of us, *her* jug emptied. She asked the two guys on my right and me if we would like a second cup. The two guys said no, but I said, "Yes, please." I did not bother to tell her that this would be my first and only cup; she was working very hard and I didn't want to bother her. Again I was told she would be right back.

So I waited—and waited—and waited. Still no coffee came.

By now my American *friends* were getting annoyed that their new buddy from Britain was getting bad service. I tried to assure them that I was okay and would just use the call button to summon a hostess to bring me a coffee.

I pushed the overhead call button—and waited. Nothing. I pushed it again—and waited. Still nothing. So I pushed it a third time, which produced the first hostess, the one who had served the initial meal. Finally, she asked how she could help me.

Again, not wanting to make a fuss I said simply, "May I have a coffee, please?"

To which she replied, somewhat condescendingly, "I am sorry, sir, but we stopped serving coffee awhile ago. We did bring it around twice, you know."

Her response started to irritate me, so I said, in my best British accent, but trying to remain polite, "That may well be, young lady, but each time coffee was served,

I was missed; so I would be grateful if you could arrange to get a cup of coffee for me."

At this point, I have to say that by now I was becoming glad of my new American friends. They became cheerleaders for the cause. They took it upon themselves to improve Anglo-American diplomatic relations by making sure that this shy Brit would get his coffee. The hostess assured me that, although they would have to make the coffee just for me, she would see to it right away.

So I waited—and waited—and waited. How long does one wait for a cup of coffee? Surely it should not take *too* long?

Well, it *was* being made "just for me" and we were in an aeroplane 30,000 feet up in the air.

So I waited—and waited—and waited.

My cheering crew was not as patient, so, with them egging me on, I pressed the call button again. Nothing.

I pressed it a second and third time. Still nothing.

Okay! That was it! Now I was angry! No more stiff upper lip courtesy! Accompanied by my crew, now in full voice, I pressed and pressed and pressed the button until the curtain separating first class from the rest of us was dramatically thrust aside and a concerned-looking head was thrust into the gap, peering frantically from side to side, searching out the cause of the panicked button pressing. This was the head hostess, who, having not been a party to anything that had so far happened, came racing up the aisle so see why I was sitting there repeatedly pushing the call button.

Somewhat breathlessly she demanded of me, "What is the matter, sir? Why are you pushing the button like that?"

To which I replied calmly and evenly in the Queen's English, "I would like a cup of coffee, please!"

Well! She nearly ripped my head off as I was lashed with strips of verbiage. "You can't use the call button just for a cup of coffee. That's for emergencies only. Don't you realize when you use the button like that, it sounds in the pilot's cabin ..." and on and on she went.

I must admit I cringed at her onslaught, but my trusty new friends were right there, going toe-to-toe with her until it all calmed down as the full catalogue of events was explained to her. Finally, this head hostess realized that my grievance was genuine.

She promised me she would rectify the situation and, very soon, with profound apologies from the airline, two of the previous hostesses, fawning over me with personal apologies for forgetting me, appeared with a cup of freshly brewed coffee in their best china cup, with real cream and a very fancy looking spoon.

I declined any further help from the hostesses and to the cheers of my team (having suffered so much together, we were truly buddies now), I proceeded to empty some sugar into my coffee and, luxuriating in the moment, I started to gently stir the aromatic brew. Considering everything, I was not going to rush this, right?

But then—and I give you my word this is *exactly* how it happened—a voice on the speaker system announced, "This is your captain speaking. We are now coming in for a landing at Pittsburgh International Airport. Please store your tray tables and place your seats in the upright positions ...."

A hostess who had not been part of anything that had happened previously briskly walked up the aisle to make sure everything was ready for landing. As she efficiently breezed past me, not even stopping, she took away my cup of coffee saying, "I am sorry, sir. I shall have to take this now."

The coffee never reached my lips. No one in the seats ahead of us on that plane had any idea why those behind them erupted in spontaneous, raucous laughter.

That's it! Now you know the famous coffee story.

CULTURE SHOCK

Culture is different and legitimate, but when we begin to feel that one culture—usually my culture—is superior to another, or sometimes somebody else's culture is superior to mine and so we feel intimidated, then the difference becomes a division.—Charles Price, April 13, 2011

Culture has nothing to do with skin colour.

We may assume that because a person's outward appearance is different they belong to a different cultural group.

Wrong!

In communities like Great Britain, which has absorbed people from countless different races over a great number of years, one can find many people who look different but are as British as a cup of tea.

To some people, that is a shock. They look at the exterior and do not expect to hear a cultured British accent—or even a not-so-cultured British accent.

Culture shock creeps up and surprises people. That is why we call it culture "shock." No one expects it!

When I, as a white-skinned Anglo, meet someone who, judging by his or her skin colour and/or facial construction, is obviously not like me, I subconsciously prepare myself for that person to be different. But when a person I meet *looks* like me, I am unprepared for the cultural differences that can eventually become apparent.

I married into a Canadian/Italian family and believe me, we are very different. In my wife's family, for instance, their concept of conversation is everyone speaking at the same time yet still managing to hear everything—or so they say. I come from the more ordered, sedate English culture where conversation involves one person speaking at a time—so much more civilized.

For ten years, my wife and I worked closely with people in thirty-three different European nations who spoke twenty-two different languages. We taught them the drama, "Heaven's Gates and Hell's Flames." During that time, we recruited, trained and mentored nine different teams.

Trust me, we encountered culture shock many times but never once on the basis of skin colour.

Culture is based on local circumstances and history. It can differ greatly within a single nation and often creates an insular attitude.

When I first came to Canada, I was accused one day of being an immigrant, which, of course, I was. But without thinking, I retorted, "I'm not an immigrant I'm British!" As soon as the words left my mouth, I realized how pompous that must have sounded. Is the capacity to be pompous in the British DNA?

Culture can nurture a feeling of superiority or it can propagate feelings of inferiority.

Culture can generate fierce loyalty and protectionism, sometimes to the degree of overlooking truth and reasonable argument.

Culture restricts growth. People ask, "Why should we change?" and say, "This is the way we do things where I come from."

Well-meaning missionaries, in the process of sharing their faith, have often been guilty of imposing their own culture on other nations.

Culture is often blind to reality. Throughout history, cultures have continuously adapted and evolved, but change is always difficult for people.

Culture affects work ethics. In Europe, they speak of the "northern European work ethic" as opposed to the "Mediterranean work ethic." The differing climate is the most obvious factor. Let's face it; it is easier to work hard in a cold climate where physical activity is essential to keep warm than in a hot, humid climate that saps your energy.

Culture affects humour. One Sunday at church, I was standing talking with a group of people, amongst whom was Ruth, a senior lady who was still very attractive and always well-dressed. The minister for seniors at this church was a charming, older gentleman who would often compliment people effusively—perhaps a little over-the-top sometimes. As we were talking, this seniors' minister approached our group and said, "Ruth, you are looking particularly beautiful today."

Without thinking, I took off my glasses and offered them to the seniors' pastor saying, "Pastor, perhaps you would like to try these?"

In England, that would have been considered funny. The reaction from an English lady would have been to playfully thump me, but my Canadian friends' jaws dropped in horror at the insult. It took me some time to extract myself from the hole into which I had inadvertently fallen. (Perhaps "jumped" would be more accurate.)

On another occasion, I was speaking at a Youth For Christ conference in Frankfurt, Germany. There were about 1,000 young people there. My wife Ginny and two other singers, Wendy and Mary (both from America), were sitting in the front row.

To help get the audience (and myself) relaxed, I decided to start by telling a joke, but in my inexperience, I did not check with my German interpreter to ensure that the joke would translate properly—or even that those of the German culture would find it funny.

So it was that, when I delivered the all-important punch line, instead of interpreting it, the interpreter turned to me and said, "I do not understand."

Out of the corner of my mouth, I whispered, "It doesn't matter, just interpret it."

The interpreter said, "I cannot interpret it; it does not make sense."

"Of course it doesn't make any sense," I replied. "That's why it's funny."

The interpreter frowned and shook his head. "I cannot interpret something I do not understand. Please explain."

And so it went on. This interpreter was like a dog with a bone that he would not let go of. Even when I said, "Okay, let's just forget it and move on," he still insisted that I explain the joke. Meanwhile, nearly 1,000 German young people were wondering what was going on. At the same time, while I was dying a slow death of embarrassment, Ginny and our American friends were collapsed in uncontrollable laughter at my predicament. Obviously, failure to properly understand different cultures can result in embarrassing situations.

Culture greatly influences worship. In some parts of Eastern Europe, drums are still not allowed in churches. For preachers to wear rings or ties is considered highly inappropriate—or even sinful.

One of my favourite experiences was at a church in Krasnodar in southern Russia, where they did not sing Russian translations of the popular Western choruses or hymns, preferring to write their own worship songs. What made it particularly interesting was that the famous Cossacks originated in this region of Russia, so their locally written "worship music" had all the energy and pulsating verve associated with Cossack music and dance. I loved it, but I fear some westerners—seeing the dance and hearing the music but not understanding the words—would have judged it to be secular music. In truth, these people had a great love for God and were worshipping Him with a passion and fervency they expressed through their own unique music—their own culture.

Sadly, missionaries have often been guilty of exporting their culture along with the Christian message.

Culture affects the interpretation of Scripture. It moulds and *can be* moulded by politics.

Culture creates exclusivity. The city of Toronto, Canada, is celebrated as being the most culturally-diverse city in the world, but the downside of this is that Toronto is probably also the most culturally-divided city in the world. It is true that we have learned to live together, but that is more in a state of refined tolerance than actually mixing in an integrated manner. To prove this point, just visit some of the ethnic pockets of Toronto, where the shops, restaurants and people in the streets could lead one to think they were in another country, or visit one of the many ethnic churches, many of which conduct their services in the mother tongue. While Toronto is a mosaic of cultural diversity, it is far from being culturally-integrated.

Culture becomes something that people hide behind. We British sometimes use our culture as an excuse for not outwardly displaying our affection, thus, the common reference to our "stiff upper lip."

Cultures can be labelled by common characteristics. I once worked in Greece, where our many good friends claim that Greek people are very "relaxed" concerning time keeping. Our good friends from the Caribbean joke affectionately about "Caribbean time." Interestingly, these are both very hot, humid climates that would have the same debilitating affect on anyone, regardless of skin colour.

While training people in Eastern Europe how to present the drama, "Heaven's Gates and Hell's Flames," I was often accused of trying to turn the cast into Americans, supposedly, by imposing North American culture. This was ironic because I am English, which is very different from being American. However, our Eastern European friends found many of our ways to be typically American.

All of this forced me to radically re-evaluate the way I did things. Eventually, I came to the realization that, although we all have distinctive characteristics based on our cultures of origin, Christians have another culture which is based on our spiritual rebirth. We are "citizens of heaven." The culture that emanates from that, as proclaimed to us by God through His Word, should always take precedence over whatever our earthly culture may require. We should be united as Christians prior to any national or cultural heritage.

Although I am from southern England, my family originated on the little channel island of Guernsey. People from the islands have a different outlook—call it culture—than people who live in large cities and land masses where they live in close proximity to people of other nations. I moved to Canada in 1978 and then back to England in 1984. I have worked all over Europe and even lived in Poland. As I mentioned, during our first sixteen years of marriage, Ginny and I lived in seventeen different places.

Strangely, it is since moving back to Canada in 2000 that I have experienced the greatest culture shock. Why? Because Canada has changed!

In the past, cultures were very static. Indeed, they provided comfort, in that they were a place to belong; they defined one's identity. But now cultures are constantly shifting. The old stability is being shaken.

The younger generations increasingly don't know who they are or where they belong. They are caught in the confusion of constant culture shift. This produces a feeling of alienation. Interestingly, young people tend to create their own culture, mainly through music and clothing styles. This phenomena started in the early 20th

century and is accelerating rapidly today, through Facebook, Twitter and other social media.

Whereas previous cultures were confined to their geographical birthplace, these new "cultures" are not confined within such geographical or political barriers. The advent of television and the World Wide Web means that these new cultures spread rapidly like wildfire across the world, leaping over borders and boundaries into new countries, with total disregard for past history or current local politics.

Now skin colour and ethnicity is less relevant. What people today seek is somewhere to belong, with people of their own "culture" who understand them, do not condemn them, appreciate them and, in their own way, love them.

Love, understand, appreciate ... are these not what Jesus encouraged us to do "to the least of these,"—especially our enemies?

I previously mentioned being accused of trying to make the people "American" whilst working in Europe. The Eastern Europeans interpreted our way of doing things as being "western" rather than recognizing it as simply more efficient.

Very quickly, I learned that, in training the casts and crews for the drama, practically and spiritually, my reasoning had to be based on Scripture rather than on my own cultural experiences.

When Jesus walked the earth, His main way of communicating with the different cultures was through telling stories, or parables, to which each different group could relate—be they fishermen, farmers, tax-collectors or prostitutes.

And so it was that the Lord led me to use just such a method in my efforts to challenge people of differing cultures on that universal church problem, *punctuality* (or rather, the lack of it).

At each church where we went to present the drama, we were always working with forty to fifty people from that church (hundreds of churches in thirty-three different countries and cultures). I would ask the following questions of all the cast: "How many of you like to go and see a movie, even if only once a year?"

Almost everyone did. "How much does it cost to see a movie here in your country?" I established that they did not mind paying for it.

For the next question I would ask that they be totally honest. "How many of you, after paying whatever the local ticket price was, go into the movie ten, fifteen or twenty minutes *after* the movie has actually started?" No one ever did this—in *any* country. When people are paying to see a movie, they make sure they see it from the start.

Then I would say, "So, when you pay to see a movie, you plan to arrive in time to find a parking space, walk from that parking space to the movie theatre box office, pick up your ticket, visit the washroom, buy your popcorn and soft drink *and* be seated before the movie starts. Right?" Everyone would nod in agreement.

"Then why," I would ask, "are you frequently—almost always, in fact—late for church or for prayer meetings or for rehearsals or other church related events? If you can discipline yourself to be on time for things that *you* want to do but not for things that you do for the Lord, what does that tell Him about your attitude towards Him?" Then I would say, "I think I'll just let the question hang there, but let me say this: If we are consistently late, if it is 'normal' for us, our actions will disappoint our pastor, discourage our co-workers and friends and, worst of all, show disrespect for God. We insult and sadden Him. Our actions speak louder than words because they say to God, 'Movies are more important to me than You are.'"

We are not talking about legalism; we are talking about *love*. If we truly love God and are not just giving lip-service to that idea, we will *want* to do our best at all times for Him. With that attitude, except in understandable, unexpected circumstances, being late will never happen—regardless of individual habits or cultures.

So, getting back to the main subject here, where have I had my most challenging cultural experiences? Without hesitation I would say it has been working with people from, and in, North America.

You may wonder why that has been the case. We speak the same language, don't we?

Yes, but the same words or phrases can have vastly different meanings according to the particular culture. For instance, in Britain, an elevator is a "lift," the trunk of a car is the "boot" and the hood of a car is the "bonnet." That universally popular game which is played by men (or women) kicking a round ball is logically called "football." Where on earth did the word "soccer" come from?

The list could go on and I will not bore you with that, but I will share with you a true story to illustrate what can happen when people of a different country use the same words and phrases but are unaware of their different meaning.

When I first came to Canada, it was at the end of January, 1978, and, as expected, the weather was extremely inclement: very cold with lots of snow, ice and strong winds. I worked as the manager of the Toronto office of a large international employment agency situated in downtown Toronto. One of my first tasks was to hire a suitable PA (personal assistant/secretary/office manager).

After exhaustive interviews, I settled on a young lady by the name of Delina from Montreal whose academic qualifications were outstanding. She also happened to be very attractive—which ordinarily should not make any difference, but it actually does have some bearing on what subsequently happened.

As I said, the weather was awful. Delina was in the process of buying or leasing a car but had not yet found one. She did not live on a subway line, but my morning route caused me to drive by the end of her street every day, so I gallantly offered— as a temporary measure—to pick her up and take her to work each day until she completed her car business, which would take a few days at the most.

Well, you may ask, what's wrong with that? Well, nothing, except the fact that I, fresh off the boat, used an expression that is common in England but has a totally different meaning in Canada. So it was in total innocence that I said to this young lady, "If you like, I'll come by and knock you up in the morning." Because this book will be read by people in different countries and cultures, please allow me to digress a little with this explanation.

The phrase "I'll knock you up" derives from the time when most people in England did not have a telephone and cell phones only existed in the minds of science fiction dreamers. If they wanted to contact someone, they knocked at his or her door. If I were to arrange with friends to give then a lift (a ride) to work, or a football game or whatever, the usual procedure upon arrival would not be to honk the car horn and risk disturbing the neighbours but to get out of my car and knock on the door. Sometimes this knocking on the door was what woke them up.

So, the expression to "knock someone up" was widely used, as it was derived from very practical circumstances. Even when times changed, the expression remained a part of our British lexicon of speech.

However, across the pond (an affectionate name for the North Atlantic Ocean), unbeknownst to me, that phrase had a totally different meaning.

For the sake of my non-English friends, and others who may not be aware of this, in North America, the phrase "to knock someone up" is a rather vulgar phrase referring to the act of causing a lady to become pregnant.

I don't think I need to get too graphic with this, other than to say it is only a male who can "knock up" a female—not the other way around. Okay, you've got the point.

Now, transport yourself back into this scenario on a cold, wet and windy February day in Toronto, 1978, as a handsome (if I may say so) young boss is offering to "knock up" a very attractive, new employee.

Although I was acting in all innocence, she was horrified. I was stunned by her reaction and she could not understand my matter-of-fact gall.

What confused her even more was that, in conversation, I had mentioned that I was a churchgoing Christian—and yet here I was, coming on to her in a most blatant way. She really wanted the job, but didn't know how to deal with the situation, so she rather stiffly declined my offer and walked out of the office. I thought her manner was a bit odd but let it go.

On the following days, when she came into the office, wet and bedraggled from the inclement weather, I would repeat my offer and was always confused by her haughty response. I could tell she really wanted to keep her job but for some reason unknown to me, she was putting personal distance between us.

This illustrates my point: two people who think they are speaking the same language may be totally oblivious to the fact that the same phrase or word may have entirely different meanings in different cultures or areas of the country. When even the sense of humour differs the situation can be disastrous.

How did this situation resolve itself? Well, Delina resigned. In doing so, she left me with no doubt as to what she thought of my rude, sexist, insensitive, crass behaviour, saying I should consider myself lucky I was not facing a sexual harassment charge. I can't put into print what her exact words were (bless her), but to say she was angry and upset would be an understatement. She finally exploded in a veritable fusillade in French leaving me understanding nothing—but it seemed to make her feel better.

I listened, stunned. Where had all this come from? I asked her to sit down, stay calm and please explain to me how I had given her the erroneous impression that I wanted to be sexually indiscrete with her.

Her response was that I had repeatedly "come on" to her. Here's how the conversation went:

Terry: genuinely puzzled, "But how was I coming on to you?"

Delina: (feeling free to give full vent to her anger now that she had resigned): You persistently kept propositioning me to have sex with you."

Terry: by now, I was *really* dumbfounded, "Delina, I am so sorry, but please, I have no idea what you are talking about. How could you possibly have gotten that idea?"

Delina: by now so upset she is almost hyperventilating, "By repeatedly saying that you wanted to knock me up in the morning."

My first thought was to say, "So what is wrong with that?" but something clicked in my brain, causing me to refrain from saying that. Instead, I went over to the door of my office, which was open (as it was my practice never to be alone in a room with a woman unless the door was open, both to protect the lady's reputation—and mine) and called in another senior staff person to sit in on the remainder of the conversation.

I then asked what she understood me to mean when I offered to "knock her up."

When Delina's misunderstanding was properly (and somewhat graphically) explained to me, my initial reaction was one of shock, but it was quickly followed by my huge smile, as the humour of the situation dawned on me.

Delina's reaction to my smile was understandable—until I explained the meaning of the phrase in England.

It wasn't long before all three of us were laughing so loudly that we drew a crowd from the nearby offices. The laughter grew louder when we considered what an embarrassingly awkward situation could have developed if Delina had not been a girl of high morals and had invited me into her home.

Word of the incident quickly spread throughout the entire thirty floors of the Manulife Centre office building, at 55 Bloor Street West, Toronto.

The amazing thing is that, as a consequence of this misunderstanding, my fame (or should it be infamy) spread rapidly throughout the organization, catapulting me to the attention of the top people. The fact that I was a born again, churchgoing Christian was highlighted as an important factor in the story. My witness was now right out there. For a while, I was a celebrity around the water coolers and in the local coffee shops.

This, of course, cannot be compared with the story of Joseph being sold into slavery and then becoming the controller of Egypt; but you know, if you live your life right before God, "things" will happen in your life. It's important to be patient and let God work these things out, because we know that *"in all things, God works for the good of those who love Him, who have been called according to His purposes"* (Romans 8:28).

Wrapping it all up: We can look the same and even speak the same words but not be prepared for the shock when we—often painfully—realize just how very different we may be. Sir Winston Churchill perhaps best summed it up. When speaking of the USA and Britain, he said, "We are two nations, divided by a common language."

Praise God that in heaven there is only one culture. If our new bodies have different coloured skin, I suggest we will all be colour blind. Seeing each other illuminated by the light of Jesus, we will all be beautiful as we spend eternity worshipping the King of Kings.

THE ROLLER COASTER

Sometimes the smallest, seemingly insignificant incidents can teach us the most profound lessons.

Many years ago, Ginny and I were staying with some friends in Winnipeg, Manitoba. One day, we went with them and their granddaughter to a small local fair, or *midway*, as some call it in Canada.

The little girl was bursting with excitement. She wanted to go on all the rides, and of course, she constantly badgered her grandparents to go on the rides with her.

For the most part, her doting grandparents did go with her, but for some reason, they drew the line at going on the Roller coaster, even though it was a very small, child-friendly version.

Now, I *love* roller coasters. Ever since I was a little boy and we went to the Blackpool Pleasure Beach in the UK, you could not keep me off whatever was the latest version of "The Big One" roller coaster there.

The current version in Blackpool is sixty-five metres high. In its three minute duration, it will hurl you up and down, inside-out and end-over-end, at gravity-defying speeds of around 120 kph that will rattle your teeth and rearrange your intestines and other vital organs.

Great! I love it! Whether it be in Canada, the USA or Europe, I have been on the best of them—or the worst of them, depending on your perspective.

So it was that I gallantly offered to accompany the little girl on this little roller coaster. Why not? A piece of cake. Right?

The two of us climbed into a car that would seat four people sitting side by side. We pulled the safety bar towards us and started the gently undulating oval ride—up and down, round and round; up and down, round and round; up and down, round and round.

Soon, I began to feel very sick—as though I was literally turning green. As the little girl squealed in unfettered delight, I fought to stop whatever was in my stomach from an unceremonious evacuation. The ride could not finish too soon. It took several hours before I regained my equilibrium and dignity.

But I was puzzled. I have punished my body on the most traumatic roller coasters that twisted minds can invent and loved every moment; so why was I brought to the point of violent sickness on this diminutive ride that should have soothed me to sleep?

In a moment of epiphany, it hit me. In the child-friendly roller coaster, the little girl and I were seated in a contraption that was designed for four adults. We had so much space, we were literally rattling around, sliding from side to side and there was no way to avoid the persistent up and down, up and down motion.

On the *big* roller coasters, on the other hand, although we might be violently thrown around, we would be firmly, tightly and safely secured in our seats.

I came to the realization that life is like a roller coaster. It *will* toss us around, but what matters is not the degree to which we are shaken and violated, but how strong is the anchor that holds us in place.

The two main anchors in most of our lives are family and faith. Both are important, but only God will never let us down.

I am not going to apologize for being sentimental. In relishing some of the wonderful new songs being written, we should not discard some of the old songs that have stood the test of time.

You may think you are familiar enough with these words, but if you take the time to read through them carefully, you may be surprised at the strength and wisdom contained herein.

WE HAVE AN ANCHOR

Will your anchor hold in the storms of life,
When the clouds unfold their wings of strife?
When the strong tides lift, and the cables strain,
Will your anchor drift or firm remain?

Refrain: We have an anchor that keeps the soul
steadfast and sure while the billows roll,
Fastened to the Rock which cannot move,
Grounded firm and deep in the Saviour's love.

It is safely moored, 'twill the storm withstand,
For 'tis well secured by the Saviour's hand;
And the cables passed from His heart to mine,
Can defy the blast, through strength divine.

It will firmly hold in the straits of fear,
When the breakers have told the reef is near;
Though the tempest rave and the wild winds blow,
Not an angry wave shall our bark o'erflow.

It will surely hold in the floods of death,
When the waters cold chill our latest breath;
On the rising tide it can never fail,
While our hopes abide within the veil.[15]

29

OH NO!
NOT SATURDAY MORNING

John Lennon said, "The Beatles are more popular than Jesus."

For a brief period of time, in some places, this may well have been true. But although the Beatles may fleetingly have had worldwide fame, it will never span over 2,000 years and will never reach into as many hearts as Jesus has touched and continues to transform.

Some may be familiar with this poem. I include it here for those who have never heard or read it before.

ONE SOLITARY LIFE

He was born in an obscure village,
the child of a peasant woman.
He grew up in another obscure village
where He worked in a carpenter shop
until He was thirty, when public opinion turned against Him.
He never wrote a book.
He never held an office.
He never went to college.
He never visited a big city.
He never travelled more than 200 miles
from the place where He was born.
He did none of the things

usually associated with greatness.
He had no credentials but Himself.
He was only thirty-three.
His friends ran away.
One of them denied Him.
He was turned over to His enemies
and went through the mockery of a trial.
He was nailed to a cross between two thieves.
While dying, His executioners gambled for His clothing,
the only property He had on earth.
When He was dead
He was laid in a borrowed grave,
through the pity of a friend.
Nineteen centuries have come and gone
and today Jesus is still the central figure of the human race
and the leader of mankind's progress.
All the armies that have ever marched,
all the navys that have ever sailed,
all the parliaments that have ever sat,
all the kings that ever reigned put together;
have not affected the life of mankind on earth
as powerfully as that one solitary life.[16]

Jesus has had more impact on mankind for good than any other person.

In our English dictionary[17], the word "religion" has several different definitions, among which are the following:

1. belief in, worship of, or obedience to a supernatural power or powers considered to be divine or to have control of human destiny

2. any formal or institutionalized expression of such belief: the Christian religion.

3. the attitude and feeling of one who believes in a transcendent controlling power or powers

---

[16] Adapted from an original essay by Dr. James Allan Francis in "The Real Jesus and Other Sermons" © 1926 by the Judson Press of Philadelphia (pp 123-124 titled "Arise Sir Knight!") Public domain.
[17] TheFreeDictionary.com

4. (Roman Catholic Church) RC Church the way of life determined by the vows of poverty, chastity and obedience entered upon by monks, friars and nuns: to enter religion.

5. something of overwhelming importance to a person: football is his religion.

So here is a question: In the UK and many other countries is football (soccer) more popular than Jesus or the Beatles?

While writing this chapter, I delved into statistical research (which I thoroughly enjoyed) and discovered that I could pretty much make statistics say whatever I wanted them to say, depending upon my own personal bias. So after hours and hours of work through which I had hoped to impress you, I decided not to use any of the statistics I found.

Were the hours I invested wasted? No—as I have learned to stay away from statistics.

Another consequence of my efforts was an unexpected directional turn in this chapter. This has caused it to become somewhat different than the other chapters, but I have decided to retain it, as it adds to the eclectic character of the book—and it does have a point I need to make.

If I were to use the word *football* to describe a sport, it would mean different things to different people, depending on the country in which they live.

To anyone in the USA, the word refers to American football, which is a huge passion to many Americans, both male and female. If, however, you cross the northern border, you will find Canadian football, which is similar to American football, but definitely not the same. Down under in Australia, you will find a distinctly different game, called "Australian Rules Football," which actually doesn't have many rules at all. And then there's Gaelic football in Ireland. The following quote about Gaelic football renders all other discussion about it unnecessary: "Players compete with a non-stop-until-you-drop attitude. A steely determination. A belief that a show of pain is a show of weakness."[18]

Ouch! I don't think you'll ever find me playing Gaelic football.

---

[18] The words of Dean Goodison who makes his living standing on the sidelines of playing fields up and down the island of Ireland.

Then there is *Rugby* football, popular in Australia, New Zealand, South Africa, France and Great Britain. Reportedly it started when some students were playing football (the other football) and one of the players decided to pick up the ball and run with it. As this took place in the town of Rugby, England, they decided to call their new game *rugby*.

American and Canadian football are more a derivative of rugby than they are of the other football. That other football, the original version, was invented long before some of the countries, in which later versions of the game are played, were even discovered.

It is now the primary sport of Europe, Central and South America, Africa and, of late, much of Asia.

It's called "the beautiful game." To quote an Internet article:

"The modern-day game we play today traces its roots from England in the 1860s. It was once played by aristocrats privately. The game became quite popular even among the common folk due to its simplicity. Many schools then adopted the game and pretty soon they held matches pitting gaming skills with other schools. This gives us a bit more modern hint as to who invented soccer (football). The slight difficulty early on came from the fact that there were no uniform rules. Thus the Football Association was established in 1863 along with uniform rules thus establishing fair games. From there the game continued in popularity among various countries around the world.[19]"

There are officially football associations in 209 countries of the world under the world-wide governing body 'FIFA'—the Federation of International Football Associations; and the Football World Cup held every four years is by far the biggest single sport event on the planet.[20]

The game as we know it now was created in England and exported around the world in the early days by traders and missionaries.

In other sports claiming the name, the ball is not kicked anywhere near as often as it is in the original. This shows practically, as well as historically, that there is only one sport that can truly claim the name football.

---

[19] http://www.whoinventedit.net/who-invented-soccer.html
[20] See http://en.wikipedia.org/wiki/FIFA_World_Cup

It is truly the beautiful game. So, is it a religion?

As a young boy in England back in the early 50s, every Saturday during the football (soccer) season, I used to worship at that altar, as did every other self-respecting Englishman (Scotsman, Welshman and Irishman, too).

To be honest, the self-respecting Englishmen were all probably faithful to that other peculiar English institution called *cricket*. It was the rest of us who were football crazy.

Football fans in England—1962. Can you spot 14-year-old Terry?

The occasion of this 1962 photo at White Hart Lane, London, was an FA Cup, Fourth Round replay between Southampton (the Saints) who played in the Second

Division, and Nottingham Forest who were, at that time, one of the top teams in the country playing in the First Division.

After first of all drawing one-to-one with Nottingham Forest at their home ground in Nottingham, a replay took place at the Saints home stadium, the Dell, in Southampton. The Saints had scored three goals in the last fifteen minutes of a truly pulsating match to force that game to a three-to-three tie. So now a second replay had to take place at a neutral stadium and that was to be White Heart Lane in London, which, at that time, had a capacity of almost 60,000. It was packed full.

In the opinion of all the football experts and the media, it was not a question of who was going to win but simply a matter of by how many goals Nottingham Forest would beat the Saints.

So what was the score of that third game? Southampton won five-to-nothing.

It was unbelievable!

This photo was taken while we were in the full flush of optimism before the game. Football supporters can display a remarkable disconnect with reality where their teams are concerned.

The extent of my passion for my religion of football decreed that I would never miss a home game. There was no football on television in those days.

I would get up early on the Saturday morning of the game, as I had to take two buses and a boat to get to the stadium. I always arrived at 11:00 a.m. for a match scheduled to start at 3:00 p.m. It used to annoy me that every week a boy who came over by boat from the Isle Of Wight was always there before me.

Why go so early? You need to understand there would be 32,000 people (mostly men in those days) squeezed like sardines into an antiquated stadium built at the turn of the 20th century—that means the late 1800s, early 1900s.

There was space for only 10,000 to be seated in what was called "the stands." (I always wondered why the place where you sat was called the stands.) That meant more than 20,000 people would be crushed together—standing on the terraces— swaying backwards, forwards and from side to side. It was a very dangerous place to be. There was no escape from the stale body odour, the bad breath, the stench of alcohol and the smoke-filled air.

To make it worse, if I didn't position myself properly, someone taller than me would always arrive just before kick-off and stand right in front of me, so I couldn't see.

Obviously I had to get to the stadium early. I made it my mission to be first in when the doors opened. Then I could stand right at the wall behind the goal so no big, tall bloke would get to stand in front of me.

It had to be a religion. What else could garner such blind devotion in such appalling circumstances?

In short (pardon the pun), if one were somewhat vertically challenged (I wouldn't go so far as to call myself short, but I am most definitely not tall) it would be impossible to actually see much without arriving early.

It was being there that mattered, belonging to that great crowd of humanity and singing all the raucous football chants (some of which were quite clever but could never be uttered in decent company, much less printed in a book). You really had to be there. Otherwise, it would be impossible to understand the intoxication of being part of a throng of 32,000 male voices chanting in unison, "The referee's a bar steward! The referee's a bar steward! The referee's a bar steward!" It was all done with friendly, good humour.

Well, that was my Saturday. That was *my* Saturday. It *belonged* to me and I cherished it. It would have helped if my team had won more games, but that's another story for another time. Anyway, an important element of religion is that it should involve some suffering, and boy—did we suffer!

In the many years of crisscrossing all of Europe in ministry, I hardly ever got to see a game of football. But then, when we moved back to Canada in 2000, I discovered that, with cable television, I could see three top English premiership football games *live* every Saturday morning on a large screen television—from the comfort of my armchair—with a nice cup of tea.

This was *my* Saturday, again. Could life *be* any better?

Until ... our church decided to have prayer meetings on Saturday mornings.

Why Saturday morning? There are 168 hours in each week. Why choose that particular one or two hours? Apparently, that was the time the church leadership decided was best.

But why on *my* Saturday mornings?

Of course, I was being faced with a choice.

Was God *really* first in my life—or was that true only when it did not inconvenience me.

I am not going to pretend it was easy because it wasn't, but for over two years (until caring for Ginny's aging parents demanded that we make some adjustments in our lives), we attended the Saturday morning prayer meetings faithfully. Even though we are now unable to be at the prayer meetings, I still retain the habit of praying on Saturday mornings (as well, of course, as at other times).

You see, Saturday mornings are *still* mine, but now I spend them with God, in fellowship and conversation with Him.

I love it!

TO THE HOOK OF HOLLAND

In the late 1980s, Ginny and I did a lot of work in Holland with Atlantic Bridge, an organization whose mantra was "building bridges, breaking down walls."

What the Dutch did was simple but extremely effective. Their education authorities were very progressive in ensuring that their young people learned English well. Because they designed the curriculum to have only English spoken in the teaching of some lessons, the teachers would invite English-speaking artists and singers to visit and engage the students in conversation—in English—about their work and their art. There was to be no Dutch spoken at all, so the students were forced to use the English they learned in other lessons.

The English visitors were not allowed to initiate the subjects to be discussed. Whatever topics the Dutch students raised were fair game and the visitors were expected to answer whatever questions the Dutch students might have.

When Ginny would enter a classroom of twenty-five to forty students, usually the first question asked by the students was "What job do you do for a living?"

Ginny's answer would be "I am a missionary gospel singer." And there it was; the door was legitimately opened for her to share her faith, always within the context of whatever searching and insightful questions the students might ask.

Ginny would then do mini lunchtime concerts at the school. At night, she would sing in the popular local coffee houses. At most of these, marijuana was freely available and openly smoked.

Inhaling the second-hand marijuana fumes was often dizzying, but this was a unique opportunity to share our faith with a great many Dutch young people.

We had many challenging conversations. They liked Ginny's music and loved Ginny, whom they said was surely a Dutch girl because of her blonde hair and beauty.

Over the course of many years, we went to Holland often, taking friends with us who were talented singers, musicians and actors. There were always wonderful ministry opportunities with extremely fruitful results.

These intimate visits taught us many valuable lessons when it came to understanding the differences between cultures. It was on one such visit that an unusual incident occurred.

We would usually cross the North Sea from Harwich in East Anglia, England, to the Hook of Holland—or "Hoek van Holland."

Because it was a six-and-a-half hour journey, depending on the rough North Sea weather and tides, we would travel by night, in the hope that we would be able to sleep during the crossing and be refreshed to start work the next day.

We would travel on a Stena Line Superferry. In the summer months, these were extremely busy, so to get a seat to try and sleep in, you had to pre-book and reserve your seat when you booked your vehicle on the ferry.

So it was that I was standing in line at the purser's office to get our seat numbers. In front of me was an older lady who was giving the Dutch ship's purser (a young lady) a very hard time. The older lady was ranting and raving, her speech liberally littered with foul language and profanities. She was rude, obnoxious, pompous and overbearing.

It was none of my business, of course, but I was particularly irked when she invoked her Canadian citizenship as a reason why she should receive some kind of preferential treatment. The Dutch purser was being very polite and professional, while the Canadian was getting under my skin. Finally, she went too far. She was bringing great shame on the Canadian name and I had to do something about it.

When an opening came in the hateful tirade, I politely addressed both women. "Excuse me, but may I say something, please?"

The Dutch lady said nothing, while the other lady was obviously not pleased with the interruption, so I hurried on. "I thought you might like to know that I, too, am a Canadian citizen."

The demeanor of the Canadian lady changed when she thought she had found an ally.

So I continued, addressing myself to the purser and nodding toward the other Canadian. "I want you to know that this lady's conduct is rude and obnoxious and is in no way a true reflection of Canadian people. I am deeply embarrassed by her behaviour and, on behalf of Canada and its people, I would like to apologize sincerely."

For a brief moment, everything stopped. The Dutch purser stared at me. And then, as if breaking a spell, the obnoxious Canadian lady snatched her ticket rudely out of the purser's hand. Giving me a withering look, she stormed off in an indignant huff.

Quickly regaining her composure, the purser turned to me, as I was next in line, and asked, "May I see your ticket please, sir?"

After looking briefly at my ticket, she excused herself, saying she needed to go to the back office for a moment. After quickly returning, she then said to me, "Mr. Bridle, it would appear that we need to upgrade you to a first class cabin. Will that be okay, sir?"

I swear to you she had a twinkle in her eyes as she spoke and I was very impressed with her poise and professionalism.

So it was that, for standing up in defence of my adopted country, Ginny and I jumped from having uncomfortable seats, in which it would have been difficult to sleep, to a cabin with a king size bed, a large television, air-conditioning, complimentary tea and coffee, an ensuite, a wake-up call and a full English breakfast.

Sometimes it does pay to speak up!

IT'S NOT SO BAD!

CAN GOD POSSIBLY USE ME?

WHAT IS THE SOURCE OF YOUR CONFIDENCE?

When I was growing up, I think my parents wished I were a girl. My mother certainly did.

They loved me in their own way, but because they—especially my mother—did not receive much affection from their own parents, they did not find it easy or natural to show affection to my brother or myself.

In other ways, they were exemplary parents, lacking only when it came to expressing affection or building confidence in me.

In my presence, as I mentioned earlier, they liked to tell people the story of when my dad first came to see me right after I was born. My mother told him I was ugly. After seeing me, my dad agreed. This is what I heard as a little boy.

They could not agree on a name for me, so I have no middle name (see the story "The Man With No Name").

My dad came to watch me play football just one time, but he often went to watch my brother's girlfriend play in a ladies' football team. One day, he walked right past the pitch on which I was playing, waving a greeting to me as he walked to another pitch where she was playing. She was good. In fact, she was *very* good, but to me, it was a snub from my dad.

What young boy does not want to see his dad cheering and encouraging him from the sidelines? It made me angry. In fact, it made me so angry that I scored a goal, which was unusual for me because I was a midfield player. Even so, I was sent off the pitch for retaliating to a bad foul on me. The disappointment, anger, and resentment that had built up had sought a place for release.

I hold no grudges against my parents; they were, as I said earlier, products of homes in which, for different reasons, they were shown no, or very little, affection. No one can give to others what they don't have inside.

That said, to this day, my Achilles' heel is my inadequate sense of self-worth. I do not understand why the Lord gave me such a wonderful person to be my wife. If I believed in reincarnation (which I don't), I would have assumed she must have done something bad in a former life to deserve being paired with me in this life.

My sense of worth, though lacking in natural terms, has been restored to me by my heavenly Father. It is not based on anything I have done or not done but on the fact that, even if I were the only sinner in the world, Jesus Christ, *the Son of God*, would still have allowed Himself to be crucified—just for me.

If I am *that* valuable to God, then I must not allow myself to believe the lie of Satan that I am worth nothing. So …

> The next time you feel like God can't use you, just remember …
> Noah was a drunk. Abraham was too old.
> Isaac was a daydreamer. Jacob was a liar.
> Leah was ugly. Joseph was abused.
> Moses had a stuttering problem. Gideon was afraid.
> Samson had long hair and was a womanizer. Rahab was a prostitute.
> Jeremiah and Timothy were too young.
> David had an affair and was a murderer.
> Elijah was suicidal. Isaiah preached naked.
> Jonah ran from God. Naomi was a widow.
> Job went bankrupt. Peter denied Christ—three times.
> The disciples fell asleep while praying.
> Martha worried about everything.
> The Samaritan woman was divorced, more than once.

Zaccheus was too small.

Paul was too religious.

Timothy had an ulcer ... and Lazarus was dead!

So now! No more excuses!

God can use you to your full potential.

Remember He does not necessarily call the equipped,

but He definitely equips the called.

Besides, you aren't the message, you are just the messenger.

1. God wants spiritual fruit, not religious nuts.
2. Dear God, I have a problem; it's *me*. Acknowledge that and you are on the right track.
3. Growing old is inevitable ... growing up is optional.
4. There is no key to happiness. The door is always open.
5. Silence is often misinterpreted but never misquoted.
6. Do the math ... count your blessings.
7. Faith is the ability to not panic.
8. Laugh every day; it's like inner jogging.
9. If you worry, you didn't pray. If you pray, don't worry.
10. As a child of God, prayer is kind of like calling home everyday.
11. Blessed are the flexible for they shall not be bent out of shape.
12. The most important things in your house are the people.
13. When we get tangled up in our problems, we must be still. God wants us to be still so He can untangle the knot.
14. A grudge is a heavy thing to carry.
15. He who dies with the most toys is still dead. [21]

Leaving the very best until last ... *God loves you!*

Did you hear that?   *God* loves you!

God *loves* you!

God loves *you!*

<u>No matter how</u> you say it, or may even want to deny it, it's still a wonderful truth.

[21] Source unknown

Have a great day!

The *Son* is shining and if He can use me, He can certainly use you.
Be encouraged.
Go on, smile.
It won't hurt.

30

ARE YOU SATISFIED WITH JUST BEING GOOD?

The best lessons in life are not necessarily learned from books but from personal experiences that, initially, may not be easy to accept.

The most profound lessons are the simplest to learn, but are sometimes so obvious, being right in front of our noses, that we don't see them.

The biggest enemy of "the best" is "the good," especially if being good is good enough.

There is a verse in the Bible that says, *"To whom much is given, from him much will be required"* (Luke 12:48 NKJV).

In over thirty-five years of ministry, I have encountered many situations where people are satisfied to get by doing the least possible, especially when being good is good enough.

With notable exceptions, sadly, the biggest culprits of this malaise tend to be those who have been given much, either materially or in terms of talent.

Over the many years we worked with people all over Europe, directing "Heaven's Gates and Hell's Flames," we would come upon situations, time and time again, where people who had talent, and knew it, would not be as effective as other far less talented people, who humbly knew they needed help from the Lord.

In gospel music I have encountered people, whose talent I envied, waiting until the last moment to decide what songs they would sing at a concert and other extremely talented people who just didn't like rehearsing. Their attitude and effort was so lax, it was embarrassing.

I have many good friends who are talented in the field of music and have no one particular in mind when I say this, but there are some in the field of Christian arts who think they are good and would consider themselves to be professional but who fall far short of what the world considers professional.

Talented people can drift into complacency because they know they can "pull it off." Whereas the less talented are much more aware of their need for God's help.

I have, on many occasions, seen talented actors and singers perform well but without the power of God's Holy Spirit. Conversely, I have witnessed many times when the quality of the acting or music may not be very good at all, but the people were doing their best and there was a powerful presence of the Holy Spirit, bringing amazing results.

What truly breaks my heart is seeing tremendously talented people doing just enough to please their audiences without effort, their trust being in their own ability rather than in God's empowerment. I think how much more powerful their ministry would be if they were truly giving their all, trusting God rather than themselves.

To those Christians who maintain it is somehow wrong for a Christian to strive to be professional, let me remind you what the word actually means. When used as an adjective, it means "extremely competent in a job, et cetera." When used as a noun, it means: "a person who engages in an activity with great competence."[22]

Why would anyone who loves the Lord—and is grateful for all He has done—not want to strive to be professional, to do anything but their very best for Him?

The trouble is we want to take short cuts in life and do the least we can for the most reward. That is a sad human trait. Where it exists, the biggest hindrance to doing the very best we can is having the attitude that we are already *good*.

Let me repeat that: The biggest hindrance to giving our best is believing that what we are already giving is good enough. Well let me tell you: It is better to be dependant on God rather than to be sure of ourselves.

---

[22] Dictionary.com

If we seek secular accolades from secular people rather than the empowerment of the Holy Spirit, we'll miss the most important element of our efforts.

If, on the other hand, we are doing something for the glory of God and hoping to see some spiritual, maybe even supernatural, response, we can't be surprised if God doesn't show up if we haven't done all we could, our very best.

In other words, if we settle for *our* good, we'll miss *His* best. If we ever stop trying to do better, we will stagnate.

Two examples of genuine professionalism, one small and one large, will serve to clarify this truth.

The first involves my wife, Ginny. When we first met, I asked her what she wanted to do with her life.

Without hesitation, she replied, "Sing for Jesus."

Since that day, I have seen Ginny sing on secular and Christian television on three continents, in churches, schools and auditoriums. She has fronted her own live band, done concert tours in Europe and Canada, sung to all ages in both indoor and outdoor concerts. Churches of all denominations have invited her to sing. There have been huge audiences of up to 20,000 as well as intimate ladies' meetings and seniors' homes where as few as twenty were in attendance. What has been common to all these situations has been her effort to practice and spend time seeking God's will as to what she should sing and share. She puts forth the same effort no matter what size the group.

Yes, God has given her the gift of a beautiful voice and a captivating personality, but she does not rely on those alone. The power and effectiveness of her ministry comes from the consistency and depth of her personal relationship with Jesus—and that can never be taken for granted. It has to be cultivated and replenished daily.

The second example involves the Toronto Mass Choir, an ethnically and denominationally diverse, multi-award-winning choir, popular not only in southern Ontario, but in the many countries in Europe and the Caribbean where they have toured.

There is no question that the Toronto Mass Choir is highly professional. I have been in many secular, non-church situations with them where the people have marvelled at how musically excellent they are, with other musically excellent choirs asking, "How can we sound like you? What is the reason for the difference we feel when you sing?"

So why is the TMC musically excellent?

1. The leaders of the choir, Karen and Oswald Burke, put God first in their lives.

2. They have worked hard to become trained and proficient in the skills needed to lead such a choir.

3. The auditioning process is tough, dealing with not only the singing ability of the applicant but also the reason why he or she wants to be in the choir and whether he or she has the backing and support of their family and pastor.

4. There is a three-month probationary period to further determine if the applicant is reliable and committed to the rigorous demands of being in such a choir.

All that is tested before an applicant can formerly become a member of TMC. Many applicants don't make it through the full process.

But for those who do, then come the hours of learning and practicing the songs. No sheet music is used because when TMC sings, the songs have all been committed, by everyone, to memory.

So that helps to explain why TMC is musically good, but where does the power for that "special something" come from? What is it that causes other excellent musicians and singers to recognize the fact that there is "something different" about them? Why do they ask, "How can we get that difference for our choir?"

The *difference* comes from the commitment as a choir, both corporately and individually, to spend time with God in prayer, sometimes even fasting. This is an ongoing choir activity. Before each concert, the choir meets to hear a testimony or Scripture reading from one of the choir members and then they pray for that concert or presentation.

It may interest you to know that when Toronto Mass Choir perform a concert, generally, the members know only what the first song will be. Sometimes they know the first two songs. After that, Karen will move to whatever songs she feels led by the Holy Spirit to do. If she has a skeleton of a program in mind, she will change it on the fly as she feels it is appropriate.

How can a choir of thirty to thirty-five singers and a live band do that? By being professionally prepared, in the truest sense of the word, and by being spiritually in tune with God. There are no short cuts to either of those two essential elements.

So what is my point?

- It's okay to seek to become the best that you can become.
- It's okay to work to be disciplined and professional.
- One should never stop trying to improve because there is always room for improvement.
- No matter how good you become, never be tempted to think that your effectiveness rests on your ability alone.

Years ago I wrote this:

> He gives the talent.
> He gives the strength.
> He gives the provision.
> He gives the opportunity.
> He gets all the thanks.
> He gets all the praise.
> He gets all the glory.
> And what do we get?
> Far more than we deserve.

And let me close with this: *"From everyone who has been given much, much will be demanded; and from the one who has been entrusted with much, much more will be asked"* (Luke 12:48).

These words of Jesus have become somewhat of a mantra in Western culture. They are paraphrased in Uncle Ben's words of wisdom to Peter Parker in Spiderman: "With great power comes great responsibility."

TO WHOM MUCH IS GIVEN, MUCH WILL BE REQUIRED

"The idea of 'to whom much is given, much will be required' is that we are held responsible for what we have. If we are blessed with talents, wealth, knowledge, time and the like, it is expected that we use these well to glorify God and benefit others.

"In context, Jesus had just told a parable about being ready for His return. His disciple Peter asked if the parable was for just them or for everyone. Jesus replied with another parable in which He defines the 'faithful and wise manager' as one who gives out food and other allowances 'at the proper time.' When the master returns and finds the faithful servant managing his resources well, he 'put him in charge of all his possessions' (Luke 12:42-44). We have been entrusted with certain things, and faithfulness requires that we manage those things wisely and unselfishly.

"Jesus continued the parable with a contrast: 'Suppose the servant says to himself, 'My master is taking a long time in coming,' and he then begins to beat the other servants, both men and women, and to eat and drink and get drunk. The master of that servant will come on a day when he does not expect him and at an hour he is not aware of. He will cut him to pieces and assign him a place with the unbelievers. The servant who knows the master's will and does not get ready or does not do what the master wants will be beaten with many blows' (Luke 12:44-47). The unfaithful servant mismanages the master's resources to satiate his own greed. Jesus warns that judgment is certain for that servant. The Lord then summarizes the point of the parable with these words: 'Everyone to whom much was given, of him much will be required, and from him to whom they entrusted much, they will demand the more' (verse 48, ESV). A related parable that also deals with stewardship is the Parable of the Talents (or the Parable of the Bags of Gold) in Matthew 25:14-30.

"It is easy to assume that only wealthy people have been 'given much,' but, in truth, we have all been given much (1 Corinthians 4:7). We have been granted the abundant grace of God (Ephesians 1:3-10; 3:16-21; Romans 5:8-11; 8:14-17), the Word of God and the gifts of the Holy Spirit

(John 14:16-21; 16:13; Romans 12:6). 'Each of you should use whatever gift you have received to serve others, as faithful stewards of God's grace in its various forms' (1 Peter 4:10).

"We should also not assume that the less we know about God and His gifts, the less we'll have to do. As evident in Jesus' parable, we are held responsible to know our master's will. God has plainly shown us what He requires (Micah 6:8).

"God gives us resources such as finances and time, talents such as culinary skills or musical ability and spiritual gifts such as encouragement or teaching. We should ask God for wisdom on how to use those resources and commit ourselves to expending them according to His will so that He may be glorified. In regards to spiritual gifts, Paul said, 'We have different gifts, according to the grace given to each of us. If your gift is prophesying, then prophesy in accordance with your faith; if it is serving, then serve; if it is teaching, then teach; if it is to encourage, then give encouragement; if it is giving, then give generously; if it is to lead, do it diligently; if it is to show mercy, do it cheerfully' (Romans 12:6-8). This is simply responsible stewardship.

"We have been given much, and God desires us to use what He has given to further His Kingdom and proclaim His glory. It's what we were created to do. 'Then Jesus said to his disciples, 'Whoever wants to be my disciple must deny themselves and take up their cross and follow me. For whoever wants to save their life will lose it, but whoever loses their life for me will find it ... For the Son of Man ... will reward each person according to what they have done' (Matthew 16:24-25, 27). We are living sacrifices (Romans 12:1), giving the things God has given us in service to others, and in that we actually find life. God, the giver of all good things (James 1:17), gives us everything we need to fulfill His will. 'Freely you have received; freely give' (Matthew 10:8)."[23]

[23] http://www.gotquestions.org/much-given-required.html#ixzz36bYHvVHg

31

REACTIONS

One of the joys in life are those unforeseen things that happen.

On one of our missionary journeys, whilst driving back from Poland to the UK, my van unexpectedly broke down.

There followed a series of misunderstandings and inefficiencies with the local roadside rescue services that caused me to be stranded for over ten hours. During that time, I wrote the following on some cheap napkins. Despite the temptation, I have resisted editing or embellishing my original notes written on December 9, 1999 at 3:40 p.m. at a roadside garage, somewhere in East Germany.

We plan our *actions*, but our *reactions* teach us more about ourselves.

Here I am—stuck on an autobahn built by Hitler, somewhere in East Germany.

My carefully planned drive from Poland to the UK is in disarray because, whilst driving at eighty mph (perfectly legal here), my gearbox decided to quit.

How could such a thing happen to me? I am living my life as righteously as I can. I cannot think of any unconfessed sin. Ginny, as usual, has mobilized a whole army of prayer support for me (bless her), so how can the enemy possibly get close to me? Do I really need to remind the Lord of just how hard I have worked for Him all year? So—again I ask—how can this be happening to me?

Of course, as I contemplate my predicament, it serves to remind me that no matter how well prepared we may be, both practically and spiritually, *things happen!* I am not going to give the enemy any credit for this inconvenience, major though it is.

However, my meticulously planned two-and-a-half-day drive from Poland to the UK has all gone wrong. Those who know me well know that I enjoy planning things and am particularly gratified when everything goes according to my plan. I don't think there is anything wrong with this way of thinking, as I am firmly convinced that the Holy Spirit can, and does, guide us in the planning process—but I have noticed that when everything does go as planned, we do not grow. We may feel some personal satisfaction and we may thank the Lord for His part in our success, but it is only when things go wrong that we get the opportunity to test ourselves—and it is only by our *reactions* to unexpected, unplanned for, unwelcome circumstances that we can really see how much we have, or have not, grown as Christians.

As I look back over the last year, I can identify several situations that were not welcome in my life. They were not a part of *my plan.* I wish I could say that my reactions in those circumstances were consistent with the maturity expected of me, but honesty does not permit me to say that. Sometimes I blew it! So guess what? I am still learning and the Lord is still working on me. I am *so* glad that He shows more patience towards me than I sometimes show towards others. I do not say that as an excuse for my reactions. I do believe we are always accountable for our words and actions and should seek forgiveness from any whom we may have wronged—but having done that, I know we do not then need to walk around burdened with guilt.

If we look hard enough, we can see the Lord at work in *all* situations. He quite definitely *does not cause* all the things that happen to us. Some of them are our own fault, while some are the fault of others. Sometimes it is the enemy trying to trip us up—and at other times, *things just happen!*

But we can take comfort in this, knowing that our wonderful Lord and Saviour, in His great love for us ...*"causes all things to work together for good to those who love God, to those who are called according to His purposes"* (Romans 8:28 NAS). Think about it!

WHAT iS A DOOR?

I started to think about doors today. What are they?

Of course I know what doors are, but why was I thinking about them?

I have learned that when a thought or word persistently sticks in my mind, this may be the prompting of the Lord trying to get my attention. And so, rather than scrounging around in dictionaries for the obvious definition of the word, I let my thoughts simmer, assuming that if the Lord is trying to show me something, whatever it is will rise to the top of my conscious thought. The following are some of my musings on the word "door."

1. A door is a flat piece of wood with metal hinges.
2. A door is an entryway to another space or an exit from somewhere else.
3. A door is a static object separating two spaces.
4. A door is a transitional object between two spaces.
5. A door is a barrier preventing the movement from one space to another.
6. A door can be a friend or a foe, depending where you want, or do not want to be.
7. A door can be an obstruction, preventing me from going where I need to go.
8. A door protects people from unwanted intrusion.
9. A door is protection from unpleasant people.
10. A door is a potential opportunity.
11. A door is our first line of defence against the outside world.
12. A door can be whatever you want it to be.

Obviously, a door can be many things. What it becomes is largely determined by one's perspective. It is an inanimate object, incapable of thinking for itself, so it can be whatever one needs it to be. In Christian parlance, we often use the expression "God opened a door" or "God closed a door."

For all the reasons listed, doors are extremely important. In thinking further, I recognized the fact that I have discovered how to deal with doors in my life.

What do I do when I am faced with a door?

I am not one of those people who believes we can get anywhere in life by sitting on our hands waiting for things to happen. Inertia leads nowhere. We need always to be moving forward, on one level or another.

Whenever I encounter a door, I don't turn away from it and sit down. I move towards it and try the handle to see if it will open for me. If it will not open, I realize that:

1. It may not be God's will for me to go through that door, no matter how much I think that what lies on the other side would be good for me.

2. I realise that it may not be the right time to go through that particular door, so I turn away from it, push it out of my mind and wait patiently.

3. I do not try to break through the door. I may have the strength to do that, but if the door is shut to me, the sooner I accept that, the better.

4. I do not try to pick the lock. This is tantamount to manipulating things to get me through the door. I might succeed, but it would not be good for me. However, if the door opens when I turn the handle, I will walk through it boldly, even though I don't know where it may lead.

If it is God who opens the door, at His perfect time, it does not matter where it leads—because the issue is not the destination; the issue is with whom one is making the journey.

Over the years, Ginny and I have stepped through many doors when we had absolutely no idea where the open door was leading us. If we had known what God had planned for us, we probably would have turned tail and run in the opposite direction.

Finally, when God opens the door, the issue of provision for where that road will lead has already been settled.

You do not have to concern yourself with what you may not have nor whether you think you are ready for what is ahead.

He who instigated your journey will always supply what you need precisely when you need it.

Do you feel unprepared for the task? Good.

Do you feel you cannot do what you are being asked unless the Lord steps in to help you? Excellent!

His strength is perfected in our weakness.

If God asks you to jump, your only question should be "How high?"

33

CRABBY OLD MAN

You will find, littered throughout this book, a few stories or tomes I have gleaned from the Internet. They have come to me uninvited, but they have touched my heart or brought a lump to my throat or tears to my eyes.

I included them because if they have touched me, they may touch you also. Sometimes I have adapted them and sometimes I have quoted them just as they came to me. Where I have been able to find the author, I have acknowledged that person, but in other situations I have had to content myself with signing the piece as anonymous, hoping I can eventually find and acknowledge the author.

The following is one such article.

When an old man died in the geriatric ward of a nursing home in North Platte, Nebraska, it was believed he had nothing left of any value.

Later, when the nurses were going through his meagre possessions, they found this poem. Its quality and content so impressed the staff that copies were made and distributed to every nurse in the hospital.

One nurse took her copy to Missouri. The old man's sole bequest to posterity has since appeared in the *Christmas edition of the News Magazine of the St. Louis Association for Mental Health*. A slide presentation has also been made based on his simple but eloquent poem.

And this little old man, with nothing left to give to the world, is now the author of this "anonymous" poem winging its way across the Internet.

I am so glad it found its way to me. I hope it blesses you as it has blessed me.

CRABBY OLD MAN

What do you see nurses? What do you see?
What are you thinking when you're looking at me?
A crabby old man, not very wise,
uncertain of habit with faraway eyes?

Who dribbles his food and makes no reply
when you say in a loud voice ... "I do wish you'd try!"
Who seems not to notice the things that you do;
and forever is losing a sock or shoe?

Who, resisting or not, lets you do as you will,
with bathing and feeding, the long day to fill.
Is that what you're thinking? Is that what you see?
Then open your eyes, nurse; you're not looking at me.

I'll tell you who I am, as I sit here so still;
as I do at your bidding, as I eat at your will.
I'm a small child of ten with a father and mother,
Brothers and sisters who all love one another.

A young boy of sixteen with wings on his feet;
dreaming that soon now a lover he'll meet.
A groom soon at twenty, my heart gives a leap.
Remembering the vows that I promised to keep.

At twenty-five, now I have young of my own,
who need me to guide and a secure happy home.
A man of thirty: my young now grown fast;
bound to each other with ties that should last.

At forty, my young sons have grown and are gone;
but my wife's beside me, to see I don't mourn.

At fifty, once more, babies play 'round my knee.
Again, we know children, my loved one and me.

Dark days are upon me; my wife is now dead.
I look at the future and shudder with dread.
For my young are all rearing young of their own;
and I think of the years, and the love that I've known.

I'm now an old man, and nature is cruel.
'Tis jest to make old age look like a fool.
The body, it crumbles; grace and vigour depart.
There is now a stone, where there once was a heart.

But inside this old carcass, a young guy still dwells;
and now and again my battered heart swells.
I remember the joys—I remember the pain;
and I'm loving and living life over again.

I think of the years, all too few and gone too fast;
and accept the stark fact that nothing can last.
So open your eyes, people—open and see
not a crabby old man. Look closer ... see *me!*[24]

This poem pierces my heart as Ginny and I spend the sunset days with her ninety-two-year old father, Gus Ambrose. Gus is definitely *not* a crabby old man, but I often see that faraway look in his eyes, and I wonder at what he is thinking.

He's probably remembering Jeannie, his dear wife of sixty-seven years, whom he misses so much. Perhaps he's thinking of that time that draws closer each day, when he and Jeannie will be reunited in Christ's presence, in that place He has gone to prepare for all of us.

We should all remember this poem when we next meet an older person whom we might otherwise brush aside, not seeing the young soul within. We will all, one day, be that person.

---

[24] Anonymous

NUGGETS

ON ~ WISDOM

We usually say that age, plus experience and knowledge, equals wisdom. But that is not necessarily true.

True wisdom comes from God. It is obtained at His discretion according to how much time we spend in His presence.

ON ~ PIONEERS

We should be careful of criticizing the past and should acknowledge the fact that many of those who went before us were radical, innovative, pioneers in their time. We should be grateful for whatever positive foundations they laid down.

At the same time, we need to recognize our responsibility to build upon those positive foundations, and not be afraid to be the radical pioneers of *our* time, never forgetting that the day will come when those who follow us will see us in terms of the past. We must be willing to give them the same freedom to be innovative that we now crave.

ON ~ WE ARE ALL THE SAME

Has it ever occurred to you that we are all the same—in that we are all different?

ON ~ POWER AND STABILITY

Power without stability is potentially destructive, not creative.

Donald Campbell was famous in the 1950s and 60s for setting new speed records on both land and water. In 1964, he set a new land speed record of 403 mph. That same year, he set a new water speed record of 276.33 mph.

On January 4, 1967, Donald Campbell died in a spectacular crash as he tried to break his own water speed record. Yes, power without stability can be destructive.

In life, the Holy Spirit is the power. The Word of God provides the stability.

ON ~ DEFINING SUCCESS

Ultimate success is determined by the fruit that *remains*, not the fruit that is harvested. If the fruit that is harvested is allowed to rot and spoil, all the hard work and effort that has gone into harvesting is diminished and ultimately ineffective.

ON ~ ADDED ROOMS

In recent years, some churches have become like houses where rooms have been added to meet certain needs. Rather than operating with cohesive, long term plans and enacting God-given visions, many congregations have just reacted to current situations. Some have adapted existing rooms to meet whatever needs emerged at the time. The results may not have been perfect solutions, but they may have been deemed relatively adequate, and that was considered good enough. Good enough is never good enough!

Sometimes real progress means taking the courageous step of tearing down elements that aren't adequately serving needs to make space for better structures that have been carefully planned for future growth and development, God-inspired plans to meet present and future needs.

This does not mean we have to discard all the components (people and materials) of "the old rooms" of our lives. Indeed, many of the existing elements can and should be incorporated into the new structure.

It takes time to deconstruct the old and build the new and there are usually a few casualties in the process, especially if the old materials will not adapt to the new structures. If not replaced, old structures fall down through decay.

Surely it is better to preempt that situation with careful thought, wise planning and the leading of the Holy Spirit.

ON ~ THE PRESENT TENSE JESUS

Although Jesus died over 2,000 years ago, nobody has ever referred to Him as "the late Jesus."

Not even unbelievers.

Nowhere in history.

Nowhere has He *ever* been referred to in the past tense.

He is the *living* God!

ON ~ GETTING UP EARLY

You know what I have discovered? When I get up early in the morning, when I am still tired and perhaps only half awake, my spirit seems to be more in tune with the Lord. I am more open to Him and more open to sharing my heart with others.

Perhaps it is because the more I wake up, the more self-sufficient I become; and self-sufficient is not how God wants us to be. He always wants us to be *God-sufficient.*

Of course I am not advocating that we go around half asleep all day, but it is helpful to realize there are certain times of the day when we are more amenable to God and hearing His voice.

ON ~ THE PEACE OF GOD

"The presence of the peace of Christ is the decisive proof that the heart is right with God."[25]

I have found this to be true—over and over and over again!

ON ~ RIGHTS VS. SURRENDER

Do I have rights as a Christian?

When one understands the true meaning of surrender—to willingly give up whatever rights one might have—the answer would have to be "no."

As a Christian, my expectation is that God knows what is best for me, so I have faith and trust in Him that whatever befalls me is ultimately for my good.

God is more than capable of doing whatever He wants to do. Truly *nothing* is impossible for Him.

The question is "Do we have the right to demand how He answers our prayers?" In light of the above, again, the answer would be "no."

When we trust in God alone, it means our trust can be nothing less than total. Anything less means we may as well have no trust at all. We don't get to pick and choose what parts of our lives we will entrust to God and what parts we will not.

We can ask whatever we want to ask of Him, but our prayers must always include the caveat "Yet not as I will, but as You will," as Jesus prayed to His Father. *"My Father, if it is possible, may this cup be taken from Me. Yet not as I will, but as You will"* (Matthew 26:39). *"And again He prayed, 'My Father, if it is not possible for this cup to be taken away unless I drink it, may Your will be done'"* (Matthew 26:42).

That is the kind of total, trusting surrender God is looking for in each and every one of us.

[25] Clarke's Commentary on Colossians 3:15

Prayer is about thanking God, praising and worshipping Him and presenting our needs (i.e. our daily bread) to Him with supplications, but it is *not* about trying to bend His will to fit our fleshly desires.

If we are completely and totally surrendered to Christ, our prayers—after giving thanks and praising and worshipping Him—should be all about seeking God's will. We should ask what He wants, what His plan is and what we can do for Him, rather than asking what He can do for us.

The following article, written for The Center For Development by Lawrence Wilson, MD, is reprinted with permission.

THY WILL BE DONE
by Lawrence Wilson, MD

"A very powerful affirmation is to say Thy will be done. This article explains why this is so, and how to use the phrase properly. It is an important phrase today. Many people fear it for the wrong reasons, and many need to use it to move on in their lives fearlessly. It is also necessary, or at least helpful, to move the world forward at this time in history.

WHAT IS MEANT BY "THY WILL BE DONE?"

"Basically, the phrase represents a type of mental surrender to a higher power than the ego mind. This is its essence. Many do not realize it, but the ego mind, sometimes also called the *lower mind, the reactive mind or the monkey mind*, runs most people. Even if one claims to be religious or spiritual, the ego mind still rules in most instances.

"This ego mind is always a conditioned, limited mind. It is influenced by its upbringing, its emotional traumas, its moods and whims, and much more, in fact. Most people have subconscious or unconscious blocks, ideas, beliefs and more that all influence the ego mind at all times and in all situations. Saying Thy will be done is one way to unblock a person from the rule of this mind.

FEAR OF LETTING GO OF THE EGO MIND

"The main reason many people do not like the phrase Thy will be done is because they are turning control over to a seemingly unknown force. This is frightening for the ego mind, which does not ever want to give up its power and control over a person. Indeed, the ego mind was set up early in life to manage one's life and one's everyday decisions and conflicts. Giving it up seems like suicide or death to many people, so they do not like this phrase.

"For example, what if 'Thy will' is that one should be poor, sick, lonely, injured, or even killed? This is the fear that always comes up when one says Thy will be done.

"This fear is very real and anyone who wishes to use the phrase *Thy will be done* must face it and think about it, or the ego mind will block the use of the phrase, at least in its most potent form.

"The most basic answer to this fear is a realization that 'Thy will' is going to be better than anything the ego mind can imagine or create. This is the ultimate answer. To get to this answer, however, many people must fail on their own, often almost destroying their lives with drugs, alcohol, illness, sexual mistakes, caving in to tyrants, or something else. Only then are most people willing to really embrace the idea of *Thy will be done.*

RELIGION AND *THY WILL BE DONE*

"Most religions realize that to progress, most people need to let go of or loosen the hold of the ego mind, which is almost always a reactive mind that is not particularly creative, is quite fear-based, and is often vicious, arrogant and full of hatred for what it does not understand or what it does not like. Therefore, most spiritual systems and religions employ various means to counteract, go around, destroy or weaken the ego mind.

"In fact, the use of the phrase *Thy will be done* is one of the main reasons for resistance against the Jewish and Christian religions, in particular. Other religions use the phrase to some extent, such as the Hindu and Muslim religions. However, none employ it to the same degree as does the Christianity, in particular.

HOW TO USE THE PHRASE "THY WILL BE DONE"

"One way is to repeat the Lord's Prayer at least once and preferably twice or three times per day. This contains the phrase *Thy will be done.*

"Other options are to use affirmations such as:
> 'Not my will, but Thine be done in this situation.'
> 'Take me, use me this day to do Thy will.'
> 'Father, what would you have me do this day, or in this situation?'

"These can be repeated as often as one wishes. I would suggest using them at least three times each day. For those with severe health issues, or any serious situation, more is better.

ARE YOU SERIOUS ABOUT THY WILL?

"Many people repeat the phrase *Thy will be done,* but they are not totally serious about it. They say the words because one reads about them or the words sound good. However, taking the phrase seriously is another story, and is still frightening to the ego mind.

"However, saying the words as an affirmation is still very beneficial, I would maintain, because conditioning the mind to use the phrase makes it a little easier to finally accept the idea into your life fully.

"Another pitfall is to accept 'Thy will' in some areas of life, but not in others. In other words, it is not a total blending or surrender of the ego mind, but rather a partial one. For example, it may be fine to ask for 'Thy will' in your studies, for example, or with your friends, but not in your marriage or with your children, perhaps. This is another common fear of the ego mind. It will allow Thy will to be done in some situations, but not in others that are more personal or more threatening to it.

ANOTHER INTERPRETATION OF *THY WILL BE DONE*

"I once saw an interesting translation of the Lord's Prayer, supposedly from the original Aramaic, which is different than the Greek translation of the New Testament. In this translation, the phrase *Thy will be done* was translated as: 'Let Your Heart's desire unite Heaven and earth through our sacred union.'

"I include this unusual translation because it has a slightly different meaning. The meaning seems to be: *Let the desire of God unite heaven and earth by my merging with God or the Creation. Said differently , please God or Creation, merge with me, and this will bring forth the true desire of God in and through me.*

"This translation of the familiar prayer is similar to, but not quite the same as the familiar phrase, *Thy will be done.* It does not imply quite the degree of surrender, so this may be helpful for some people. It also reminds me of another Bible phrase spoken by Jesus of Nazareth that 'I and the Father are One.' Again this does not imply surrender as much as it implies a union or blending process with the Holy Spirit or with the Father energy. Some people may prefer this interpretation of the phrase *Thy will be done* for this reason."[26]

If Jesus, when He prayed to His Father said, "Not My will, but Thy will be done," that's good enough for me.

Lord, in everything I say, do, desire or think ... let it be not my will, but Thy will be done. Now, *that's* surrender!

[26] By Lawrence Wilson, MD © December 2011, The Center For Development—Used by permission.

THE BRICK
Author Unknown

"A young and successful executive was travelling down a neighbourhood street, going a bit too fast in his new Jaguar. He was watching for kids darting out from between parked cars and slowed down when he thought he saw something. As his car passed, no children appeared.

"Instead, a brick smashed into the Jag's side door! He slammed on the brakes and backed the Jag back to the spot where the brick had been thrown. The angry driver then jumped out of the car, grabbed the nearest kid and pushed him up against a parked car shouting, 'What was that all about and who are you? Just what the heck are you doing? That's a new car and that brick you threw is going to cost a lot of money. Why did you do it?' The young boy was apologetic.

"'Please, mister...please, I'm sorry but I didn't know what else to do,' he pleaded. 'I threw the brick because no one else would stop...' With tears dripping down his face and off his chin, the boy pointed to a spot just around a parked car. 'It's my brother,' he said. 'He rolled off the curb and fell out of his wheelchair and I can't lift him up.'

"Now sobbing, the boy asked the stunned executive, 'Would you please help me get him back into his wheelchair? He's hurt and he's too heavy for me.'

"Moved beyond words, the driver tried to swallow the rapidly swelling lump in his throat. He hurriedly lifted the handicapped boy back into the wheelchair, then took out a linen handkerchief and dabbed at the fresh scrapes and cuts. A quick look told him everything was going to be okay.

"'Thank you and may God bless you,' the grateful child told the stranger. Too shook up for words, the man simply watched the boy push his wheelchair-bound brother down the sidewalk toward their home.

"It was a long, slow walk back to the Jaguar. The damage was very obvious, but the driver never bothered to repair the dented side door. He kept the dent there to remind him of this message: **'Don't go through life so fast that someone has to throw a brick at you to get your attention!' God whispers in our souls and speaks to our hearts. Sometimes when we don't have time to listen, He has to throw a brick at us. It's our choice to listen or not."**[27]

Thought for the Day:[28]

If God had a refrigerator, your picture would be on it.

If He had a wallet, your photo would be in it.

He sends you flowers every spring.

He sends you a sunrise every morning and a sunset to end your day.

God did not promise days without pain, laughter without sorrow, sun without rain, but He *did* promise strength for the day, comfort for the tears and light for the way.

Remember, if God brings you to it, He will bring you through it!

---

[27] Author unknown

[28] Adapted from the Internet—Author unknown

HUMOUR

I love humour, not in the same way that I love my wife, of course, but I cannot image life without it.

Whether one spells it "humor" or "humour," the dictionary and thesaurus are unsatisfactory in their attempts to define it. I did find the root of the word, but it is so gross I don't want to sully this book by trying to explain it. Suffice to say some humour is a throwback to the word's origins.

Try looking it up. You may be surprised at what you find.

In my extensive travelling, I have found humour to be very different in different countries; it even differs in regions within the same country.

However, I have noticed some similarities, or constants, where humour is concerned.

Some of these are:

- Humour is used as a way of disparaging a nation or group of people that is considered to be inferior to another group; whether intellectually, socially, or financially. Consider the plethora of jokes aimed against the Irish, Jewish, or Newfies. All over Europe, each country has jokes aimed against their neighbours, to the extent that many jokes can easily be transposed onto another nation, gender, or social class. For example, "have you heard about the Irishman who ..." can easily be transposed to "have you heard the one about the Newfie, Mexican, or blonde who ..."

- Humour is used to bring other people who are better off intellectually, socially, or financially down to one's own level. Consider jokes by the indigenous peoples of the Caribbean against their white former slave masters, or similar jokes told by Polish people against Russian people during the days when Poland was under the thumb of communism.

- Humour is a way to make comments about a particular social situation. These types of jokes are often told within a certain culture to make a social comment that would otherwise be deemed inappropriate.

- Humour is a mechanism to subtly insult other people. This one walks a delicate balance because it is only funny if the target of the joke does not realize they are being made fun of. There are obvious in-your-face jokes that are easy to understand. These are often favoured by the people of North America. Then there are the subtle, insulting jokes favoured by the British. Political jokes are appreciated or understood by only a small circle of people.

I am going to share with you here just a few of my favourite jokes, which will probably reveal a few things about me.

Not a fictional joke, this actually happened to me in London, England.

I was in a taxi going down the A3 road out of central London on my way to a training centre situated in a former mansion where there were extensive gardens, ornamental ponds and exquisitely designed flower beds.

The taxi driver was a cheerful, animated Irish man who chattered a lot, most of which I could barely understand.

The grounds were very large so that the mansion house itself could not be seen from the main road. We left the main road and started down the driveway that meandered between the flower beds, ponds and beautifully sculptured lawns. I said conversationally to this Irish taxi driver: "Goodness me, this is an awfully long driveway."

To which the taxi driver replied in his best Irish brogue, "Ah, to be sure. But if it was any shorter, it wouldn't reach the house."

Now we go to Texas where a Texan rancher is discussing with an English farmer the relative sizes of their properties.

"So," said the Texan rancher to the English farmer, "how big is your farm back there in England?"

"Well," said the English farmer modestly, "it is quite large by English standards ... about fifty acres." He then politely asks the Texan rancher, "And how large is your ranch?"

Puffing out his chest in pride the Texan rancher boasts, "Well, my ranch is *so big* it would be hard to explain just how big it is. Put it this way: If I were to get up in the morning before the sun comes up and drive my car all day long in a straight line from east to west, by the time the sun goes down at night, I still would not have reached the other side of my ranch."

"*Really?*" said the English farmer incredulously. "I used to have a car like that."

And now let's go to Moscow, Russia. This is a joke told to me by a Russian businessman whilst I was in Moscow.

There were three businessmen in a hotel bar discussing what is the most pleasurable experience in life.

The Englishman says, "Definitely the most pleasurable experience is Sunday in England. In the late morning, I take a leisurely walk to the pub and have a few pints with my mates as we discuss yesterday's football results. Then I amble on home where my wife will have waiting for me a superb English roast meal: roast beef, Yorkshire pudding, two kinds of potatoes, three kinds of veggies and, of course, apple pie with custard to finish it off. I then sit by a nice roaring fire with my feet up, read the Sunday paper's sports page, puffing on my pipe and downing a nice cup of tea. Now that is the world's most pleasurable experience."

"Huh!" grunted the Frenchman. "You English have no idea what real pleasure is. I will tell you. I have a beautiful young woman on my arm and lots of money in my pocket. We dine in the best Parisian restaurant, eating the most exotic food and drinking the very best aged wine. Then we dance the night away under the beautiful stars of Paris. Now *that* is the most pleasurable experience in the world."

"No, no!" says the Russian, shaking his head. "You decadent westerners have no idea of what real pleasure is. I will tell you. I am asleep in my Moscow apartment. At two o'clock in the morning I am awakened by very heavy knocking on my door. A very angry loud voice screams, "Gregor Ivanovich, this is the KGB. We have come for you!" When I can say, "Gregor Ivanovich lives next door; you have the wrong apartment," that is the most pleasurable experience in the world.

The humour is based on the unpleasant reality.

And finally, let me leave you with the wit of that venerable politician, Sir Winston Churchill.

Winston Churchill's scathing put-down of Britain's first female MP has seen the wartime Prime Minister voted king of the witty insults. Churchill frequently butted heads with Conservative Prime Minister Lady Astor. His acerbic (and sexist) riposte is voted number one by 2,000 Britons in the top ten list of the funniest insults in history.

When accused by the lady of being "disgustingly drunk," the Conservative Prime Minister responded, "My dear, you are ugly, and what's more, you are disgustingly ugly. But tomorrow I shall be sober and you will still be disgustingly ugly."

Some of my North American friends don't quite get English humour. One of the classic British sitcoms stars John Cleese as Basil Faulty in *Faulty Towers*. It is hilariously funny from start to finish, but one of our Canadian friends thinks it is cruel. How can one person find something funny and yet another person find the same thing to be cruel? That's humour for you.

One final word. Telling jokes can have its pitfalls. Elsewhere in this book, I shared a story of a great embarrassment that I suffered in Germany. On another occasion, I was asked to be a comedian at a Christmas dinner for an accounting company. The evening was going well, with all my jokes eliciting the desired laughter, when suddenly, at that critical moment at the end of one joke, I could not remember the punch line. It was just not there.

I told the audience I had forgotten the punch line, but they thought I was kidding. The more I tried to convince them that I *had* forgotten the punch line, the more they laughed. So, in desperation, I asked the audience, "Does anyone out there know the punch line of the joke?" At which time, a lady came on stage and perfectly delivered the punch line.

I have never known if the uproarious laughter was for the punch line or for the circumstances leading to its delivery. Perhaps the funniest thing was that the audience thought it was an intentional set-up and deemed it to be brilliant. Like the magician who never gives away his tricks, I never let on.

37

TO CONCLUDE ...

So, now we have reached the end of this book, but most definitely *not* the end of the journey.

People from most religions like to believe there is a heaven and that hopefully, at the end of their lives, whether good, bad or ugly, they will end up there.

Cynical people might find some kind of solace in the depressing views of John Lennon, who writes of imagining there's no heaven, only sky above with no hell below. To be fair to Mr. Lennon, the premise behind his song was not all bad; it was just that he had no hope, no concept of a loving God who had gone to prepare a place in heaven for him and for all who would put their trust in Him.

So let's imagine ... what *will* heaven be like?

In contrast to the words of John Lennon, the wonderful lyrics of "I Can Only Imagine" by Mercy Me, lead the listener to consider what it will be like when we walk by Jesus' side in heaven—what we will see when we look into His face, what we will feel when surrounded by His glory and whether we will dance before Him or stand in silent awe. "Will I stand in your presence, or to my knees will I fall? Will I sing hallelujah, will I be able to speak at all?"[29] The rapturous conclusion is that we will forever worship Him in fullness of joy.

Because of Him, I can say with confidence that I do know where I am going. I know with whom I am making this journey. But as for the journey itself, it is to be continued ....

---

[29] "I Can Only Imagine" by Mercy Me

A WORD OF THANKS

Towards the end of writing this book, I began to think of all the wonderful people whose lives have intersected mine; people who have contributed to making me who, and what, I am today. Tears came to my eyes as I thought of you all.

I wanted to write the words of gratitude that began to well up in my heart, but I had to remind myself to stay focused on the original vision for this book and the fact that this book is really not about *me*; it's about how God has moved and directed my life. Thus, I needed to refrain, as much as possible, from writing anything that pointed to me personally; I needed to stay with the "God stories." I am not sure how successful I have been with that; you will have to be the judge.

Nevertheless, I do want to thank all those people who have impacted my life in so many different and diverse ways. There are so many of you, in so many countries, that if I were to try to list names, I would most certainly forget some people.

So, I hope you will trust my sincerity when I say, "God knows your name and *His* is the *only* book where you need to make sure your name is included."

Thank you and God bless you.

Terry

"Nevertheless do not rejoice in this, that the spirits are subject to you, but rejoice that your names are recorded in heaven" (Luke 10:20).

"Indeed, true companion, I ask you also to help these women who have shared my struggle in the cause of the gospel, together with Clement also and the rest of my fellow workers, whose names are in the Book of Life" (Philippians 4:3).

"He who overcomes will thus be clothed in white garments; and I will not erase his name from the Book of Life, and I will confess his name before My Father and before His angels" (Revelation 3:5).

"Your eyes have seen my unformed substance; And in Your Book were all written the days that were ordained for me, When as yet there was not one of them" (Psalms 139:16).

Nore: A very special thank you to my publisher and friend (still) Diane Roblin-Lee (now the newly married Mrs. Roblin-Sharp) whose patience with this rookie author guided this book to become what you now see in your hands.

The inspiration is from God. The words are mine but the presentation is all Diane. Thanks again!

Terry

Photo by Reynold Mainse

To book

Terry and/or Ginny

or for information on our ministry

Please e-mail

terenceb@rogers.com

or call

905-426-1816

Websites:

www.terryandginny.com

www.afunnythinghappenedvolumeone.com

I'M HERE

Perhaps you would like to make this your prayer.

I'm here.
I'm waiting just on You,
It took some time to do, but now I'm listening Lord to You.

I'm here.
It took a long, long time,
but now the water's wine.
A miracle has happened and I'm listening this time.

I've been so long and so headstrong in going my own way;
and only when the storms set in did I take time to pray.
I talked a lot, but then I forgot, that You, too, had a say.
But now I'm here and I'm listening today.

I'm here.
I've much to say to You,
but more, I know it's true, have You to say to me.
And You're here, the still and silent voice
that waits to hear my choice – to rush away, or listen.

Lord, I'm here.

Will you rush away – or will you listen?

Words & Music – John Daniels
(Reprinted with permission)
Sung by – Ginny Bridle

CPSIA information can be obtained at www.ICGtesting.com
Printed in the USA
LVOW02*1953221014

409655LV00001BA/1/P